CONQUISTADORES DE LA CALLE

Conquistadores de la Calle

CHILD STREET LABOR IN GUATEMALA CITY

Thomas A. Offit

UNIVERSITY OF TEXAS PRESS
Austin

Requests for permission to reproduce material from this work
should be sent to:
    Permissions
    University of Texas Press
    P.O. Box 7819
    Austin, TX 78713-7819
    www.utexas.edu/utpress/about/bpermission.html

♾ The paper used in this book meets the minimum requirements
of ANSI/NISO Z39.48-1992 (R1997) (Permanence of Paper).

Library of Congress Cataloging-in-Publication Data

Offit, Thomas A., 1968–
    Conquistadores de la calle : child street labor in Guatemala City
/ Thomas A. Offit. — 1st ed.
        p.   cm.
    Includes bibliographical references and index.
    ISBN 0-292-72150-1
    1. Child labor—Guatemala—Guatemala City.   I. Title.
    HD6250.G953G836   2008
    331.3′10972811—dc22

                                                    2007045838

For my father, Benson Israel Offit, and my mother, Suzanne Gerber Offit

CONTENTS

Acknowledgments   ix

ONE   *Introduction*   1

TWO   *Street Work in El Guarda and 18 Calle*   27

THREE   *Jobs and Income of Child Street Laborers*   60

FOUR   *Child Street Laborers, Their Families, and the Household Economy*   90

FIVE   *The Social Nature of Economic Success*   115

SIX   *Child Street Laborers and Education*   152

SEVEN   *The Futures of Child Street Laborers*   161

APPENDIX   *Summary of Guatemalan and International Legislative Responses to Child Labor*   171

Notes   179

Bibliography   193

Index   217

ACKNOWLEDGMENTS

Anyone working on a monograph is indebted to many people for support that varies from continuous to occasional, from emotional to financial. I am no exception, and indeed have relied upon the support of too many people to adequately name them all in this short space, though I shall give it a go.

First and foremost, this work would not have been possible without the friendship extended to me by the children with whom I worked. This is their story, filtered through my own imperfect lens. Without their collaboration, I would have failed. I hope a fraction of their light shines through in my work.

I was also aided greatly by the many students I taught at the Universidad del Valle in Guatemala City, who taught me far more about Guatemala and anthropology than I ever taught them. Special recognition goes to the students who participated in my summer field methods class and gathered much of the information about the children of El Guarda found in this work, especially Andrés Alvarez, Aaron Argueta, Eileen Cunningham, Isolda Fortín, Daniela Galíndez, David García, Tatiana Paz, Luis Velásquez, and Deimy Ventura. Dre, David, and Tatus also gave me some idea about how to be cool on the streets, leading of course by example. Dr. Didier Boremanse and Dr. Marian Hatch also gave me advice and counsel that made teaching at Del Valle a wonderful experience.

Friends such as Tomás Simonsen, Ileana Bustamante, Ian and Kuka González, Jenny Mahyer, and Garrett "Boo" Martin also helped make my time in Guatemala a wonderful experience. Josh and Bridget Sarubin, Carl and Rylan Hutzler, Nick and Liz Baldick, Ken Turnbull, Leslie Spiegel, and Jackie Baldick provided emotional support while I was writing. My sister Meg, her husband, Marc, and my uncle Sid also provided encouragement when my energies were flagging.

I am also indebted to the staff of Programa Educativo del Niño, Niña y Adolescente Trabajador (PENNAT) of Guatemala City, who provided me with constant support during the course of my research. *Mi héroe* Jairo González was my guide in all that I did, and Marie Román de Tejada introduced me to El Guarda and those who work there, allowing me to piggyback on her fine name and teaching me a great deal in the process. Ximena Paredes was also a fine research companion during my early days in El Guarda, and through her fund-raising and organizational efforts, the children of El Guarda have a schoolroom that will serve their needs for generations.

Academically, my debts are equally vast. Dr. William Taft Stuart, Dr. Erve Chambers, Dr. Michael Agar, Dr. Tony Whitehead, Dr. Mark Leone, and Dr. Alaka Wali first exposed me to the world of anthropology at the University of Maryland. Dr. Munroe Edmonson, Dr. Victoria Bricker, Dr. Robert Hill II, and Dr. E. Wyllys Andrews made me a Mesoamericanist at Tulane. Dr. Garrett Cook, Dr. Charles Tolbert, Dr. Paul Froese, Dr. Christopher Bader, Dr. Sara Alexander, Dr. Carson Mencken, and Mrs. Donna Grelle at Baylor University mocked me sufficiently (in a loving way) to get me to finish this book. My greatest debt goes to the three people without whom this work would never have been initiated much less completed, namely, my trifecta of advisors, Dr. Justin Rudelson, Dr. Judith Maxwell, and Dr. Nancie González. Without the constant emotional and intellectual guidance, and the occasional kick in the pants, provided by Nancie González, I would never have made a career in anthropology in the first place. Without Justin Rudelson, I would never have made it through graduate school, *punto final.* And I hope that Judy knows that throughout this process, she has been a mentor, a friend, and, most importantly, an intellectual and ethical guide.

Financial support for my research was provided by the Fulbright-Hays Dissertation Research Fellow Program, Tulane University; the Tinker Foundation; and my brother, Andy, who never stopped giving until it hurt. Baylor University provided me with a summer sabbatical and an ideal milieu for revising my manuscript.

I am also indebted to the staff at the University of Texas Press, especially Theresa May, assistant director and editor-in-chief; Megan Giller, assistant manuscript editor; and Nancy Warrington, copyeditor, for providing me with immeasurable help during the publication process, and to the anonymous reviewers of my manuscript for all of their suggestions and comments.

My final thanks go to those who gave the most of themselves to me during this project: Julio Héctor Cutzal, who was my teacher and friend, a long-lost brother who guided me. What Julio could not teach me, Don Emiliano Herrera did, and our friendship and our collaboration has made my work and my life richer. My parents, Suzanne Gerber Offit and Benson Israel Offit, always believed in me. They believed. I miss you so much, Dad. And finally, nothing I do would be possible were it not for my wife, Oriel Jane, and my children, Benson, Anya, and Bobby. Oriel Jane, you are all my dreams.

CONQUISTADORES DE LA CALLE

One

INTRODUCTION

REY'S STORY

Rey[1] is fifteen years old, and he shines shoes for a living. He'll also repair a broken heel, restitch a bad seam, or even change the color of your shoes if you can give them to him overnight. Rey is good at what he does. He works hard, he takes his job seriously, and he's been doing it since he was six years old. He spends six days a week, twelve hours a day working underneath an overpass, sitting on a stool seven inches by five inches in size, about six inches off the ground. He sits there, a few feet from perhaps the most traveled street in all of downtown Guatemala City, shining shoes from the time the sun rises until it sets.

If it is raining and you have a little time on your hands, or if you decide it's time to get a shine, you might stop and learn a little bit more about Rey. If you manage to catch him early in the day, say around 7:00 AM, his clothes and his body will be clean, but after a few hours, shoe polish covers his hands and forearms, and the dirt of the sidewalk and of the black clouds of exhaust from buses, trucks, and cars paints his clothing with soot. If you or someone else does need a shine, you might notice that Rey has a full complement of shine brushes, rags, and different-colored shoe polish laid out in front of him, along with a well-built foot stand and a chair for his customers. He works fast and confidently, and he lets the customer initiate any conversation; his replies are good-natured. He is quick to laugh at a joke or smile, but his manner is not obsequious. You would appreciate that when he is doing the final buff job on your shoes he makes his rag pop, and that in the end you have a quality shoeshine for only one quetzal, or about fifteen cents.[2]

Rey is not only a shoeshiner; he also handles the sale of newspapers and cold drinks for an older man who sits on a chair at a portable cart a few feet away, selling cigarettes, candy, and cookies. Sometimes the older man, Don Fernando, may be engrossed in a conversation with someone, or not there at all, and you might think that Rey works for the twelve-year-old girl, Don Fernando's daughter, Roxana, who is then sitting in the chair by the cart. Nevertheless, it's obvious that Rey is working for them, because all the money he gets from the newspapers and cold drinks goes immediately into the hands of Don Fernando or Roxana, and Rey looks much different from both Don Fernando and Roxana.

If it's a slow day, and neither you nor anyone else is in need of a shine or a Pepsi, you might see Rey reading a newspaper or chatting with Don Fernando or Roxana, and you'd realize that Rey has no difficulty reading or conversing in Spanish. But perhaps Rey will be talking to someone else, and he will speak in a much different language that you might recognize as K'iche', a Mayan Indian language. In only a couple of minutes, you will have learned a good deal about Rey: who he is, where he's from, what he does for a living, how well he does it, who he works for, and how much he makes. But most people never notice Rey at all.

For two years, I spent my time working with hundreds of children like Rey, children who work on the streets of Guatemala City, Guatemala. Working children are ubiquitous in the streets of Guatemala City, as they are in most cities of the developing world. They are so common that they go about their lives and labors largely unnoticed. If Rey were to be shoeless and dressed in rags, passed out beneath his overpass with a bottle full of paint thinner or glue dangling from his hand, people would take notice. If he and four of his friends were gathered beneath the overpass wearing similar clothing, with sleeves rolled up and arms displaying tattoos with expressions such as *"puros vatos locos"* (crazy boys) or *"Mami, perdóname por esta vida loca"* (forgive me, mother, for living this crazy life), people would take notice. But Rey does not fit the popular conception of street child, and he's not in a gang. He is a member of the working poor, a population that makes up about half of all the children of Guatemala City yet fails to captivate the imagination of the public, government officials, international aid agencies, or academic researchers the way a much smaller percentage of the city's children do.

Because Rey and others like him are everywhere and therefore not exceptional, we feel as if we know and understand them. They perform small tasks and sell us small things that we purchase every day. They and their lives hold little mystery. If we do think about why they, as children, are working on the street rather than being in school or at home, we are quick to blame their families or an indifferent government for their plight, bemoaning the fact that in a poor country like Guatemala, everyone must work. Like virtually everyone, their lives are defined by their own and their families' struggle to survive, and as children working in the city, they are forced to work in the least hospitable job site—the streets—and perform tasks that contribute little to the larger economy and bring in only meager wages. We believe that child street laborers are victims of exploitation who have little hope of ever exiting the vicious cycle of poverty that brought them to the streets in the first place, and that most will be irreparably damaged by their labors.

The purpose of my time spent working with children like Rey was to delve deeper into their lives, to take them and their labor seriously, and to see if what we think about them and their work matches both what they think about themselves and what can be called the "objective truth" of the matter. It is my contention that, in the case of Rey and other children who work in the streets of Guatemala City, common beliefs about child street labor are incorrect. Child street laborers are not merely victims of poverty and exploitation; they are active agents in fighting these conditions. For Rey, and almost all of the other children working on the streets of Guatemala City, child labor works.

CONQUERING THE STREETS

Over the course of nearly two years, I conducted research among child street laborers working in two different areas of Guatemala City, the 18 Calle (Eighteenth Street) area of Zone 1 and the El Guarda market of Zone 11. My work was conducted on the streets, with the children themselves, while they were working and playing, indeed living their lives on the streets. From hundreds of hours spent working with the children, their peers, bosses, family members, and others, the results of my research indicate that the popular conceptions of both child street labor and of street children are erroneous.

Children who work on the streets provide a present and a future for themselves and their families. Over 70 percent of the children with whom I worked made a wage above the Guatemalan national minimum adult wage for urban workers, and the minimum wage is far above what many workers, rural and urban, actually receive. This income is not only essential for the children's and their families' immediate survival, but is often a vital part of the capital accumulation that allows children and their families to improve the conditions of their lives. While the economic activities of a porter, shoeshine boy, or informal street vendor may appear to be disorganized and marginal, the earnings that street work provides are far from being so.

In addition to the money that is to be made by children who work on the streets, through their labors, children also gain knowledge and make connections that allow them to move up the ladder of street jobs as well as find work outside the local street environment, be it a formal-sector job in the city or opportunities outside of Guatemala. For children who forsake school for street work, the streets provide many lessons that are integral to their future. A street education, while including lessons in immediate survival, also provides children with the opportunity to learn the ins and outs of running a business, from the importance of locations, profit margins, and where the best suppliers are, to contacts with non-related adults who can aid them in furthering their personal and economic development. A street education is applicable to both street and nonstreet settings.

The education that child street laborers receive is complementary to the benefits of a formal education. Virtually all of the children with whom I worked were born in poverty and have worked since their earliest years, yet most have attended school and left because they found many disadvantages to formal school attendance, most notably the high cost and low return of "free" public schooling. Most child street laborers have a great respect for formal learning, which many continue on their own while they work, yet they left schools because the schools were failing them.

While familial poverty is a contributing factor to why children work on the streets, it is only one aspect of the overall forces that drive them to work. The moral and ethical importance of work is a value that is heavily engrained in the child street laborers that I worked with, and virtually all believe that work is what has saved them from the fate of their "pathological" peers in their midst. Children work because of the poverty they and their families face, itself a result of national and global inequalities in the distribution of wealth. While the developed world tries to use legislative means of eradicating child labor, it is these same nations that, through their control of the global economy, consign children to the bottom rung of the ladder.

It is my contention that child street laborers are prospering from their time spent working on the streets and are making the best of the dire poverty that brought them to the streets in the first place. Global and national economic injustices force children onto the streets to work, yet the children actively respond to this by transforming the streets into a place where they can contest their poverty. They are providing for the survival of their families and are gaining the skills and the knowledge that will allow them to provide for themselves as adults in the future. As I demonstrate, child street labor works, unlike the legislation that attempts to help them, the schools that are provided to educate them, or the national and international economic forces that contributed to them being on the streets.

THE DEFINITION OF
CHILD STREET LABOR

As I believe that child street laborers are incorrectly understood in the popular and academic literature, it is necessary to define child street labor and to explain how the confusion regarding this definition is central to the general misunderstanding of child street labor. I define child street laborers as children under eighteen years of age who are engaged on a full-time basis in a variety of occupations—primarily the sale of foodstuffs and dry goods and the provision of basic services—that take place in the public streets and parks and for which the children are paid. This definition therefore sets child street laborers apart from the two other groups of children with whom they are usually confused: street children and child street workers.

Street children are children who have become, to varying degrees, estranged from their families for a variety of reasons, usually having to do with neglect, abuse, and insufficient emotional and financial resources for their maintenance (Wright, Kaminsky, and Wittig 1993a). They spend much of their time on the streets, engaged in a variety of activities that range from odd jobs and begging to theft and prostitution; occasionally, they sleep on the streets. Although most street children, like child street laborers, do manage to earn their keep on the streets, the irregular nature of their work and their opportunistic and ephemeral choice of occupation and work site make them incomparable to child street laborers. Original estimates in the late 1970s to early 1980s placed the number of street children in Latin America at 40 million, 7 million of whom lived in Brazil (Tacon 1981). Yet as numerous studies have since pointed out (see Hecht 1998; Rizzini et al. 1994; and Scheper-Hughes and Hoffman 1998, to name but a few), these figures and most others from that same era were greatly inflated. More recent estimates indicate that there are only about 40,000 true homeless street children in Brazil (Hecht 1998). While no comparable estimates exist for Guatemala, the results of my own cursory investigations lead me to believe that the number hovers around 1,000, and the local office of Casa Alianza (Covenant House, an international NGO and the most prominent advocate and service provider for street children throughout Central America) estimates that it serves some 1,235 children a year (Casa Alianza 2007).[3] That there are any children living in this manner is a cause for serious concern. At the same time, researchers obscure investigation into the lives of child street laborers by failing to distinguish them from "true" street children. Although the distinction between street children and child street laborers has been emphasized in previous studies (Thomas 1995; Wright, Kaminsky, and Wittig 1993a, 1993b), confusion still results. Because of the shock value that descriptions and photos of true street children provide, most researchers tend to write about street children. Sometimes mention is made that they are far outnumbered by child street workers and laborers, yet statistics and descriptions are offered that include child street laborers and child street workers under the rubric of street children.

In addition to differentiating child street laborers from street children, a distinction must be made between child street laborers and child street workers. Child street laborers engage in remunerated employment. Child street workers, while often working as hard as laborers, work with family members and are not paid for their labors. Many child street workers do receive pocket money, given at the discretion of their family members, but they do not receive compensation commensurate with the work they perform, as child street laborers do. The work that child street workers perform is usually combined with other tasks, such as childcare and the running of errands, which, though tremendously important to the running of a street business, are considered either as an apprenticeship in street work or as their roles in the familial division of labor. Most often, relatives or parents will not even identify their child as working, but rather as coming to work with them. Child street work, and the nature of the unremunerated work that urban children, especially girls, perform, is itself a largely understudied phenomenon, though a few excellent studies on this phenomenon in rural settings do exist (Loucky 1988; Nieuwenhuys 1994; Reynolds 1991). By failing to differentiate between these two groups, existing research leads to confusion, especially with regard to such topics as earning power and contribution to family income.

Children who belong to the middle- and upper-class families of Guatemala City, like their economically less advantaged peers, are to be found en masse on the streets of the nation's capital. These children, known as *fresas*,[4] frequent the theaters, cafés, retail stores, and street kiosks that dominate the 18 Calle area, often without adult supervision. They also visit El Guarda on big shopping days. All of them attend school full-time, most in private schools that offer a full day's curriculum of academic and other courses. Although they may dress and behave in ways that distinguish them from the youth actually working on the street, it is difficult to determine who they truly are without knowledge of the symbols that differentiate youth subcultures and socioeconomic classes in Guatemala City (see Hebdige 1979 for a classic statement on youth subcultures and dress). Needless to say, though these youths may at times be difficult to distinguish from other children in the street, the fact that they do not engage in any type of work or labor in the street excluded them from my research.

An intermediate group of children who are frequently in the streets are part-time child street workers and laborers. These youths, like *fresas,* all attend school on a full-time basis, though most attend public or parochial schools that generally require only half-day attendance, either morning or afternoon. Some perform street labor for pocket money on an opportunistic basis (much like the child hawkers of Nigeria profiled by Beatrice Oloko (1991)).

Children whose primary means of income came from illicit street activities, such as prostitution, thievery, and drug sales, do meet my criteria for child street laborers, but they will not be addressed extensively here.[5] These children, like street children, are a small minority of the total number of urban child street laborers. Nor will child street laborers who attend formal schools and work part-time be addressed extensively in my work, for they, too, are few in number in Guatemala City relative to the number of child street laborers who do not attend schools (this does not seem to be the case elsewhere; see Oloko 1991; Porio, Moselina, and Swift 1994). Within the estimated 137,000 child street laborers and workers in Guatemala (Villarreal and Peralta Chapetón 1997), my own survey and ethnographic research indicates that the child street laborers of the type I shall describe here make up the majority.

RESEARCH PERSPECTIVES
AND METHODS

My first memorable experience in Guatemala was with a child street laborer. In 1990, I was a twenty-one-year-old undergraduate with a small research grant to study the history of the development of the export *típica* (Maya weavings and fabric) textile trade in the town of Panajachel (Offit 1993). Upon my arrival in Guatemala, I decided to spend a few days in the capital before setting off for the Western Highlands, and I spent the day walking around the downtown area. While admiring the *huipil* (blouse worn by Maya women) market set up in the Parque Central (Central Park), a child in clown face who entertained on the streets for money spotted me. My command of the Spanish language was meager at best, and that child proceeded to lure me in and ridicule me for more than fifteen minutes as a huge crowd of onlookers laughed and threw money into his hat.

Once I recovered from the embarrassment of this encounter, I began to appreciate the guile with which the child had drawn me into his act and turned the appearance of another gringo (foreigner, white person) in the Parque Central into a fine moneymaking opportunity.[6] After I completed my research in the highlands, I decided to make child street laborers the focus of my anthropological research. Through a grant from the Tinker Foundation, I had the opportunity to work with homeless street children and child street laborers in Guatemala City and Tegucigalpa, Honduras, in the summer of 1994. During the course of this trip, I visited many of the nongovernmental organizations (NGOs) in each city that worked with urban "street children" and ended up working closely with the renowned Proyecto Alternativos (lit. the Alternatives Project) in Tegucigalpa and with Childhope in Guatemala City. I made another trip to Guatemala City in the spring of 1997 to continue my preliminary research and choose the site for my research, again with the aid of Childhope.

When I returned to Guatemala City in the fall of 1997 to begin my doctoral dissertation research, my planned research site, the Parque Concordia, had been unexpectedly razed by the municipality in order to construct an underground parking garage and to remove the many undesirable elements, such as street vendors and homeless street children, who used the park as a workplace or a home. I therefore was at a loss for where to begin my work and sought help once again from my friends at Childhope. They then put me in touch with the largest local NGO working directly with children in the streets of the capital, the Programa Educativo del Niño, Niña y Adolescente Trabajador, or PENNAT (Educational Program for Child and Adolescent Laborers).

PENNAT's aim was to provide a flexible education program for child laborers that would allow children who could not attend public schools an opportunity to receive their elementary school diploma. They had independently devised a primary school curriculum that had received approval from the Guatemalan Ministry of Education and was designed to permit students to work at their own pace with only minimal (thirty to forty minutes per week) instruction from a street educator. Therefore, students could receive this instruction either while at work (common in the case of child street laborers) or during their daily breaks (which was the case with children whose work entitled them less liberty). At the time of my research, PENNAT employed nearly fifty educators who worked in twenty-two areas of the capital and taught almost three thousand students. I had the opportunity to visit most of the PENNAT projects and with their counsel chose the 18 Calle area of Zone 1 and the Trébol area of Zone 11 as my research sites.

Of the more than one hundred thousand children working informally on the streets of Guatemala (Villarreal and Peralta Chapetón 1997), the majority of them work in Guatemala City. The two areas on which I based my study both rank near the top of the list of neighborhoods characterized by a high quantity of child street labor. Each area is a popular shopping destination, as the Trébol hosts the capital city's largest retail market (El Guarda) and the 18 Calle area of Zone 1 contains the largest agglomeration of street vendors and retail and wholesale shops in the country and is home to another large retail market, the Mercado Sur 2. In addition, both areas have tremendous pedestrian traffic and are major city centers for bus transportation within the city and from the city to all points throughout the country.

While working in both neighborhoods, my research site was the street. Many other researchers, working either directly with child street laborers or with homeless street children, end up basing their research of street populations on data they gathered from these children in nonstreet settings, such as health clinics (Wittig 1997; Wright, Kaminsky, and Wittig 1993a, 1993b), advocacy programs (Tierney 1997), and even in some cases state reform institutions (Aptekar 1988; Patricia Márquez [1999] spent part of her time in a state-funded institution). Though these areas are undoubtedly safer and more conducive to long-term interviewing and testing, as an anthropologist, I found it impossible to justify the study of a population that is largely defined by the public nature of their workplace in any type of private, off-street setting.[7]

By choosing to focus my research in the street, some limitations were placed upon my research. Though I chose Zones 1 and 11 as the focal points for my eighteen-month-long study, I did not live in either area. Granted, this is contrary to the traditions of ethnographic fieldwork, but it was a practical and necessary condition for my research. Unlike most traditional village-based ethnographic research, the heterogeneous nature of the city makes it difficult to reside exclusively with one's research group, unless the study being undertaken is of a specific residential neighborhood. In the case of child street laborers, at virtually any point in my research, the children I worked with were living dispersed over the entire city, as well as in the outlying *pueblos* (hamlets) or *colonias populares* (shantytowns) located on the *periferia* (periphery) of the city.

Over the course of my research, I lived in four different locations, from an apartment located only minutes from both the Trébol and 18 Calle, to a small house in the colonial city of la Antigua, about twenty miles outside of the capital. I did visit many of my subjects' homes, which ranged from single-family dwellings on the *periferia* to apartments in the heart of the city that housed eight to ten workers to a room and doubled as workshops and *bodegas* (warehouses), so I was well aware of the conditions in which they lived, though I never shared the same quarters with them.

I also limited the majority of my research time to the daylight hours. The children I was studying worked almost exclusively in the daytime hours, from as early as six o'clock in the morning to as late as eight in the evening, and the latter only on days of extreme economic opportunity such as during holiday shopping seasons. While the streets of El Trébol and 18 Calle presented many dangers during the daylight hours, they were a much more dangerous environment at night. Much as in many environments, the whole landscape of predators and preyed upon transforms when the sun goes down, and the streets were too dangerous for work or leisure except in exceptional circumstances. I did spend some late nights in the 18 Calle and Trébol areas both to confirm the working and socializing schedules of my informants and to observe the radical change in environment, but these nights were few.

During the initial stage of my research in each area, I would assist the local PENNAT educator and work with children on the PENNAT educational curriculum, as well as any other educational concept, including the study of my own language, which the children wished to learn about. I believe that by working on education, both the children and I became much closer than would ordinarily have been possible. Education was my introduction to each area, not only among the children but with the local adults and authorities as well. Any adult, especially a foreign one, would not last very long on the streets of Guatemala City by being known simply as an unaffiliated researcher who spent his time talking to children. Fears of abduction and abuse of local children by adults, particularly foreign ones, were always high in the neighborhoods where I worked,[8] and without my affiliation with PENNAT and my accepted role as "Profe Tomás," I myself would not have been able to conduct my research, much less survive.

My early work as a "street educator" was also vital to establishing a true relation of reciprocity between the children and myself, as we were both benefiting from my time spent on the streets as opposed to the often-criticized one-way exchange that occurs between an anthropologist and his/her informants (recent work by Carey [2001] and Little [2004] point out similar reciprocal relationships in their fieldwork in Guatemala). Contrary to the traditional teacher-student relationship in which power flows one way, my own childlike errors while speaking Spanish, as well as my near total ineptitude in the many Indian languages that the children also spoke fluently, frequently placed me in the role of the student. My constant questions concerning the nature of their jobs and what it took to become a street worker and move up the ladder within the street economy also placed them in the role of the learned elder, with me as the novice.

SELECTION OF INFORMANTS

Once I had spent a few weeks in my field site assisting the PENNAT educator, I created a map of each neighborhood area and identified which areas contained high concentrations of child street laborers. At the same time, I compiled a list of all the different street occupations in which children were engaged. Then, with the aid of the PENNAT educators and Guatemalan university students, I gathered basic data (name, age, job) on as many individual child street laborers in the area as possible. Unfortunately, I was unable to obtain an exact population of all child street laborers residing in each neighborhood because, much as the Greek philosopher Heroclitus remarked that one can never step twice in the same river, so, too, no informal market area is ever the same from hour to hour, much less day to day.

To gather a pool of informants that met my requirements (i.e., children working full-time in one of the many street occupations), I needed to try to distinguish full-time child laborers from their part-time peers. As Oloko (1991) and others have remarked, street sales or hawking is an activity undertaken by many adults and children on a part-time basis, from only one or two days a week to only three or four weeks a year. In addition, many children who attend school full-time and belong to a socioeconomic stratum in Guatemala that would correspond to "working class" engage in street work on a very opportunistic schedule.[9] Thus, to make my possible pool of informants representative of children for whom street work is a true vocation, I chose to work only with full-time child street laborers. I devoted two weeks to making rounds of the neighborhood twice a day (at 9:00 AM and 2:00 PM to eliminate children who attended school full-time in the morning or afternoon sessions) and noting which children worked in the same area doing the same job for at least eight of the fourteen days. Once this was accomplished, I had an idea of the relative population of full-time child street laborers in the area as well as their distribution by age and occupation. I then further introduced myself to those children and discussed with them my research as well as the PENNAT educational program.

I next developed a typology of the categories of jobs that child street laborers performed consistent with the existing classification of street work in Latin America devised by sociologist Ray Bromley (1997; see Chapter 3). This was done to determine which particular categories of jobs were most common and what the gender and ages were of those engaged in them based on my population estimates. I then used the principles of quota sampling (Bernard 1994, 94–95) to choose informants representative of each of the largest occupational groups. I chose my principal informants, who numbered 112 (66 from 18 Calle, 46 from El Guarda), according to the relative distribution of children by vocation, age, and gender, as well as by their inclination to work with me. While I am confident that my informants do represent the typical child laborer working in these two neighborhoods of Guatemala City, my final subject pool, due to the nature of research on the street, was not a true random scientific sample.

DATA GATHERING AMONG CHILD STREET LABORERS

My first data-gathering technique was participant observation, that is, getting to know the child and the ins and outs of his/her job simply by hanging around. While I did not shine shoes or sell gum as the children did, I watched them work and even had them teach me about the techniques that made them good at what they did. At times, I did also help by carrying a *bulto* (bundle of merchandise) or watching a *puesto* (kiosk), but I did not become a child street laborer, as this would have been impossible, not to mention ridiculous to all concerned. From this participant observation, I gained information not only on the child in question but also about the other children and adults with whom the child interacted.

Time spent with the children on the street was my most useful technique, but I also conducted and tape-recorded semistructured interviews with the children during a time when the child could get away from his job, which usually involved buying lunch for the two of us. I conducted these interviews along with substantial help from my two principal research assistants, Julio Héctor Cutzal in 18 Calle and Marie Román de Tejada in El Guarda. Julio and Doña Mari both worked as PENNAT educators and assisted my research on their own time by scheduling and aiding my tape-recorded interviews of the children and their peers, parents, and employers. Often their existing relationships with adults with whom I was only vaguely acquainted allowed me access to interviews I would not have been able to secure otherwise. Topics covered included the children's past history, their experiences in the capital, their histories as workers, as well as their opinions on their current and future situations. These semistructured interviews, which usually lasted between one and two hours, served as a means to further validate information I had compiled through my informal talks with the children and to introduce other topics of interest.

I also spent significant amounts of time with the adults with whom many children worked, including bosses, family members, or mentors. Information gleaned from these conversations again served to confirm or deny reports on all topics that I had heard from the children themselves; it also significantly furthered my education on what it takes to be a successful street worker in Guatemala City. My assistants and I also conducted and tape-recorded semistructured interviews with some adults in order to obtain their opinions on the nature of street labor and its effect on children, as well as to provide insight into their own careers on and off the streets to see what likely awaited the children with whom I worked.

My final methodological tool was pure observation. One of the advantages of working in the street is that there is so much activity going on that one is hardly noticed, even if standing a few feet away. The hustle and bustle of the flow of people; the rumble of trucks and motorcycles; and the endless visual stimuli coming from display windows, street kiosks, and other pedestrians isolate the individual to the point of invisibility. Though most people try to be aware of those around them so as to protect themselves, those intent on not being visible usually succeed in doing so. I was a true beneficiary of this invisibility and was therefore able to gather data on the children I worked with in a variety of instances where my direct interaction was unnecessary.

I performed time-allocation studies based on spot observation of what my subjects were doing at various points in the day when I encountered them. This technique was especially useful in documenting the relatively low labor intensity of street labor as well as the social nature of street work in general. I did encounter difficulties performing these observations when it came to children who either were nomadic in their workplaces or combined a variety of jobs in different areas during the course of their day, but I was nevertheless able to gather data concerning the time they devote to work using behavioral stream analyses combined with spot observation. I am confident that, in the end, I gathered a sufficient number of observations for all my vocational categories of child street laborers to verify my data with only a relatively small degree of error.

Through observation, I was also able to get a grasp on the practical economics of child street labor and use my observations as a means of confirming the veracity of the children's responses to many of my queries concerning the number of customers they had in a day and how much they earned. Perhaps the best-guarded secret of all street laborers, especially those involved in street sales, is the amount of income that is available to the street laborer. As one adult vendor in the 18 Calle area told me (and a near-identical quote is available in another brief study of the street vendors in Zone 1 [Porres Castejón 1995]): "If people knew how much one could earn selling, they would never leave us in peace." Only through the use of multiple techniques such as informal and formal interviewing and intensive observation can a true picture of the economic benefits of any informal sector endeavor, much less street work, emerge.

My time spent on the street also allowed me to observe the way the children interacted with their customers, their peers, and the many adults they encountered while working on the streets. Although interviews can provide responses to questions such as "Is your boss nice to you?" and "What friends do you spend the most time with while working?" only extensive observation can allow the researcher to emerge with a true idea of whether or not the ideal behavior often expressed in interviews matches the quotidian reality of a life spent working on the streets. Observation of the children interacting with others, both with my presence known and when I was "invisible," also revealed perhaps the most important strategy that children use to succeed on the streets: their situational manipulation of their social identity.

DATA GATHERING AMONG OTHER GROUPS

In addition to my time spent on the streets with the child street laborers, I also worked with individual children who are often on the streets, and therefore may be erroneously identified as child street laborers, but who in fact belong to such groups as homeless street children, child street workers, market children, and part-time child street laborers who attend school. Homeless street children were not the subjects of my research, but I nevertheless interacted with them regularly. From the talks we had, as well as the talks I had with my informants concerning their perceptions of homeless street children, I saw the cultural line that separates these two groups, as well as the various factors that would lead, albeit only rarely, a child street laborer to become a true street child.

Child street workers are another group of children to be seen on the streets that I came to know well. I worked directly with many children who worked with their parents without pay, or in exchange for pocket money, as they, too, were part of the PENNAT program. There are often differences between these children and child street laborers with regard to age, gender, and family situation. It is also true that many child street laborers began their careers as child street workers and became true laborers when they began to run their own microbusinesses.

I also had the opportunity to work for five months as a volunteer teacher at one local public elementary school, where I saw the many problems with public school education in Guatemala City. I had daily contact and informal conversations with hundreds of students and conducted semistructured interviews with educators concerning the difficulties they encountered as teachers and the difficulties faced by their students. By working in a public school, getting to know many of the students and their teachers and observing what went on, I became well versed in the many realities of "free" public schooling in Guatemala that led children to either stay in school or abandon it.

ETHICS

As many other researchers who have worked in street settings have testified (see Bourgois 1996; Hecht 1998; and Márquez 1999 for recent examples), the streets present many ethical quandaries to the participant observer. Though my research subjects were largely engaged in legal work, hearing about and witnessing crimes, from petty theft to the murder of an adolescent by an angry mob, were all part of my work. The violence of the streets was never far from the children or myself, and coping with it was part of their everyday experience as Guatemalans and mine as a researcher working on the streets. Fights between children were common but rarely serious, and physical confrontations between children and adults were uncommon. Similar to Tobias Hecht (1998), in my role as researcher and friend to the children, I merely tried to help the few times I was involved in these disputes, or stood by silently when I felt there was little I could do to help. In my role as an outsider, albeit a well-known and well-liked one, I was in a precarious position and therefore offered only aid and sympathy, rarely acting as judge or moral arbiter. Perhaps the greatest threat to child street laborers' welfare was public traffic, and two children that I worked with were badly injured by automobiles that hit them while they were working. Both suffered dire injuries that will leave them scarred for life.

As far as my research is concerned, I have done my best to protect the identity of all the child street laborers presented here by changing their names and altering the exact location of where they work in order to prevent easy identification. One advantage of doing research on the street is that these measures, while vitally important, are often unnecessary because of the difficulty of quick identification in a population that is so vast in an environment that is constantly changing.

Money was also a vital ethical matter in my research. Regardless of how much I tried to minimize the differences between the children and myself—dressing in a similar manner to them, traveling exclusively by public bus or on foot as they do, and eating at the same *comedores* (food stalls) and street kiosks as they did—my status as a foreign researcher from the land of plenty was nevertheless quite obvious. Children were continually asking me for small loans for food, clothing, medicine, and other needs. Parents of the children generally refrained from such a practice, though there were one or two who believed that my particular interest in their child or ward would result in my adopting the child and providing for his or her family. In the end, I tried to act as a friend would, helping out when the need was dire and genuine, but ignoring the vast majority of the pleas. As a researcher, it was vital not to pay for information, as the practice can become quite tiring and expensive in the long run. I never paid anyone, child or adult, for information. In the case of extended interviews, if the respondents were forced to remove themselves from work in order to work with me, I almost always paid for a meal for both of us. This was a means of compensating the informants for their time without actually buying information.

The ethics of writing about those deemed the underclass is itself a complicated matter, and it only gets more complicated when the subject is the children of the poor (see Bourgois 1996 for an excellent description of this dilemma). My work makes a point, namely, that child street laborers use hard work to gain skills and income that provide for them and their kin in the present and the future. I focus on how children take what are thought to be marginal occupations in a dangerous environment and transform them into a means for survival and even prosperity. Such a picture of the lives of these children could lead to the conclusion that child street labor, or indeed all child labor, is a good thing. It is not, though most of the children I worked with would beg to differ.

Just because children can survive on the streets, earn a decent income, and likely develop skills that will allow them to continue to do so in the future *does not mean* that this is an ideal or even acceptable state of affairs. It is a testament to the children's intelligence, work ethic, and social skills that they can work to overcome the disadvantages of their birth, but while they can ameliorate their own and their families' immediate and (perhaps) future situation, they are in no way able to exercise their full potential. The streets of Guatemala are littered with adult street vendors who can provide for their families, yet have the intelligence and drive to have risen to far greater heights had they not been denied the opportunity to study full-time and been driven to work instead. I realize that some may fail to grasp this point and will conclude from my work that child street labor is acceptable, perhaps even beneficial. It is not. The fact that child street labor offers some children and their families greater income and perhaps a brighter future does not mean that much is not lost when a generation of the working poor is denied the chance for an education and driven to the streets instead.

Children are driven to street labor to survive because of the poverty in a nation that has a substandard and underfunded educational system and gross economic inequality. The Guatemalan government and society, while truly victimizing the children of the poor, is itself a victim of a global economic system that is characterized by gross inequality between the rich developed nations and the rest of the world, and that sees the developing world only as a market for its goods and a source of cheap, flexible labor and raw materials. Ironically enough, it is the developed world that calls for the poor nations to eliminate child labor while itself bolstering the cause of the free market that drives more children to work each day.

While I believe that the children with whom I worked were prospering from their time spent on the street, other children, namely, street children and children working in clearly exploitative and illegal industries such as drug selling and prostitution, were not. It is truly a tragedy that children live in this way, and the removal of children from these lifestyles should be a top priority for all concerned. Yet these children, while being part of the mass of poor children in Guatemala and throughout the world, are only a small part of all children working on the street. The children with whom I worked represent the vast majority of the world's poor, the hardworking nonpathological poor, about whom I believe too little is written. It is these children whose words and experiences are to be found throughout what follows, and my ethical desire is to represent their reality in as honest and complete a form as possible.

Photographs are the most common vehicle for our apprehension of what the lives of others are like, especially those whose situations we view as extreme or alien.[10] I had originally expected to take hundreds of photos of children while at work, dirty, or overburdened yet nevertheless with smiles or looks that belied their inner fortitude and resilience. The literature on child labor is replete with such photos, and I hoped to add to it. However, once I began to take out my camera, after months of getting to know the children and of working with them, I found that while they were excited to have their pictures taken, it was not in the context that I had perceived. I first showed my camera to a bunch of shoeshine boys who worked the most crowded thoroughfare in the city. I explained to them why I wanted to take the pictures, and told them that I would of course give them copies of the photos. Most of the boys consented immediately, but said that tomorrow would be a better day. As I did not want to pressure them, I readily agreed.

The next day, at about ten in the morning, I came strolling up and took out my camera. The boys then immediately took small mirrors out of their shine boxes and combs out of their back pockets. Over the next few minutes, they proceeded to groom themselves as if for a formal portrait. A few of the boys even changed their shirts on the street, taking a clean T-shirt out of a plastic bag, and all tucked their shirts in their pants. They then suggested that we walk to the nearby Parque Central, which had a fountain that would make a better backdrop for the photos. I ended up taking over two rolls of film that day, all of child street laborers. The photos were of individual children, pairs, and groups. Some of the boys smiled, but the majority kept stern looks on their faces, as if posing like criminals who appeared in the paper on a daily basis.[11] In lighter moments, they smiled, playfully fought with each other, and made the hand signals that are common among the Guatemalan youth street gangs. What I failed to get that day, or any day thereafter, were pictures of these children studiously at work, unaware of or ignoring my camera. The pictures presented in this book show children at work, but photographed in a way that did not compromise their wishes as to how they were depicted.

The reason I did not take any pictures of the children surreptitiously was because the children did not want their pictures taken while they were working. They wanted pictures of themselves hanging out with friends and family, playing soccer, or wearing their finest clothes. I then thought back to all the pictures I had of my wife and myself, and in all of them we were doing similar things. I of course could have taken all the pictures I wanted of these child street laborers and others, as they were constantly in public plying their trades, and a little misdirection and a zoom lens could transform a seeming picture of a monument or hotel into a snapshot of a child street worker, but once I got to know these children, to have taken their pictures without their consent would have been tantamount to exploitation. The exploitation of child street laborers comes easily when one does not know them, or when one offers them compensation in the form of a few dollars for their time. My true ethical consideration throughout my research was to honestly represent the lives of the children I worked with, to listen to what they had to say, and to observe how they really worked and interacted with those around them. I believe that this is the correct and ethical way to present their reality and is worth more than any picture could provide. Nevertheless, to give a face to some of the children I worked with, I do include some of the photos I took that day in the Parque Central and other similar days, pictures that I know reflect how my friends wish to be pictured.

Pictures also have served as a means of confusing if not outright misrepresenting the lives of child street laborers. Of course, the camera can lie, and photographers may not be aware of the uses that their employers will dedicate their pictures to, but the image presented in Figure 1.1

FIGURE 1.1. *Child working at a street shoeshining stand in Ecuador (UNICEF/ICEF 8917/B. P. Wolff)*

stands out in my mind as a photograph that communicates a great deal, little of which has to do with the lived reality of its subject. While I doubt that the authors of the books that utilize the photo intended to misrepresent their subjects, and likely believed that the photo provided visual representation for their well-meaning objectives, by misrepresenting the truth, the photo robs children of their agency as individuals performing meaningful valuable labor.

Figure 1.1 shows a picture from the book *Combating Child Labour*, an edited volume published in 1988 by the International Labour Organization that details the plight of child laborers in different industries in countries throughout the developing world (Bequele and Boyden 1988). The picture is presented with a caption that states "Child working at a street shoe-shining stand in Ecuador," and also credits the photographer and the organization that provided the photo. Despite the ambiguity of the caption (is the child the shoeshiner and therefore the child laborer, or is she merely working there performing some other task?), the image presented does not equivocate. Of the six chapters in the book that discuss specific types of child labor in specific countries, neither Ecuador nor street labor is specifically addressed, yet the photo appears in the book as a means of accompanying the text. It is an excellent and provocative photo, showing a very young girl with a shock of hair and large eyes looking meekly up at the camera while supporting herself by grabbing onto the shoeshine bench, shoe polish at her side. On the edge of a frame is a cropped image of an unidentified seated adult, presumably a customer. One image and a few words convey to the reader the grave injustice of child labor. I was so struck by the photo when I first saw it that I posted it on the wall of my office as a means of inspiration during the grant-writing stage of my research.

This photo was also reprinted in the book *Child Labor* by ex-UNICEF and Oxfam Education specialist Alec Fyfe (1989). The caption in this book reads only "Girl shoe-shining, Ecuador" and credits UNICEF as the source. The ambiguity concerning what job the girl is performing is resolved, and as shoeshiners are directly compensated for their labor by their customers, we know that the girl is a child laborer and not a child worker merely helping out a family member. In this photo, only the child and the shoeshine bench are visible; the older adult has been edited out of the picture.

Based on my experience, both versions of this photo are misleading, and the second borders on deliberate misrepresentation.[12] In my two years of research in Guatemala, I never saw a girl or a woman shining shoes on the street. While this may be more common in Ecuador, it is rarely reported in the literature on the topic, and I believe it to be anomalous, as shoeshining in Latin America is a male-dominated street occupation. Second, it is also rare that a child as young as the girl pictured, regardless of sex, would be engaged in this task, as it demands a good deal of strength and dexterity that a child of her age would not be likely to possess. If a child her age were to be engaged in child labor, she would be far more likely to be selling newspapers near a family member or engaged in a less physically demanding task. Third, as anyone who has seen a street shoeshiner is likely to observe, the hands and forearms of anyone performing this job, child or adult, are covered with shoe polish even after one or two shines, and the girl in the photo shows no evidence of having shined shoes that day. She looks quite clean, especially considering the grime that surrounds her. Finally, as anyone who knows the intricacies of shoeshining can attest, the purported shoeshine girl is sitting on the customer's side of the shoeshine bench! The sloping footrest that she holds is meant to be facing the shiner so that the toe of the customer is elevated to allow for easier access to the shoe. Based on this photo, it is far more likely that the adult whose image is cropped in the first photo and deliberately eliminated in the second is the shoeshiner, and the young girl, though sitting near him, is either a child street worker engaged in some other task, or simply a child accompanying an adult to work. This photo, reprinted here in its first version and many more times in similar volumes as a definitive image of the injustice of child labor, does *not* picture a child laborer!

THE ORGANIZATION OF THE BOOK

In Chapter 2, I return to Rey and present a more complete description of his life and his place of business, the Eighteenth Street area of Zone 1 in Guatemala City. Zone 1 is the traditional downtown of Guatemala City and historically has always been the major site for street vending in the capital. It still retains this distinction and therefore was my primary field site. I also introduce Velásquez, a child street laborer with whom I worked in my other field site, the Trébol area of Zone 11 of the capital, and provide a current description of this neighborhood as well as a history of street work in the area. My description of Velásquez's life and labor provides a contrast to much of the information presented concerning Rey, as they work very different jobs and have very different living arrangements. Where the two boys are similar is that both of them are vital participants in their families' struggle to survive and are loved and respected by their parents and kin. They are also both representative of child street laborers in general, especially with regard to their occupations, family household arrangements, income levels, and demographic characteristics.

In Chapter 2, I also place Rey, Velásquez, and other children like them in the context of the available academic research on all child labor within anthropology and other disciplines. My aim is to describe where child street labor fits into our current knowledge about child labor and its historical evolution. I also focus on the anthropological literature concerning the roles of child labor and child play as forms of cultural learning or socialization for life in peasant farming or hunting-and-gathering societies, and explore how urban child street labor fits similar patterns among groups that have become enmeshed in the current international capitalist economy.

Chapters 3 through 5 represent the primary ethnographic focus of my research, namely the economics of child street labor. In Chapter 3, my emphasis is the income earned by child street laborers. I begin by providing a list of the occupations that the children are engaged in, as well as demographic data concerning the age, sex, ethnicity, birthplace, family life, and place of residence of the children with whom I worked. Based on these data, I develop my own typology of child street laborers and introduce descriptions of individual children whom I find to be representative of certain categories. Of primary importance is the income that the children bring in—which is much more substantial than other research and popular opinion would suggest—and what they do with their money. The notion that children contribute to their own and their families' survival is not a new one, yet it is the extent of that contribution that my research documents for the first time.

In Chapter 4, I examine the roles that the children play in the economies of their households. Child street laborers live in a variety of domestic arrangements, but most are integral contributors to the households of their parents. Drawing on the work of David Cheal (1989) and Winnie Lem (2002) on household regimes of control, my research shows how, through income derived from street labor, children are able to be both dutiful members of their households' traditional moral economy as well as individual agents pursuing their own present and future interests.

The parents of child street laborers are rarely present in the literature on the topic because they, too, are seen as helpless victims of poverty, and it is generally assumed that poverty, if not family pathology, forces them to allow their children to labor on the city streets. My research indicates that the opposite is true. The majority of the children I worked with came from two-parent homes, and most parents themselves had been child laborers and felt that child labor has many benefits aside from the purely economic ones. This was especially pronounced among the Maya parents of kids I worked with, who strongly believed that work was essential to maintaining family cohesion and discipline, contrasting their hardworking and dutiful children with the gang-affiliated and drug-addicted children with whom they share the streets. And though some of the children I worked with were separated from their parents due to family discord or a combination of neglect and abuse, the vast majority were involved in loving relationships with their parents and siblings. Each child has a large group of friends where he works, and they enjoy an active social life that is an often-overlooked benefit of street labor. From what I learned about child street laborers through the course of my research, one of the most objectionable beliefs about them is that prolonged experiences working on the street alienate children from their families and their peer groups, transforming them into anomie-filled delinquents.

In Chapter 5, I depict the social nature of economic success for child street labor. Unlike adults, children must capitalize on their social skills to make street labor both safe and productive. Success at work for children also has far more to do with their ability to project a satisfactory identity[13] to their clients than with the quality of the goods and services they offer. Following the seminal work of the ethnographically oriented sociologist Erving Goffman (1959, 1967, 1971), I employ a dramaturgical model of social interaction to analyze the behavior of child street laborers and those with whom they interact. In his description of his dramaturgical model, Goffman emphasized the ways in which individuals act to foster impressions of themselves that allow them to get what they desire from social interactions, be it social approval or something more concrete. My research indicates that street children have multiple social identities that they utilize in front of different audiences so as to survive and prosper on the streets. In this chapter, I document these multiple identities and illustrate how the situational use of each is directly tied to the needs of the specific child and the particular resource that the other individual (be it another street child, a potential shoeshine customer, or a street educator from an international organization) has to offer. I also present the results of time-allocation studies that I performed on selected children that show how hard the children work and how relatively flexible their schedules are—one of the primary advantages of street labor. The dangers inherent in child street labor are also included here, along with the actions the children and their families take to minimize them. The streets of Guatemala are a profitable place for children to work, and children work very hard to make them that way.

Chapter 6 details the reality of public education in Guatemala, offered by national and international governments as the antidote to child labor. Through the course of my study, I had the opportunity to do research in a public elementary school in Guatemala City, located in the immediate environs of my Zone 1 field site. There I observed numerous classes and spoke with students, teachers, and the school principal about their views on the public school system. I also spoke with hundreds of parents of child street laborers concerning their opinions of the public educational system, its strengths and its limitations. The most telling thing I learned was that while almost all of the subjects interviewed believed that schooling was an essential part of childhood and key to rising out of poverty, because of the poor quality of the education students received and the difficulties of attending school on a daily basis, very few thought that the prospects for completing even the first level of secondary school were possible for most children. I also performed my own study of the actual costs of sending a child to school, based on the cost of the mandatory uniforms, utensils, and other items requiring outlays of cash, such as transportation and supplemental activities. When factored in with the hours of work that children lose while attending school, the cost of "free" public schooling makes education beyond the reach of most poor Guatemalans, those whom the public schools are most intended to serve.

I conclude in Chapter 7 by addressing three related issues: what skills and knowledge child street laborers gain from their time spent on the streets, how they hope to utilize these skills as adults, and how this relates to the ultimate structural causes of child labor. My research has illustrated the agency that poor children and their families have in abandoning school; choosing street work; and making street labor a safe, nonexploitative, and ultimately productive job that provides vital income for immediate survival as well as future opportunities. Yet it is also important to view child street labor as a response to larger political-economic structural conditions that poor children and their families have little control over. The most local of family decisions are responses to the most global of phenomena. From the age of exploration onward, the countries of the South have suffered at the hands of the countries of the North. In our current age of the global economy, the evenhanded market is deemed to be the ideal control mechanism for economic growth for all, yet the poor only seem to grow in numbers while the same nations, and the multinational firms whose headquarters they house, are the beneficiaries. As this market-based philosophy continues to dominate the world stage, child labor will grow, not recede, in the future, and the streets of cities like Guatemala will be filled with more children like Rey. Ultimately, what is objectionable about child street labor is the dire poverty that forces children to work, and not the responses that the children and their families make to this poverty.

Two

STREET WORK IN
EL GUARDA AND 18 CALLE

RETURN TO REY

Rey begins his day at five in the morning, when he wakes up; after a quick wash, he gets himself dressed and heads off to work. If the morning is not too cold, or if he wants to save a little money, he walks the three miles from the little apartment he shares with his older brother in Zone 9 to where he works in Zone 1. If he's tired or in a hurry, he catches one of the many buses that run directly to where he works, paying either seventy-five centavos for a gypsy minibus or one quetzal twenty-five centavos for a red municipal bus, or *gusano* (worm). Either way, he should arrive under the overpass by six o'clock sharp to help Don Fernando retrieve the two carts that make up his kiosk from the nearby parking lot where he pays to have it stored. While Rey could set up his shoeshine operation in a manner of seconds, since he works for Don Fernando, he should be there at the start of the day to help with the heavy work of moving and setting up the kiosk.

Once the kiosk is assembled and in place, stocking it is relatively quick work, as the candy, gum, and cigarettes stay in the cart all the time. Should these items need to be replenished, Don Fernando will send Rey to one of the many nearby *distribuidores,* or wholesale shops, to purchase bags of candy and gum or cartons of cigarettes. While Rey and Don Fernando are setting up, the deliveries begin, with local newspaper company representatives dropping off the hundred or so copies of the four Guatemala City newspapers Don Fernando stocks. A truck from one of the local soda companies will also pull up to the kiosk and deliver to Don Fernando his daily quota of sodas, bottled water, and orange juice to be stored in his Coleman coolers. Once all this is in place, usually by 6:30, the kiosk is fully stocked and Don Fernando and Rey are ready to begin catering to their customers.

From 6:30 until about 8:30, the time of the morning "rush hour," Rey will have his hands full with both shoeshine customers on their way to work and the many other individuals purchasing a paper or a soda. Newspaper sales are almost exclusively the responsibility of Rey, as the papers lie in stacks on the pavement next to his shoeshine chair. Customers will either reach down for themselves, pick up the paper, and hand their money to Rey, or else just blurt out "La Prensa," "El Día," or "Diario" and wait for him to retrieve the paper and hand it to them in exchange for their payment. Unless he is engaged in doing a shine, Rey will immediately place the money for the paper in Don Fernando's hands.

Sales of sodas and other beverages can be a bit more time consuming for Rey, especially if Don Fernando's daughter, Roxana, is not around to handle the bulk of the work. Don Fernando keeps his drinks in a chest full of ice left open to entice the passersby. Orange juice, fruit drinks, and water are easy sales because they all come in either plastic bottles or plastic bags and therefore require Rey or Roxana merely to hand the customer his or her drink and a straw and collect the money. Sodas, on the other hand, come only in glass bottles or cans. Cans of soda, which at the time of my research cost about three quetzales (about forty-five U.S. cents at the time), were out of the price range of most of Don Fernando's clientele. Most customers would instead opt for a twelve-ounce bottle of the same soda for about half the price. Customers could choose to drink the bottle of soda under the overpass and return the bottle to Don Fernando, but most preferred to have their sodas poured into plastic sandwich bags and take the drink with them, mindful to never set the bag down. The process of uncapping the bottle, pouring it into the bag, and serving it to the customer was not difficult for Rey or Roxana, but it nevertheless required a bit more time and effort.

Rey receives no cash payment from Don Fernando for his help setting up in the mornings or for his aid in the sale of newspapers and sodas, but he does receive a free breakfast and lunch in exchange for his work. Even though this saves Rey eight to ten quetzales a day, many would insist that Rey is being exploited by Don Fernando. If these two meals were truly all that Rey received for his help, such a charge might have validity. But what Rey really receives for his efforts is the right to work under Don Fernando's overpass, which is a very worthwhile exchange.

Don Fernando pays for a municipal street vendor's license for the right to sell his sodas and candy under the overpass, though his kiosk does not occupy the full extent of the covered area. Nevertheless, it is a rule of the street economy that the area, measuring perhaps twenty feet by fifteen feet, is his exclusive domain. Don Fernando's claim to exclusive use of this area is based on his long-standing occupancy of the area and the fact that the man from whom Don Fernando himself purchased the business had occupied it exclusively for years as well. Should others seek to encroach on Don Fernando's area, he himself would be responsible for repelling this invasion, but he would certainly muster all his contacts in the area, from the parking lot attendant he pays to keep his kiosk overnight, to the beat cops who receive free cigarettes and small "loans" from Don Fernando in exchange for their protection and their help in maintaining Don Fernando's exclusive use of the area underneath the overpass.

Don Fernando's *puesto,* which is under a pedestrian walkway that leads from one side of 6a. Avenida to the other, is an ideal spot for street vending and shoeshining. During the rainy season, it is the only area for blocks where one can wait to catch a bus from Zone 1 to points north without getting drenched. During the dry season, it has the similar benefit of keeping pedestrians out of the hot sun. It is a perfect place to while away a few minutes with a newspaper, a smoke, or a shoeshine. The pedestrian traffic along the sidewalk is one of the heaviest in the city, as the *puesto* sits opposite the large municipal office plaza of Zone 4 where birth records are registered, water bills are paid, and a variety of other vital municipal service offices are located. The kiosk is also steps away from a large indoor shopping mall—the first all-indoor structure of its kind in Guatemala City—that caters to the many municipal employees who work nearby.

Such an ideal location enables Don Fernando to be a very successful vendor, and it also helps Rey be a very successful shoeshine boy. Rey has a steady place of work, and this allows him to build up a regular clientele who use him exclusively when they need a shine and also when they are in need of more extensive services, such as the stitching of a loose seam or the dyeing of a complete pair of shoes, both of which Rey performs at his home and necessitates that the customer leave his or her shoes with him for a day or two. Because Rey is always there, and because it is known that he works for Don Fernando, who is a neighborhood fixture, people can be confident that he will return their goods. They can save a few quetzales by patronizing a street laborer rather than someone with a formal shop or market stall.

While we may note that Rey earns one quetzal for a good shine, it may not occur to us that over the course of a month the income he makes from his job is more than twice the Guatemalan minimum wage for an urban worker (Q520 or about US$75 per month during the time of my research[1]), and that the majority of his fellow Guatemalans would be envious of his wages, if not necessarily of the way he goes about earning them. As I detail later, a variety of other factors make Rey such a successful child street laborer, but the cornerstone to his success is the location where he works: at a major pedestrian point in the heart of the busiest section of the entire country of Guatemala, namely the 18 Calle area of Zone 1 of Guatemala City.

GUATEMALA AND ITS CAPITAL

As a citizen of Guatemala, or *chapín* in the local slang, Rey is a member of one of the poorest nations in the Western Hemisphere, a small country that has suffered the consequences of protracted civil conflict, corruption, natural disasters, and ownership of much of its economic infrastructure in the hands of a few elite families or foreign-owned corporations. Recent estimates put per capita annual income at $2,640 (World Bank 2007), with inflation one and a half times greater than the gross domestic product (GDP) growth rate (ibid.), a vast improvement over the situation in the late 1980s and early 1990s, when the annual average growth rate of inflation was roughly ten times greater than the annual average growth rate of GDP (IADB 1990). The top 40 percent of Guatemalans account for more than 80 percent of the nation's total income, while the rest of the nation's populace lives in poverty (IADB 1990). This situation is especially dire for the bottom quintile of the population, which receives only 2 percent of the total national income (World Bank 1999).

It is no coincidence that the vast majority of this bottom quintile in income are members of the numerically dominant yet politically and economically oppressed Maya Indian population, who have endured centuries of exploitation by the Ladino elite. Whereas the Maya were almost exclusively rural agriculturists who accounted for only 6–7 percent of the total urban population from 1880 to 1973 (Gellert 1995, 96), over the last quarter of the twentieth century they nearly tripled their representation in the municipal area to around 20 percent (CITGUA 1991).

Growth in the Maya population of the capital has paralleled the massive overall growth in the city itself. Between the years 1973 and 1987, the population of Guatemala City nearly doubled, going from 890,000 to 1,638,000 (CITGUA 1991), and at the time of my research the figure was close to 2,500,000 for the entire metropolitan area. This dramatic growth was and is the result of rural-to-urban migration, itself a product of in-equitable distribution of arable land and a thirty-year civil war. Life in the villages and small towns became either too dangerous or economi-cally impossible, and the bright lights of the city beckoned. Guatemala is considered a unique case of urbanization in the region because the percentage of its population living in urban areas is so low (39.3 percent as of 1998, compared to an average of over 60 percent in the hemisphere, according to the World Bank [1999]), but as Carol Smith (1985) has pointed out, this is offset by the fact that almost all of Guatemala's urban population resides in one overdeveloped city, Guatemala City. Thus al-most all of the child street laborers in Guatemala live in Guatemala City, belong to the Maya ethnic group, and are recent migrants themselves or the children of first-generation immigrants [2] (Villarreal and Peralta Chapetón 1997). Based on my sample of child street laborers, most begin their street careers in the Zone 1 downtown area, the epicenter of street work in Guatemala City.

The History of Street Vending in Zone 1

If Guatemala City is the social, economic, political, and cultural heart of the nation of Guatemala, then the area known as Zone 1 is the heart of Guatemala City.[3] Historically, it was home to the first area of public construction and housing in what became the fourth and final capital of the Spanish-controlled colonial kingdom of Guatemala (Gel-lert 1995). It is home to the Plaza Mayor, or Central Plaza, which is always the central spatial construction in any prominent Spanish colonial town and which may in fact have pre-Columbian antecedents in the area (see Low 2000). From the Guatemalan President's House to the Congress, the National Cathedral, and the Central Post Office, most of the major metropolitan and national civic and religious structures that dominate the nation are found in this area. But Zone 1 is not just the historic or bureaucratic center of the city; it is also the popular center of the city, and as the popular center, it has been and continues to be the center of street work.

The history of street work in Zone 1 dates back to the earliest occu-pation of the city. The Plaza Mayor, constructed immediately after the founding of the new capital in 1775, was the first public space available to the inhabitants of the new capital, and street vendors, adults, and chil-dren alike were ubiquitous in the plaza, offering the necessary goods for daily life for the rich and poor inhabitants of the area; "the products of daily life were provided by a small trading system in the hands of street vendors and peddlers" (Langenberger, cited in Porres Castejón 1995, 22). Once the Portal de Comercio, consisting of fifteen rented storefronts all bordering the Plaza Mayor, was established in front of the house of Juan Fermín Aycimena y Irigoyen on the southern side of the Plaza, formal retailing joined the informal public vending in the area and cemented the reputation of the Plaza Mayor as a commercial hub of the new capital (Gellert 1995).

This arrangement was the predominant means for the residents of the capital, virtually all of whom lived in what is now Zone 1 and who numbered only about 35,000 during the middle of the nineteenth century, to acquire the goods they needed. In 1871, the Mercado Central was inaugurated as another formal market area to complement the shops of the Portal and the street vendors of the Plaza itself. The municipal authorities constructed the market in hopes of removing the many informal vendors from the Plaza; however, both areas were soon occupied by vendors (Porres Castejón 1995, 22). As the city grew, commerce itself spread southward away from the Plaza Mayor and toward 18 Calle, the southern boundary of the city at this time. This development was brought on by the construction of offices and warehouses in the 18 Calle area to link the capital with the new Pacific port of San José in the 1870s and the national railroad in the 1880s (ibid., 23). As this part of the city grew in importance as a hub for both people and merchandise, two more markets were built around 18 Calle at the turn of the century to accommodate the growing populace, and from the overflow of these markets began the tradition of street vending along 18 Calle.

As Guatemala as a nation developed in the early decades of the twentieth century, so did its capital. The city began to expand in size and population, growing from 55,000 inhabitants in 1880 to double that number by the conclusion of the First World War. The Zone 1 area itself was transformed, since the area could no longer house the new migrants *and* serve as a commercial center. The homes of the city's elite along the avenues connecting the two primary commercial centers of 18 Calle and the Plaza Mayor were rapidly transformed into retail stores catering to the upper classes. A series of earthquakes in 1917–1918 also leveled many of the older homes in the city center and led to the construction of municipal buildings such as the Central Post Office and more retail stores to meet the needs of the expanding city. Zone 1 had lost much of its residential character and had become a commerce center catering to all classes of Guatemalan society.

At the same time, new lands to the south of 18 Calle were slowly expropriated from their indigenous Maya inhabitants and developed to house both the elites who vacated the downtown area and the many poorer individuals who worked for them. The growth of the city was still a relatively slow process during the interwar period, and migration to the capital city would only begin en masse with the fall of the dictatorial regime of Jorge Ubico in 1944. Ubico's repressive mandatory work laws tied poor peasants to their rural homes in order to guarantee a cheap exploitable agricultural labor force for national and international plantations. With the fall of Ubico, Guatemalans began migrating in huge numbers to the capital to work. By 1950, the population of the capital city had grown to nearly 300,000, and while the Zone 1 area was still the undisputed center of the city, the massive development of the surrounding areas led to the commercialization of other parts of the city. The deluxe retailers of Zone 1 soon followed their clientele out of the downtown area and into the surrounding neighborhoods.

In the twenty years after the fall of Ubico, migration to the capital increased the city's population another 120 percent, so that by 1964 the city counted nearly 600,000 inhabitants, representing an annual growth rate of more than 7 percent (Gellert 1995). During this period of unparalleled growth, the construction of markets throughout the capital city met the majority of the needs of these new urbanites, and street vending maintained its strength only in the 18 Calle area of Zone 1. Two major events followed that would transform the nation of Guatemala and radically alter patterns of migration to the capital city and the nature of street labor and the entire informal sector in Guatemala City. These events were the earthquake of 1976 and the Guatemalan Civil War.

The massive earthquake that razed many parts of Guatemala City on February 4, 1976, not only devastated the capital and the surrounding region, it also marked the entry of an inflationary cycle that further debilitated the nation's economy (Porres Castejón 1995, 16). The earthquake left tens of thousands of Guatemalans homeless throughout the countryside and the capital. Many of those from the countryside left for the capital and landed in the crowded Zone 1 area in search of basic provisions. There they encountered Guatemala City residents who had experienced similar destruction; all were in dire need of food, clothing, and temporary shelter. The Mercado Central, constructed in 1871 only one block from the Parque Central, was also leveled during the earthquake, forcing the vendors to establish their *puestos* on the streets and avenues extending from the Parque Central to 18 Calle (ibid., 41). Natural disaster, economic crisis, and massive migration to the capital city combined to make street vending a necessary and principal means for the populace to acquire the goods needed for survival, which in turn created a way for those displaced by the earthquake, from either their market vending locations in the city or their homes and livelihoods in *el campo,* to earn their bread. The combined events also forced the municipal governments, which had traditionally been hostile to street vending, to allow the practice to continue and develop.

The final factor that altered the size and nature of street work in Guatemala City was Guatemala's notorious thirty-year civil war. The war, begun in the late 1960s, took an especially bloody turn in the early to mid-1980s as the government waged a brutal campaign against those suspected of being in league with the leftist guerrilla movements. This campaign consisted of the seemingly random massacre of tens of thousands of Maya agriculturists living in the Western Highlands of the country and made economic survival a virtual impossibility for those fortunate enough to escape the bloodshed with their lives (for full treatment of the issue, see Carmack 1988; CEH 1999; REMHI 1999). Many of the victims fled into Mexico, but many also sought refuge in the capital city (see AVANCSO 1991; Bastos and Camus 1995; Camus 2002; Jonas 2000). Although the capital was rife with political repression and the assassination of suspected leftists, it was nevertheless relatively peaceful compared to the areas from which the migrants had come. The Guatemalan Army was much more inclined to slaughter civilians in the Maya-dominated Western Highlands as opposed to the Ladino capital city. Left homeless and with only the few possessions they carried, many of these displaced persons began to work and live on the streets of the capital. As most were familiar with the street markets in the city as places to buy or sell goods, they often set up quarters and businesses in and around the 18 Calle area. It was during this time that both the number of street vendors in the 18 Calle area expanded and the government's efforts to curb this phenomenon were largely put to rest.

The 18 Calle Area of My Research

Virtually every local bus and most interurban ones stop somewhere along 18 Calle, and disembarking passengers are immediately greeted by a symphony of sights, sounds, and smells that assault the five senses. *Salchicha* vendors grill their hot dogs on small braziers as the smell wafts through the streets. Shoeshine boys tug at pant and skirt hems and shout out "Lustre, jefe, lustre un quetzal" (Shine, boss, shine for one quetzal). Salsa, merengue, and lunchtime marimba music blasts from speakers lying out on sidewalk tarpaulins or hanging on the posts of kiosks selling bootleg cassettes and compact discs. Walking vendors carrying baseball hats with the logos and colors of virtually all North American baseball, basketball, and football teams shout simply "Una choca, una choca," the street and Indian slang for twenty-five centavos, which in this case actually indicates 25 quetzales per hat. Young men and boys block traffic and gesture right or left as they chant "Dale, dale," telling their customers to keep giving it gas as they usher them into the few available parking spots in the area. Finally, smog-belching buses, themselves painted in a myriad of eye-catching colors, drive up and down the avenues honking their horns to attract customers. The 18 Calle area was my primary field site, and it is the undisputed center of street work in Guatemala City. As shown in Map 2.1, I limited my research area to where concentrations of street labor and vending were the highest. Municipal markets, governmental offices, nonstreet cafés and retail stores, bus and taxi depots, and even a small public park all contributed to making this area the bustling backdrop for the street work that was my focus. It is these particular features of the 18 Calle area that I highlight next.

The Intersection of Sexta Avenida and 18 Calle

The center point of the 18 Calle area is located at the intersection of 18 Calle and Sexta Avenida (Map 2.2). The Mercado Sur 2 (MS 2 on map), an enclosed market that sells everything from food products to clothing, household appliances, tools, and religious paraphernalia, occupies virtually the entire southwest quadrant of the intersection. The Mercado is home to over five hundred formal vendors who rent *puestos* either inside the market or fronting the street on a daily or monthly basis. The Mercado also is home to a public elementary school, the Escuela Sur 2, that caters largely to the children of the vendors. Street workers patrol all the borders of the market, especially the 6a. Avenida side, which has by far the most pedestrian traffic.

The small horizontal strip of land between the southern border of the pedestrian alleyway and 18 Calle contains various small shops, warehouses, and apartments on the market side; small stores that sell shoes, luggage, and sporting goods border the streets. The only sizable formal enterprises in this quadrant are a Chinese restaurant, a wholesale and retail sporting goods distributor, and a Burger King (BK), all of which are

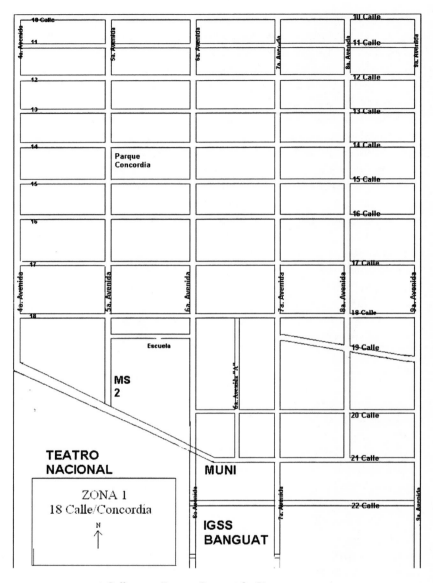

MAP 2.1.   *18 Calle area, Zone 1, Guatemala City*

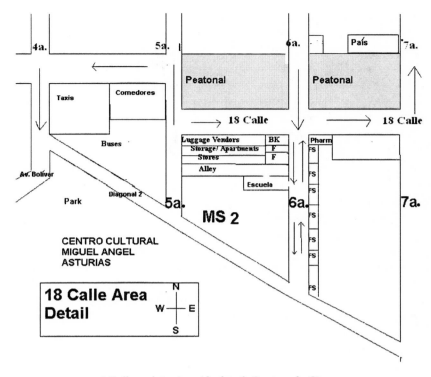

MAP 2.2. *18 Calle and 6a. Avenida detail, Guatemala City*

located on the corner of 18 Calle and 6a. Avenida. This corner is home to only a few street workers, who occupy perhaps the most prized location in the city. A newspaper vendor regularly carries all six of the daily papers available in Guatemala City. His *puesto,* usually constructed of milk cartons and odd planks of wood to allow for easy assembly and disassembly, is often manned by two workers to meet the customers' needs. In a small ring in front of Burger King are shoeshine boys, all of whom are migrants from Huehuetenango and very particular about those they will share their space with. Two other Huehuetecos operate portable *puestos* where they sell gum, candy, cigarettes, and soft drinks. The only other vendors working the corner are a few older women selling prepared sandwiches and sweets, as well as walking vendors who are permitted to work the corner as long as they do not stay too long. The rest of 18 Calle is packed with street vendors.

The other quadrants of the intersection are dominated by cafés and stores. Here one can find many of the most popular names in Guatemalan retailing: the Pais supermarket, a very popular chain of Italian food restaurants known as Macaroni, the ubiquitous fried chicken fast-food store Pollo Campero, as well as a multitude of smaller operations, especially shoe stores. What makes this area so unique is the Mercado Peatonal, or "Pedestrian Market," that occupies a large part of what was once 18 Calle. The Peatonal consists of three different roofed spaces located in what were once vehicular traffic lanes of 18 Calle, each of which provides shelter for three rows of vendors and occupies a one-block area. Vendors on the northern side of the three buildings face onto the traffic lanes of 18 Calle, whereas those on the southern side virtually front upon the shops and restaurants of 18 Calle with only a small sidewalk separating them.

The majority of the vendors of the Mercado Peatonal sell the same goods as their street-vending peers in the area, namely clothing and shoes. But these vendors differ from true street vendors; their *puestos* are relatively fixed, and many of them pay rent to the municipality for the privilege of vending in a specific kiosk in the Peatonal. Most vendors of the Peatonal maintain a somewhat difficult relationship with the municipality because they combine their authorized vending of clothing with the offering of other nonauthorized specialties such as illegal street telephones and pirated cassette tapes and compact discs. Many Peatonal vendors, especially those who sell contraband, move from one *puesto* to another on a daily basis and never actually pay any rent at all. This practice is especially suited to the Peatonal because although the area is considered a formal market by the municipality, vendors are not permitted to store their merchandise overnight in the market and therefore must store their goods elsewhere and set up their stalls anew each day. Many walking sellers also make the Peatonal their de facto home, occupying the periphery of the buildings that border the streets so as to maintain their status as walking vendors yet have the advantage of occupying a relatively fixed business location where they can sell their wares.

The Parque Concordia

The northernmost point of my research in the 18 Calle area was 14 Calle between 5a. and 6a. Avenidas, the border of Parque Enrique Gómez Carrillo, better known as the Parque Concordia. The Concordia, a public park that occupies only one small block in the downtown area, has been synonymous with street life in the capital since its inception. It was constructed as a public plaza in 1825 and after having been briefly converted to a private cemetery for the Franciscan order at the turn of the century, was rebuilt following the earthquakes of 1917–1918 as a green area amid the development of the downtown area (López Ovando 2000, 1). During the pre-WWII era, the park served as a relatively peaceful gathering place for urbanites in the downtown area and was host to public concerts on Sunday afternoons (Góngora 1998, 5).

As the Zone 1 area grew, the Concordia soon became a capital for street vending. Beginning in the 1960s, *comedores* (food stalls) and shoeshine and newspaper boys began to occupy the benches and paths of the park. At the beginning of my research, the park was still popular among the aforementioned street workers but also became known as a center for street children and hustlers, leading one popular guide book for adventuresome tourists to comment: "Sizzling comedores dot the periphery of the grimy Parque Concordia . . . You can sit and watch the preachers, magicians, tin-pan musicians and fortune-tellers that make this park a happenin' spot. At night it becomes even seedier than during the day, and you should avoid it" (Berkeley Guides 1996, 111).

The Concordia's reputation as a capital for vice led the municipal government to "remodel" the park in March of 1998. A solid barrier of sheet metal was built to surround the area, and the parks, trees, sidewalks, benches, and monuments were uprooted to allow for the construction of an underground parking garage. The destruction of the park was part of the "Plan 2010" initiated by the municipal government of Mayor Álvaro Arzú (1986–1990). Enacted by the subsequent mayoral regimes of Óscar Berger (1991–2000) and Fritz García Gallont (2001–2004), the "remodeling" was justified as a means of reducing congestion in the area by providing more parking spaces (López Ovando 2000). Although parking and congestion are indeed dire problems in the area, virtually all the street vendors and other denizens of the park felt that the remodeling was done merely as a way to "cleanse" the area by removing the city's working poor and underclass from such a visible point in the downtown area.

The vendors of the Concordia were then allowed to relocate to the sidewalks immediately surrounding the park, namely along 14 Calle and 5a. and 6a. Avenidas. All these areas were already home to other vendors. With the closing of the Concordia, the sidewalks became wall-to-wall vendors. Other vendors and street workers, particularly food sellers, shoeshine boys, and street entertainers, abandoned the area because of lack of suitable space for their particular trades and the loss of the audience that the many benches of the Concordia once provided. The municipality has promised to aid the vendors in reestablishing their businesses again in the Concordia once the garage has been completed and the street-level area again becomes a public park, but most vendors mention that they have little faith in these promises (Arellano 1998, 16). Mayor García Gallont even offered the vendors the first level of the parking garage as a space for a pedestrian market similar to the Mercado Peatonal, but this promise was soon discovered to be either an oversight or a lie on the part of the mayor, as the municipality had guaranteed the company building the parking garage a fifty-year contract in exchange for their assistance with the construction (López Ovando 2000).

The homeless street children who once called the park home were also promised a new place to sleep as well as vocational training. With the exception of the construction of a tentlike structure on the grounds of a municipal fire station, the promises were never realized (González Díaz 1998). Some of the street children have relocated to other small public parks and abandoned buildings in the area, but many have followed the street vendors and child street laborers to the sidewalks surrounding the park, a focal point for my research.

La Sexta and La Quinta

The vendors of the Concordia were not pleased to be forced off what they viewed as their territory and onto the already crowded avenues of the Zone 1 area. While 14 Calle was itself only sparsely populated by vendors before the razing of the Concordia, both 5a. and 6a. Avenidas had long been known as key spots for street work. The origins of street vending on each of these avenues can be traced back to the mid-1970s, specifically to the earthquake of 1976, which destroyed the hundred-year-old Mercado Central located on 7a. Avenida behind the Metropolitan Cathedral. The destruction of the market forced many vendors to seek new locations for their businesses. In the general chaos that reigned after this disaster, the old vendors of the Mercado Central set up their stalls along 5a. Avenida from 18 Calle down to 14 Calle. The 5a. Avenida of that era was known for its multitude of retail shops and cafés that catered to the popular classes, offering everything from clothing to books, hardware, and appliances, and vendors of like products from the destroyed Mercado Central set up shop on La Quinta with little initial resistance from the municipality (Porres Castejón 1995, 41). Through the subsequent years, various municipal governments would attempt to remove the vendors from their new location, but the vendors' intransigence and effective political mobilization resisted every onslaught, and the vendors of

La Quinta eventually earned their right to occupy and sell on 5a. Avenida when they were issued permits and required to pay rent to the municipality during the rule of Mayor José Ángel Lee Duarte (1982–1986; ibid., 45).

Unlike 5a. Avenida, 6a. Avenida was not initially viewed by street vendors as an ideal thoroughfare for vending. While 5a. Avenida was largely known for popular-class retail shops, 6a. Avenida had long been known for its exclusive boutiques lining the blocks north of the Plaza Mayor and its cinemas and cafés that ran from 18 Calle to 13 Calle, just one block short of the Concordia (ibid., 44). Street vendors began to occupy only the part of 6a. Avenida that bordered 18 Calle in the 1960s, but they never ventured farther south. In the words of one longtime vendor, "We didn't think that La Sexta could be a place of business" (ibid., 45). Walking vendors, however, would regularly sell peanuts and candy to the movie patrons of the grand cinemas, and street *taquerías* (taco stands) and vendors of small gifts targeted the many youths who made the "Sexteo" a stroll where adolescents would flirt with one another (ibid., 45), but large-scale street vending did not begin there until after the earthquake. Earthquake damage to the stores and theaters of 6a. Avenida was more extensive than that suffered by the more modest stores of 5a. Avenida, and the buildings of 6a. Avenida never regained their former splendor. Popular-class retail stores and malls replaced the older elite-centered businesses, and as the popular classes took over La Sexta, street vendors followed in numbers even greater than along 5a. Avenida. At the time of my research, street vendors on 6a. Avenida were not only recognized by the municipality and granted usufruct rights in exchange for rent, but La Sexta itself, from 18 Calle to the Plaza Mayor, was closed to vehicular traffic during the key shopping times of the Christmas and Easter seasons.

Municipal Offices

In addition to the markets and shops, the presence of the many municipal and national government offices located in the 18 Calle area also make it an ideal location for street work. While 18 Calle and Quinta and Sexta Avenidas are the prime shopping districts for the popular classes of the city and nation, they are also home to many of the places where the populace must deal with urban and national authorities. At the corner of 6a. Avenida and 14 Calle is the headquarters of the municipal police. Any crime that occurs in the area is reported here. Parking fines as well as other pecuniary police matters are also handled in these offices, making it a busy location for foot traffic the whole day through. The block of 18 Calle and 5a. Avenida is the home of the Municipal Office of Public Records, where those wishing to document or amend a birth certificate or land title must wait in line for hours. Shoeshine boys, newspaper vendors, and prepared-food sellers all fight for a prime location on this block to cater to the many Guatemalans waiting for hours in line. Itinerant street typists set up their old manual typewriters on milk crates and offer to type up vital documents for those waiting in line.

The bulk of activity occurs in the Municipal Plaza that fronts Sexta Avenida above 21 Calle, forming the border between Zones 1 and 4. The Muni, as it is popularly called, is likely the most visited public office by residents of Guatemala City. It is there that *cédulas,* or identification cards, are issued, and by law all adult Guatemalans must be in possession of their *cédulas* at all times. The local water office is located in the basement, and it is there that people come and wait in hours-long lines to pay their water bills. Most of the main municipal offices are also located here, and the clientele needing to make an appointment with someone at the MUNI is not limited to poorer Guatemalans. The vast foot traffic that is generated here makes it an ideal spot for all types of street workers, from car parkers and washers to shoeshine boys, food vendors, and those selling umbrellas during the rainy season.

The Buses

As mentioned previously, 18 Calle has long been a center for public transport within Guatemala City as well as throughout the entire nation. The first railroad depot that linked the city center and the Port of San José was located on 18 Calle and is still there. Though the train system is no longer in service, the depot still exists and is known today as a popular hangout for homeless street children and gang members. Nowadays, buses are the primary means of transportation, and 18 Calle still reigns supreme as a point of departure and arrival. Virtually every urban bus that runs downtown has its biggest stop along 18 Calle, with stops along 18 Calle and 6a. Avenida being the most prominent ones. Most intercity buses carrying individuals and their goods from the rural areas to the capital city also stop somewhere along 18 Calle, with many routes originating in the immediate area. The most frequent of these buses link the capital city to the tourist area of Antigua Guatemala and the city of Chimaltenango, and arrive and depart every fifteen minutes from 5:30 AM until 8:00 PM from a parking lot located on 18 Calle between 4a. and 5a. Avenidas. This same parking lot is also home to a taxi depot where anywhere from ten to thirty taxis regularly congregate to find fares. The number of individuals coming and going in this city block is so great that over eighty street vendors hawk their goods here. In addition, a small concrete structure is home to twelve small food stalls, or *comedores*, catering to the travelers and the transportation workers.

Considered in isolation, each of the aforementioned features of the neighborhood, from the Parque Concordia to the municipal buildings and the bus depot, would make 18 Calle an area that would lend itself to the heavy pedestrian traffic vital for street work. Together, they combine to turn the streets of the area into a bustling marketplace and principal place of business for most citizens of the capital. Rey, from his small stool under the overpass on Sexta Avenida, is a prime beneficiary of the opportunity for street work in this part of the city. Although 18 Calle is the center of street work in Guatemala City, it is in no way the only popular location for street work in the capital. Opportunity for enterprising and hardworking children like Rey abounds in other areas, such as El Guarda, where a boy named Velásquez works.

VELÁSQUEZ'S STORY

Much like Rey, as a child street laborer, Velásquez must begin his day very early. He wakes up at around 4:30 in the morning every day, rain or shine. After a quick breakfast of beans and tortillas left over from the previous night, he washes his face and brushes his teeth. Velásquez is usually the first member of his household to leave the house in the morning, though he is occasionally accompanied by his older brother Juan or his mother. Unlike many of the other children and adults who work in the El Guarda neighborhood, Velásquez is not a resident of the capital, but lives outside the city in a small canton near the town of San Juan in the neighboring department of Sacatepéquez. He does not have the luxury of a brief walk or a mere ten-minute bus ride to work, as his commute to El Guarda usually takes him at least an hour by bus. So he tries to leave the house by 5:30 at the latest. Velásquez learned to catch the bus to El Guarda by himself at the age of ten, and just two short years later he is a seasoned commuter.

Velásquez's bus drops him off on the corner of the Calzada Roosevelt and Quinta Avenida in Zone 11. If he gets to El Guarda early, he walks through the relatively empty streets of the neighborhood and arrives at a spot midway between 3a. and 2a. Avenidas on 3a. Calle, where only some rather faint lines on the street indicate the limits of what will soon be Doña Yoli's place of business. If he is late, this previously tranquil street and those around it will be full of activity as the over two thousand street vendors of El Guarda lay out their wares and prepare for the day's business.

Velásquez's first responsibility is to set up the wooden boards and metal scaffolding that make up Doña Yoli's *puesto*. Usually, Doña Yoli is present to help Velásquez with the setup, unless she is at La Terminal market buying supplies. Next, Velásquez walks a few blocks to the small *bodega* where Doña Yoli's goods are stored overnight and begins bringing out the four or five *bultos* full of the soaps, detergents, and household goods that make up the majority of Doña Yoli's stock. A few days a week, Doña Yoli will send Velásquez to a corner a few blocks away to pick up a few dozen eggs from the middleman who sells eggs to the vendors wholesale from the back of his pickup truck. For the rest of the day, until four o'clock or so, Velásquez and Doña Yoli will arrange these goods while catering to the many shoppers who come to the streets of El Guarda to buy their daily groceries. At four o'clock in the afternoon, Velásquez and Doña Yoli will reverse the morning setup process and take down the *puesto* and store the goods for the next day.

While Velásquez is most visible to others as he works setting up and taking down Doña Yoli's *puesto* and helping her bag up items for customers, his central task for her is to run the many errands that are necessary for the efficient operation of the stall. It is Velásquez who has been taught the locations of the many wholesale distributors (*mayoristas*) in the area whom Doña Yoli uses to augment her stock when she is running low on certain items. He knows where toilet paper and individual bags of detergent can be found the cheapest, and it is his responsibility to go and purchase these items when needed. He is also frequently sent to find another vendor who is able to change a large bill or who can supply a product that Doña Yoli does not normally sell but will provide at cost to a good customer with a special request. Velásquez's knowledge of the streets of El Guarda is encyclopedic, and it is his ability to navigate these streets efficiently that makes him such a valuable asset to Doña Yoli.

Velásquez's intimate knowledge of the streets and its vendors as well as his close relationship with Doña Yoli also afford him the opportunity to pick up extra money doing tasks for other vendors, such as taking their trash to the neighborhood dump located adjacent to the interior market. Velásquez uses Doña Yoli's old wooden cart to haul the remains of a full day's labor from the *puestos* of the many nearby food sellers. Depending on the quantity of garbage they have, he can earn between one and two quetzales per vendor per day. On days when Velásquez is not working for Doña Yoli, usually Sundays and Tuesdays, he can work for as many as thirty vendors and make Q30–Q40 per day. Even when things are busy and Doña Yoli needs him every moment, he has four regular customers nearby from whom he can make about Q6 without shirking his regular labors.

When the *puesto* is disassembled and the goods are back in the *bodega* and his trash-collecting duties are complete, Velásquez gets on another bus back to his rural home. By about six o'clock, he returns home after a hard day's work and is quick to bathe to cleanse himself of the smells and stains of the products he deals with. In an average month, based on Velásquez working every day—a schedule that he usually maintains—he makes Q300 from Doña Yoli, who also buys him his lunch and snacks, and an additional Q350 from his work hauling trash. This income of Q650 for a month's labor only works out to be a little more than $3.00 a day, but in a country where the minimum wage for rural work was $2.60 a day, and that for urban work only twenty cents more, Velásquez earns more than many working adults. The money he earns, which he gives directly to his mother, is essential to their small family's survival. That Velásquez can provide for his family has much to do with his own strength and determination, his mother's prodding, as well as his bosses' consideration and indulgence. But it is the nature of street work, and the particular opportunities for it in El Guarda, that make Velásquez's many achievements possible in the first place.

THE GROWTH AND DEVELOPMENT OF EL GUARDA

Technically, El Guarda is a municipal market. Established in the early 1960s after the destruction of "El Viejo Guarda," another municipal market located two miles away, it occupies about eighteen square blocks all located in Zone 11 in the western part of Guatemala City (see Map 2.3). It is bordered by 5a. Avenida and Calzada Aguilar Batres to the west and east, respectively, and the Calzada Roosevelt and 6a. Calle to the north and south. But to consider El Guarda as merely another municipal market among the twenty-five that exist in Guatemala City is to ignore what it really is. It is the second-largest market in the city,

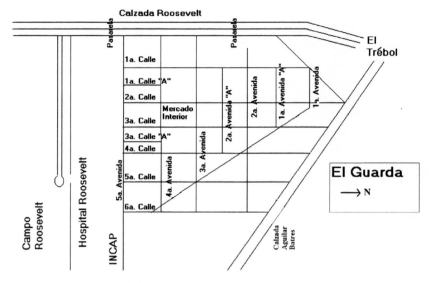

MAP 2.3.   *El Guarda area, Guatemala City*

the largest retail market, the most notorious black market in the city for stolen goods and contraband, and the second-largest area for street work in all Guatemala City.[4]

Unlike most markets in Guatemala City, vending in El Guarda is not limited to the interior of a single uniform structure and the sidewalks that immediately surround it. El Guarda is in fact a neighborhood whose streets have been taken over, bit by bit, by commercial activity that is purportedly regulated by the municipality. But there are hundreds of houses that occupy the market area and hundreds of retail shops and formal businesses that operate independently of the market structure. Within the confines of the market there is a bank, a supermarket, four churches, many bars and cafés, and some of the most infamous night-clubs and houses of prostitution, or *prostíbulos,* in the city. El Guarda is an urban working-class neighborhood that has become a bazaar.

The 18 Calle area has a long history of being a commercial center and vital point of transit in the capital, but only since the middle decades of the twentieth century has El Guarda grown from a quiet suburb of the capital to one of its vital focal points of transit and commerce. Beginning with the population expansion that saw the number of inhabitants of the city double from 284,000 in 1950 to 586,000 in 1964, the neglected western part of the city, once an undeveloped semirural extension, filled up with middle- and working-class neighborhoods (Gellert 1995, 79). These new urbanites, almost all ethnic Ladinos from the southeastern part of the country, needed markets that were closer to their homes than the existing structures in El Centro and other public works such as roads and medical services. The Hospital Roosevelt was constructed in the 1940s and became the second-largest public hospital in the city. New roads such as the Calzada Roosevelt linked the area to both the downtown and to the developing satellite city of Mixco, which grew from 11,784 inhabitants in 1950 to 346,000 by 1990 (Gellert 1995, 87). A new clover-shaped interchange, the Trébol (clover), that connected the major roads leading in and out of the city in all four directions was built in 1958. The construction of the Trébol made the area around El Guarda, specifically bus stops at the intersection of the Calzada Aguilar Batres and the Calzada Roosevelt, a central crossroads for Guatemalans on the move. In a matter of a few decades, El Guarda, a sleepy neighborhood, was transformed into a focal point for urban and interurban transit.

As the neighborhood grew, so did the market. From its inception until the earthquake of 1976, the indoor market slowly expanded to fill up the sidewalks immediately surrounding the structure. But the transformation of the market from a small local shopping venue into a neighborhood bazaar came in the aftermath of the devastating earthquake. According to my informants, the first true street vendors to descend upon the neighborhood were sellers of scavenged or stolen goods who set up around 1a. Avenida and 1a. Calle near the Aguilar Batres bus stop immediately after the earthquake. As was the case in the 18 Calle area, the municipality was powerless to control the phenomenon, considering both the chaos that descended upon the city and the need of its inhabitants to earn a living and purchase the wares they needed to survive. Residents of the area initially seem to have reacted calmly to this usurpation of the streets in front of their homes, as they, too, were aware of the dire straits of themselves and their countrymen. Many recalled the days when vendors would move their carts of goods from out of the street to allow residents to pass in their cars and then once again take their operations to the center of the streets.

Over the next five years, street vending in El Guarda was transformed as opportunistic vendors of merchandise of questionable provenience were replaced by full-time street vendors offering all types of food and dry goods. Street vendors became so entrenched in the neighborhood that conflicts soon arose between vendors and neighborhood residents. For example, when the many vegetable vendors who lined 2a. Calle began to sleep in their *puestos* and block the streets on a twenty-four-hour basis, residents found this usurpation of their streets intolerable, and after an extended skirmish with the vendors, in which human feces became the weapon of the day, a municipal ordinance decreed that the vendors selling in the residential streets had to be gone by 5:00 PM or risk the seizure of their goods and kiosks. In less than twenty years, the market was transformed from a one-block neighborhood to a pedestrian bazaar that extended for blocks and catered to the entire city.

El Guarda Today

Based on a census of all market vendors undertaken by myself and my students, we found that El Guarda was typically home to over two thousand vendors, not including the hundreds of walking vendors and those who make their living providing services, such as porters and shoeshine boys. While it can be said that all the markets in Guatemala City have at least as many vendors located on the outside as on the inside (Porres Castejón 1995), only the Zone 1 area has comparable amounts of street vending. The ratio of inside vendors to those located on public streets is regularly one to five, and during the peak retailing seasons such as Christmas, Easter, and "Back to School," this ratio soars as high as one to twelve. Though the market developed without any sort of plan, as most things do in Guatemala City, the entire bazaar now exhibits a detailed structure that informs who sells what and where, and that makes El Guarda an environment full of many niches, a complex and seemingly chaotic, yet nevertheless well-ordered, marketplace.

At its center is the indoor market that occupies one square block between 3a. and 4a. Avenidas and 2a. and 3a. Calles. The indoor market consists of a single-story split-level rectangular bunker that regularly houses 430 vendors selling small livestock, clothing, groceries, prepared foods, and all classes of household goods. The market also includes a few small storage lockers, or *bodegas,* the market administration offices, and the restrooms. But the indoor market is not limited to commerce, as it also houses two religious shrines, an informal school run by a local NGO, and an entertainment area where fiestas are held and music is broadcast all day long. The vendors who first came to El Guarda from El Viejo Guarda, the largest sellers, and those who maintain key positions on the vendors' committee, such as its formidable President Doña Gladys, are all to be found in the interior market.

Of the 435 stalls that made up the interior market during the time of my research, less than 10 percent were manned by full-time child laborers. Compared to the street vendors, those of the interior market had been working in El Guarda far longer and were generally more prosperous individuals. These vendors rarely needed to employ children to help them with their labors. Certain types of stalls concentrated in the interior market, such as butchers (*carnicerías*), are by custom worked only by adult males, and this also limited the presence of full-time working children in the interior. Except for a few rare cases, the only full-time child laborers working in the interior market were young girls working in the 50 or so food stalls, or *comedores*.

Even though the presence of full-time child laborers was relatively small in the interior market, the presence of children was far more common, as many of the vendors did care for their young children or grandchildren at their *puestos,* and in the afternoons it was a common sight to see children dressed in public and private school uniforms doing homework, playing, or helping out in the stalls of their families. Most of the vendors of the interior market had come to El Guarda from El Viejo Guarda, and because of their extensive history as market vendors in the area, were usually not dependent on the labor of nonrelated children and were fortunate enough to send their own children to public or private schools. This fact also correlates with the relatively high percentage of ethnic Ladinos in the interior market (over 70 percent) compared with the outside stalls and *ambulantes* (walking vendors), who overwhelmingly identified as Maya Indians.

The streets that border the interior market are by far the most crowded of all the exterior areas. Between 3a. Avenida and 4a. Avenida and 2a. Calle and 3a. Calle there were 517 regular vendors, more than in the entire interior market. Most of these vendors sold new clothing and shoes, the category of goods that made El Guarda known as the retail clothing capital of Guatemala City. Whereas the majority of streets in El Guarda are home to one or two rows of street vendors, usually facing each other and located just inside the sidewalks, here the streets were packed with three and sometimes four rows of vendors. Other goods that were found here included prepared foodstuffs, kitchen supplies, and fruits and vegetables (particularly in the block of 3a. Calle), as well as livestock and exotic animals—parrots, toucans, iguanas, small crocodiles, and even owls!—most of which were illegal to trap and sell. Child laborers were plentiful in this area, especially young girls working with older women in the sale of foodstuffs, and young adolescent males selling small stocks of clothing such as T-shirts, soccer cleats, and pants. Vendors in this area were also largely Maya Indians.

All the border areas of El Guarda share much in common with respect to the types of goods and services offered as well as the characteristics of their vendors. In general, radiating outward from the center of El Guarda, one begins to see younger and less seasoned vendors. The Calzada Roosevelt and the areas on and around the two overpasses, or *pasarelas,* that offer pedestrian access to and from El Guarda are dominated by younger vendors, about half of whom are child laborers. The Roosevelt sidewalks and the *pasarelas* are key vending points because of their locations as entryways into El Guarda and as a major bus depot for passengers changing buses. The products sold by these vendors are tremendously diverse, but the majority can be classed as consumer-oriented knickknacks that are sold by vendors known as *achimeros.* *Achimeros* sell youth-oriented small consumer goods, such as portable radios, watches, sunglasses, wallets, pocketknives, combs, and playing cards. Many *achimeros* also sell contraband cassettes and compact discs. In El Guarda, *achimeros* are almost exclusively young Maya Indian men and boys, mostly first-generation migrants to the capital, and many divide their time between the city and their rural homes. In these same areas, vendors also sell candy, soda, and cigarettes in small stalls, many of which are manned by children, again, usually Maya boys who are first-generation migrants to the capital.

Farther along the Roosevelt, at the intersection with the road that leads into both the Hospital Roosevelt and the offices of the Instituto Centro-Americano de Nutrición (INCAP), there are a number of street vendors who cater to the hospital staff, the patients, and their families. Manning mobile carts, the vendors serve sodas, hot dogs, and the ubiquitous sandwiches known as *mixtas* (a mix of some type of sausage with abundant amounts of cabbage and guacamole) to the captive "audience." The sidewalks are also littered with vendors displaying a variety of goods in demand by hospital visitors, such as small toys for children, slippers, robes, as well as basic medical and hygiene products that are not readily available at the public hospital such as diapers, toilet paper, and Handi Wipes.

The eastern border of the market, formed by the Calzada Aguilar Batres, is also the site of a major bus depot, and consequently attracts many of the same types of vendors as the Roosevelt, particularly *achimeros,* *chicleros* (gum and candy merchants), and many walking vendors and shoeshine boys. What distinguishes this area is the presence of a fleet of gypsy trucks. This area serves as the principal loading and unloading zone for the entire El Guarda area. These trucks, or *fletes,* make repeated trips from La Terminal wholesale market in Zone 4 to El Guarda full of vegetables and fruits that will be sold by the street vendors and *comedores. Cargadores* (porters) also congregate in this area to meet the *fleteros* and contract to carry the bundles of produce (*bultos*) to their respective stalls. While the drivers of the *fletes* that congregate on Aguilar Batres are obviously adults and almost exclusively Ladinos, the *cargadores, lustradores* (shoeshiners), and many of the other vendors who work the Calzada and the blocks of 1a. Avenida and 1a. Avenida "A" are child laborers.

There are also areas in El Guarda where the principal activity of street vending mixes with vice, another aspect of this bazaar that is famous throughout Guatemala City. On first inspection, the various stalls and car parks located along 5a. Avenida seem to be worked by T-shirt vendors, almost all young Maya men and boys selling contraband or gray-market designer goods sporting the labels of some of the most famous names in Western casual clothing, such as Tommy Hilfiger, Levi's, adidas, and Fubu. Some of these goods are indeed authentic, but they were stolen off trucks hijacked on their routes from the maquiladoras (assembly factories) in the Western Highlands while on their way to the Pacific port. The vast majority, however, are fakes, made up in home workshops where fake labels and designer accents are stitched onto cheap domestic and imported clothing. While Guatemala does have strict intellectual property laws on the books, the prevalence of this contraband as well as the generalized level of corruption among those who are meant to enforce these laws, mainly the police, make the eradication of these "pirated" goods a virtual impossibility.

Alongside these clothing vendors is a gang of young and middle-aged men, virtually all Ladinos, who run the most notorious car repair service in the city. Customers drive their cars up and park along the wall that separates El Guarda and 5a. Avenida from the INCAP and hospital grounds. They are then met by men who appear at first to be mere car parkers and guarders, who find out about the nature of the problems the individual is having with his or her car, and quickly contact nearby hidden warehouses to find the stolen parts necessary for the vehicle's repair. These individuals specialize in cosmetic repairs, such as windshields, lights, mirrors, and exterior piping, and customers can count on having their vehicle repaired at a fraction of the cost of a repair in a dealership or legal auto shop. Once again, although this illegal activity occurs in broad daylight in view of thousands, a few quetzales well placed in the pockets of local police make it all go off without a hitch.

Contraband also dominates the nearly four hundred street vendors who sell their wares on 4a. and 5a. Avenidas between the Calzada Roosevelt and 2a. Calle. In this area, pirated cassettes and compact disks are the most valued goods, selling at between eight and ten quetzales for a tape and thirty-five and forty quetzales for a compact disk, less than 40 percent of the cost of legal recordings. The sale of these items is done by individuals of all ages and ethnicities, with child vendors representing about 20 percent of the total number of vendors. According to many of my informants who sold these items, young people dominate the supply chain for these goods, which usually come through southern Mexico on the backs of young smugglers known as *hormigas* (ants) who physically carry these items across the border.

Nearby, along 1a. Calle between 5a. and 3a. Avenidas, another type of contraband dominates, namely, stolen goods. This tightly packed two-block area is filled with only adult male vendors selling a huge variety of stolen tools, car parts, home electronics, and housewares. Here, vendors were very threatened by any foray my students or I made into the area, and all attempts to elicit survey information were met with blank stares or looks of hostility. This area was one of the few in all of the market that was exclusively run by adult males, and there were rarely any children present, either as workers or as bystanders. One of my informants said that his mother instructed him never to enter the area, as it was only a cave of thieves where one was never safe.

The final area where vice was king did, unfortunately, employ far too many children, namely, the *bares* (illicit bars) and *prostíbulos* (bordellos) of the blocks of 1a., 1a. "A," and 2a. Avenidas between the Calzada Roosevelt and 2a. Calle bordering Calzada Aguilar Batres. I first became aware of these establishments when two of my student fieldworkers alerted me to a group of young shoeshine boys and car parkers I knew who were gathered around a street corner and looking up to the sky. When I asked them what they were doing, they pointed to a nearby rooftop where a group of young girls were bathing on the roof of a hotel/ *prostíbulo*, offering a free "show" to those passing by.

While prostitution has long been a reality in Guatemala City, and is found in Zones 1, 4, 9, and 10 of the capital, it is most concentrated in these few blocks of El Guarda. Prostitutes work out of small bars with bedsheets covering the entrance, small hotels known as *pensiones,* and big nightclubs such as the "Bar Trébol Show" and the "Buho" (Owl), all located in these few blocks. The vast majority of the prostitutes are women and young girls, though one or two small bars do cater to transvestites. Most of the children who were my informants are well aware of these bars, as they are located in the same blocks where street vending was common and where the most popular video game arcade (*maquinitas*) in the entire area can be found. It is widely known that a woman can be had for as little as twenty quetzales (about three dollars). One of the most prevalent rumors concerning the prostitutes of this area, many of whom were girls as young as twelve or thirteen, was that they were all *salvadoreñas*, or women from El Salvador, known to be of low morals. I did meet a few prostitutes while working in this area, and they commented that while some of the women and girls were from El Salvador, most were in fact Guatemalan.

Taken as a whole, like 18 Calle, El Guarda is a neighborhood full of commerce and all of the opportunities and problems that come with it. These hazards, in the form of shady characters selling stolen goods, drugs, and prostitution, are all an everyday part of Velásquez's workplace. Nevertheless, the opportunity that El Guarda provides children like him and the thousands of adults who work the same streets far outweighs the dangers. Of course, the need to earn money is the primary reason why all these disparate elements have come together in this small neighborhood. As Velásquez and Rey and their families would attest, their street jobs are vital to the current struggles and future dreams of all concerned. Yet it is easy to forget that these children who spend their time on the public streets, who work and earn like adults, are still children: sons, daughters, friends, and peers. Besides being good earners, besides spending most of their days in the company of strangers amid the bustle of the streets, they are also connected to many others, and these connections define who they are just as much as any label such as "child laborer" does.

CONTEXTUALIZING CHILD STREET LABOR

Children like Rey and Velásquez are easy to label with terms such as "child," "street child," "child laborer," or simply "poor child." While each of these labels does have some surface applicability to their lives, they are merely labels, capturing only a small part of who each particular child is and what his or her place is in the larger sociocultural order. Much has been written, from varying perspectives, on children like Rey and Velásquez, yet a great deal of this literature has failed to penetrate the reality of such children's lives. From Lewis Henry Morgan's classic study of life among the Iroquois (1962; orig. pub. 1851) onward, ethnography has taken children to be part of its focus on aboriginal cultures, yet children are not a prominent focus of Morgan's account, for while they were obviously continuously present during his research, they merit no extended description. This omission, typical for the nineteenth century and indeed for most of the twentieth, relegates children to the margins of ethnographic accounts, present but in no way central to the ethnographer's focus on the true bearers of culture and society, namely adults. As the anthropologists Nancy Scheper-Hughes and Carolyn Sargent (1998, 13) succinctly put it: "Children generally appear in ethnographic texts the way cattle make their appearance in Evans-Pritchard's classic, *The Nuer*—as forming an essential backdrop to everyday life, but mute and unable to teach us anything significant about society and culture." While research on children in anthropology did obviously occur during the twentieth century (see discussion below), the topic did not truly come of age until the turn of the twenty-first.

Reevaluation of Childhood, Child Work, and Child Labor

As the millennium approached, anthropological research on children truly exploded. Owing largely to the collaborative work of British social anthropologist Allison James and sociologists Chris Jenks and Alan Prout, Charlotte Hardman's 1973 call for a true anthropology of childhood was answered with a new body of research that focused on children's agency in cultural production (James and Prout 1990; James, Jenks, and Prout 1998; Jenks 1993, 1996). These authors sought to develop the links between childhood and social theory. They reintroduced the topic of children and the social construction of childhood in scholarly debates on issues such as globalization; the cultural construction of morality; and the role of the state in regulating behavior, the body, and political action.

Whereas once children had occupied only the margins in anthropological research, they now moved to the center of the field. Children and childhood were the focus of only one review article in *Annual Review of Anthropology* from 1970 to 1990 (Schwartzman's 1976 "The Anthropological Study of Children's Play). In the past decade, however, themes as diverse as child labor (Nieuwenhuys 1996), infant-parent cosleeping (McKenna 1996), street children (Panter-Brick 2002), youth and cultural practice (Bucholz 2002), and infant feeding research (Van Esterik 2002) have all been the subject of review. Helen Schwartzman's *Children and Anthropology: A Century of Studies in Children and Anthropology: Perspectives for the 21st Century* (2001) includes a review of all research on children published in the pages of *American Anthropologist*, as well as various papers that emphasize the role of archaeological, linguistic, and biological anthropology in developing a true "four-field" approach to the anthropology of childhood. Anthropologist Tobias Hecht edited a book entitled *Minor Omissions: Children in Latin American History and Society* (2002), which presents fascinating historical case studies of childhood and children in Latin America in an attempt to contextualize our current understandings of childhood and issues such as child labor and street children.

In North America, three cultural anthropologists have combined this newfound interest in children's agency with edited volumes that highlight both children's actions in the construction of their own lives and the larger political-economic constraints that they and their families face. Sharon Stephens's *Children and the Politics of Culture* (1995) contains articles on themes as diverse as the politics of identity among British-Sikh teenagers (Hall 1995) and the disappearance of childhood in Japan as it relates to the logic of global capitalism (Field 1995). Nancy Scheper-Hughes and Carolyn Sargent's *Small Wars: The Cultural Politics of Childhood* (1998) is an extended critique of neoliberal economic policies as the cause of a variety of social ills that affect children, including the starvation of children in South Africa (Lerer 1998) and infant and toddler anxiety over the loss of their mothers and the political action (known as *mamitas*) in Mexico City (Gutmann 1998).

This newfound approach in which children's own words, deeds, and feelings were used to help anthropologists understand how children constructed their own lives within current political-economic realities also radically affected research on child work, child labor, and street children. In the most recent literature on the topic of poor children, the descriptive term "street child" is rarely present. Researchers are now interested in studying all poor children. This change is even reflected in the revised United Nations terminology, which now refers to all poor children as CEDC, or "children in especially difficult circumstances" (Szanton-Blanc 1994). Anthropological studies of street children by Hecht (1998) and Rizzini et al. (1994) have attacked the erroneous assertion that there are forty million homeless street children in Latin America, although the figure still appears on page one of a recent ethnography by Patricia Márquez (1999). Much more attention is being paid to the relationships between street children and their families; researchers have discovered that even those seen as the hardest cases have frequent interactions with their families. Both Hecht and Márquez also underscore the role that the political economy has played in the creation and definition of the street child problem in Brazil and Venezuela. Rather than blaming the poor, they have demonstrated how the problem stems from global economic processes and local political responses.

Olga Nieuwenhuys (1994) made substantial contributions to the study of child exploitation in work and the role of gender in child work. She found that while child labor has been routinely targeted as a form of child abuse, those children who often work the hardest and receive the least compensation are child workers, usually girls who perform child care and domestic work and subsistence endeavors, often from fourteen to eighteen hours a day. Pamela Reynolds performed similar work among the Tonga of Zimbabwe. Using methodology similar to that employed in the time-allocation research of the 1970s, Reynolds demonstrated how vital child workers are to subsistence agricultural endeavors. In addition, she explicated the "clear disciplinary function in labor that differentially affects boys and girls and introduces them to patterns to be fully realized in the experience of adulthood" (Reynolds 1991, 161). The work of both anthropologists was instrumental in drawing clear boundaries between child work and child labor, and in demonstrating that child work, especially girls' work, constituted a major contribution to family survival.

Nieuwenhuys also strongly challenged the view of child labor as inherently backward and morally destructive, pointing out that "the moral condemnation of child labor assumes that children's place in modern society must perforce be one of dependency and passivity" (1996, 238). With the reduced role of the state in social programs among neoliberal economic regimes, children are increasingly choosing to labor as a means of supporting themselves and their families. Considering the economic need of these families, Nieuwenhuys questions the relevance of the International Labour Organization's traditional program to eradicate all forms of child labor (ibid., 245). Unfortunately, Nieuwenhuys's research is the exception rather than the rule. While studies detailing the worst and most abusive forms of child labor have appeared regularly (Bales 1999; Black 1996; Brett and Specht 2004; ILO 1999a; Seabrook 2001), very few works have examined child street labor and other types of child labor that do offer children the opportunity to be involved in the production of value while at the same time maintaining a large degree of agency and control over the terms of their labor and its proceeds.

The past ten years have been truly exceptional, for never before in the history of anthropology have children been taken this seriously as social, political, and economic actors. The anthropology of children and childhood has become a reality. Yet there is much work to be done, for even the most nuanced recent attempts at restoring agency to children often fall back upon reducing child work and child labor to merely socialization, marginalization, or exploitation, a tendency that I hope to avoid in my own research.

Child Street Laborers and Anthropology

Despite the flourishing of anthropological research on children in the past decade, child street laborers have received very little attention. Two brief studies of child street laborers in Africa do exist: a monograph on child newspaper vendors in South Africa (Moerat 1989) and a study of child street vendors in Lagos (Oloko 1991). Neither of these works focuses on full-time child street laborers. Instead, these researchers studied children who work the streets either intermittently or only after attending school.

One of the largest obstacles to the development of a substantial body of literature on child street labor is the lingering methodological confusion over what distinguishes full-time child street laborers from child street workers and homeless street children. When child street laborers do appear in the literature, they are still grouped with other poor children who use the street as a home of last resort (true street children), as a site of child care or participation in family economic endeavors (child workers), as a place to prey on the unsuspecting or engage in illicit commerce (child prostitutes, gang members, and thieves), or as an opportunistic work location (part-time child street laborers). This methodological confusion obscures both the income to be earned through full-time labor and the strategies that children use on the street to rise up the ladder and obtain even better income-generating street work. My research is the first to separate full-time child street laborers from these other groups and devote intensive and extended research into how and why children labor in the city streets.

Although my research is innovative in its subject matter and its approach, aspects of older perspectives do have significant relevance to my work. Child street labor is certainly part of the socialization process.[5] The children with whom I worked did not invent the idea of working in general or working in the street in particular. As I shall detail later, save for a few rare exceptions, they are all contributing members of extended family economic networks, and most are guided into their jobs and "taught the ropes" by older family members or landsmen. They were all child workers who participated in family work endeavors either on or off the streets long before they began their own street businesses or hired themselves out to nonrelatives. Especially among the Maya, children believe that to be good and responsible sons or daughters, they must do all they can to aid in the survival and future economic success of their families. Children are taught the value of work at a young age, and alongside this lesson come many others about what it takes to be a contributing member of the family and of village society. The enculturation process often takes place while a child is working, and as many parents of child street laborers told me, if a child does not have a good work ethic, it is the fault of the family. The culture and personality school of research is itself largely a thing of the past, but the idea that its researchers advanced concerning the role adults play in modeling attitudes and behaviors for children is still relevant today.

The view of child labor as marginalization,[6] despite the repeated attacks on the culture of poverty concept, still lives on. The idea that the poor have somehow developed a set of attitudes and survival strategies that ultimately explain their failure to "get ahead" is still proffered daily as an explanation for global poverty. As evidenced in the recent editorial by Becker about bribing poor parents to send their children to school (see note 6), a perverse common-sense logic still blames the victim for poverty, ignoring the failure of states to provide adequately for the health, security, and education of their children. It is national and international political and economic structures and policies, from the IMF-mandated neoliberal "package" of reforms to national and international unequal distribution of wealth, that marginalize the poor. As my research illustrates, the use of street labor by children and their families is an ingenious and positive response to these externally imposed conditions. Poor children take advantage of the opportunities available to them and through much hard work and dedication, use the streets to make a better life for themselves and their families.

Of course, not all children do advance as far as they might hope, and homeless street children, child prostitutes, and child slaves and bonded laborers do exist. The view of child work and child labor as exploitation is often valid,[7] and a focus on the worst forms of child labor is necessary and vital if such practices are ever to be eliminated. But a limited focus on only these practices obscures the fact that they are exceptional and creates the impression that all child labor is akin to slavery, which it clearly is not. Projecting recently created images of a Western protected childhood onto all the world's children, most of whom live in countries where such a view of childhood is both culturally chauvinistic and economically infeasible, does little good. In fact, as Nieuwenhuys (1996) has pointed out, excluding children from the production of value only serves to marginalize them more, to deny them any right or ability to actively contest their socioeconomic reality. It is important to study and publicize children who are victims of unscrupulous adults, but as recent theoretical perspectives have pointed out, children must have their agency restored in anthropology and be taken seriously as social, economic, and political actors. This recent dual focus on both children's agency in shaping their reality and the role of larger political economic forces that radically affect the lives of children throughout the globe is a current perspective that has influenced my work greatly and has served as a model for my study of the lives and labors of the children with whom I worked.

Three   JOBS AND INCOME OF
CHILD STREET LABORERS

D̲espite the myriad national and international efforts that attempt to keep children from having to work, child street labor is an omnipresent reality in the cities of the developing world and will continue to be so. Children work on the streets because the streets are a workplace full of opportunity for children who must work. These opportunities come in many different forms, yet the most important, to both the children and their families, is the opportunity to earn incomes that will provide for the children's and their family's immediate and future survival.

Pizarro, Reina, Perla, and Cortez are all child laborers. They all come from families in which poverty beats down the door. They are also very different in ages and sexes, they come from families of very different composition, and they belong to different ethnic groups. They work diverse jobs and earn varied incomes; some are self-employed, while others work for adults. But all share the streets as a workplace and the skills and discipline needed to become reliable economic assets to their families at an age when most of their peers are simply economic liabilities.

PIZARRO'S STORY

Pizarro, who is fourteen years old, works two jobs and gives most of his earnings to his mother. When I asked him what his mother does with the money that he gives her, he said in a matter-of-fact tone, "Well, that's what we use to eat." Perched on a concrete square that forms part of an elevated walkway (*pasarela*) that connects the El Guarda Market and the northern side of the Calzada Roosevelt, Pizarro sells playing cards, combs, toothbrushes, and other assorted goods. When sales are few, or he is too short of money to replenish his stock, he also works in a car park on 1a. Avenida in El Guarda, washing cars and running errands for the men who run the lot. He likes his job selling, as he shares the *pasarela* with many of his friends, who sell similar items. His major complaint is that during the rainy season, he is forced to stop selling when the daily rains come, and when it is excessively hot, he feels as if the sun is focusing all its energy on him alone. He enjoys his work at the car park far less, because he is not in charge of his labor and his income is in no way guaranteed. But he keeps going back because it keeps him working and earning when his job selling is not possible or sufficiently profitable.

Pizarro remembers that he began working at the age of five. He helped his father and uncle cut wood and cultivate the small milpa that they owned in the village of Concordia, Totonicapán. His recollections of his father are all positive, though his father abandoned his family when Pizarro was only eight. Soon after, Pizarro began to come to El Guarda with his grandfather to find work. Together, they performed odd jobs. He reported being excited to be in such a bustling place compared to his hometown, but he was also a bit afraid, as he felt that while El Guarda was fun, "I didn't know where the entrance was and where the exit was." In time, Pizarro learned the neighborhood, and he was aided by the fact that soon after his arrival, his mother and older sister left Concordia and came to live and work in El Guarda.

After the family set up quarters in El Guarda, Pizarro began helping his mother sell vegetables from a tarpaulin on the sidewalk. Once they became known in the neighborhood, the boy was offered a job helping out in a small restaurant, where he cleaned tables, swept the floor, and took out the trash. But he left this job after only a few months because his wages were low (Q300 a month) and he had to work from seven in the morning until six in the evening, with only one day off a week.

His mother then suggested that he begin selling for a living, and she allowed him to spend his entire final month's salary on buying goods for his *venta* (retail sales business). Pizarro had been studying what the *achimeros,* or vendors of small electronic and personal goods, carried in their stock, and where would be the best place to sell. He spent Q200 on a small tarpaulin and an assortment of combs, brushes, locks, and playing cards and began his career as an *achimero* on the same *pasarela* where he now works. Since his first week as an *achimero,* two years before I met him, Pizarro's stock has grown considerably, and now includes portable radios and cassette players as well as leather belts, pocket knives, and stick-on

ɔs. When the weather does not get in the way, he makes a profit of
ɛen Q25 and Q50 every day, but most of this profit he puts back into
ʋusiness by expanding the quantity and quality of the goods that he
ʋɛɪɪs. The money he makes from the car park, usually Q10 or Q15 a day, he
gives directly to his mother. He takes money out of his business only to
buy his clothing and for a movie or a trip to the arcade with his friends.

This boy of fourteen makes about Q40 a day, a salary of about US$140
a month. While this only comes out to approximately $5 a day, and less
than $1 an hour—wages that are indeed indecent by North American
standards—Pizarro is a "good earner" by Guatemalan standards, bringing in more cash than many adults working twelve to fourteen hours a
day in the countryside. Nevertheless, Pizarro is in no way satisfied with
his earnings and hopes to continually expand his *venta* until he can double or triple his income. Although he will need to work years to achieve
this goal, all the while keeping a tight rein on his personal budget, avoid-
ing illness and family catastrophe, and adapting to periodic municipal
ordinances that attempt to eradicate street vending, such a dream is
indeed possible. Most importantly, while he pursues this ideal of self-
sufficiency and economic success, he provides for his mother and siblings every day.

REINA'S STORY

While Pizarro earns his Q1,000 each month and is a good
earner for a child street laborer, his contribution to his family's coffers
only makes up about Q300, or 30 percent of his income. Reina, a ten-
year-old girl who lives and works in El Guarda, manages to contribute
even more to her family, Q400, month in and month out. This money is
perhaps even more vital to her family's survival than Pizarro's, as Reina
is one of three girls and one boy whom her mother is raising alone, and
two of her siblings are too young to work. Like Pizarro, Reina must provide for her own needs, but since Reina also lives with her employer, her
mother spends little or no money to provide for her. All of her income
goes directly into her mother's pocket. As a ten-year-old girl, she is a
complete economic asset to her family, contributing regular earnings
and costing them nothing in return.

Reina works for and lives with Doña María in her café located on a corner opposite the interior market of El Guarda. As the *comedor* is located
in a small apartment with a sidewalk entrance, Reina is not technically

employed by a street worker, but the nature of her work compels her to spend most of the day outside the *comedor* and in the street. Reina begins her workday at six in the morning, when she walks all around El Guarda soliciting breakfast orders from the vendors as they set up their kiosks. She has a group of regulars who purchase meals from her every day but is always on the lookout for new clients, as nothing makes Doña María happier than having new clients. She then returns to the *comedor* with the orders and is almost immediately sent back out to deliver the meals to the vendors.

Once this is accomplished, she returns to these same vendors to pick up their dirty dishes, as disposable plates and utensils would make the breakfast more expensive and therefore less popular with vendors and less profitable for Doña María. Reina is also responsible for collecting the funds from the vendors at this time, tucking the money into her tiny apron to give to Doña María upon her return. When the breakfast rounds are completed by 10:00 am, Reina is given the responsibility of doing the shopping for the lunch crowd and for the family dinner. She has an expert's knowledge of the hundreds of butchers and vegetable vendors located throughout El Guarda, and she is depended upon to find what is necessary and purchase it, all with an eye toward economy and quality, and transport it back to the *comedor*. She is often accompanied in this task by a young relative of Doña María's, who is not so much a helper to Reina as an agent of Doña María's, there to assure that Reina is doing her work with efficiency and not pocketing any of Doña María's funds.

Once the shopping is done, Reina will repeat her breakfast routine of soliciting orders, delivering food, and then collecting the utensils and payment, only this time for the lunch crowd. After this is completed, usually by about three thirty in the afternoon, Reina will return to the *comedor* and help with the afternoon cleanup and the herculean task of washing the dishes and silverware. By five thirty, once things have been tidied, she will usually attend a nightly evangelical Christian worship service with Doña María. Upon her return, she will begin to cook dinner for Doña María's family and herself, no small task, as Doña María has a husband and two older children of her own as well as relatives and friends who occasionally eat dinner with her family. Once dinner has been served and consumed, Reina will help clean up the *comedor* and the living quarters. Only then will she attend to her personal affairs, such as washing her clothes or doing a bit of homework for her informal classes. She reports usually falling asleep to the television, along with the other members of Doña María's family, at about nine o'clock in the evening.

During the fourteen months that I knew Reina, she did not change jobs. This type of stability is rare for a child street laborer, especially a very young one. Reina stayed working for Doña María because she was relatively happy with her job, and because her mother let it be known to her that any interruption in her regular income would not be welcome. Reina is clearly a victim of exploitation by both her mother and Doña María, but her attitude does not demonstrate unhappiness much of the time. To say that a girl of ten could be happy in a job where she works twelve hours a day, six days a week, not including the cooking and domestic responsibilities, is difficult to believe. But Reina is not a typical ten-year-old girl, though her situation may be considered typical for girls of her background in Guatemala City.

The first time I met her, she had stopped by the small informal classroom located in the interior market to visit with the PENNAT educator, with whom she had occasionally studied. Reina was tremendously shy around me and the other children who attended the informal school on a regular basis. She was wearing a dirty apron over a soiled T-shirt and skirt, and she would make eye contact only with the teacher. After this brief visit, the teacher confided to me the details of Reina's life. I quickly came to the assumption that as a young girl exploited in her labors by her family and her employer, Reina was without any hope of developing the self-esteem and confidence necessary to assert herself inside or outside the classroom. But the next time I saw her, the reverse seemed to be the case. As I was walking around El Guarda searching for a vendor of flowers, Reina tugged at my backpack and gave me a big smile. She chatted with me animatedly as she continued about her collection rounds. When I told her of my search, she took my hand and led me to a street vendor and told me to keep quiet while she bargained for the flowers. After a brief exchange, they agreed upon a price, and I paid for the flowers while the vendor and Reina talked and the vendor patted her on her head. Once this was over, she confidently trotted away and told me to come find her the next time I needed help. Reina's big smile and supreme confidence on the streets of El Guarda was the exact opposite of her shy demeanor inside the classroom.

While at work, either cooking, shopping, or delivering meals, Reina seemed to be much older than she was. She spoke with pleasure of the many dishes she could skillfully cook, from *caldo*, a meat soup that was a common lunchtime meal among all Guatemalans, to other *comedor* favorites such as *pollo dorado* (fried chicken) and *carne guisada* (a spicy beef stew). She also prided herself on her knowledge of the prices of foodstuffs and her bargaining abilities. She spoke of these things much as a young woman who was a full-time *ama de casa* (homemaker) might, not as a ten-year-old girl working for wages that made her closer to a slave than an employee. She was also proud of the money she made, though she saw little if any of the proceeds and was well aware of the vast insufficiency of her wages. Like Pizarro, Rey, and many other children I worked with, she was very proud of the fact that she was a good worker and provided well for her family.

Reina's dream was to one day have a *comedor* of her own so she could put her vast array of skills and knowledge to work for her and her family, not for others. Though she had been a wage earner for over two years, it was plain to her that the money she was making offered little present or future benefit for her. Her mother expressed great affection for Reina, but she showed little regret at using her daughter for her wages. Reina's mother echoed a refrain common among the *comedor* owners who employ girls like Reina at such low wages: that these girls have few skills, and work gives them the chance to "go forward on their own in the present and the future, without depending on anyone else."

Despite the cynicism at the heart of such comments, Reina might yet prevail. Like most child street laborers, Reina must sacrifice much of her future for the time being. Yet her job and the skills, knowledge, and connections she has attained as a worker are far better than those of most girls in her socioeconomic class, many of whom work as domestics for other families and rarely see any wages or the light of day at all (see Bossen 1988 and Menchú 1987 for a description of the conditions under which child domestics labor in Guatemala). While Reina works all day for someone else, she does have a degree of freedom, albeit earned through her skill and closely monitored. To say that Reina is a fortunate child would be ridiculous, but considering her young age, her sex, and her family circumstances, Reina does relatively well. Through considerable hard work and intelligence, she has made herself a success in street labor.

PERLA'S STORY

Perla is a seventeen-year-old child street laborer, descended from another child street laborer, and likely to be raising a child street laborer. Usually, these three generations can be found in the same spot, under the small canopy of a kiosk on the corner of one of the busiest intersections in all of the 18 Calle area. Perla sells lottery tickets, as does her mother, Doña Susana, who also sells newspapers and phone cards,[1] and both women share in the responsibility of looking after Jordán, Perla's infant child. Much of Perla's work, social life, and family life is conducted on this makeshift collection of boards and stools amid the continuous flow of cars and pedestrians around 18 Calle. Though Perla and her family would seem to present a typical portrait of the family chaos and dire poverty that typify life in cities of the developing world, their story is far more complex.

Doña Susana earns nearly four times the Guatemalan minimum wage from her labor, and Perla herself earns from Q1,100 to Q1,300 a month, an enviable income for a teenage mother working on the streets of Guatemala City. Perla is married and has a husband three years older than her who works construction and, according to Perla, makes nearly as much as she does. They are in the process of building a home in a *colonia popular* (working-class barrio) in Zone 7 of the capital, on an adjacent lot to her mother's and on land that they own. Though their home currently only has two rooms and electricity but no running water or an indoor toilet, things are going well, and they plan to add these amenities and another two rooms in three years. While this may not sound like much, for Perla, and indeed for most girls in Guatemala City who share similar circumstances, things are going quite well.

Perla's and her mother's relative good fortune is no accident, as Perla has been working since she was eight years old. Doña Susana had Perla when she was a teenager, and Perla's father abandoned her soon after. Both girls were then living with Doña Susana's mother, with Doña Susana providing for the three of them. Perla grew up alongside her mother in a variety of street settings and jobs, from market vending to working as a café delivery girl like Reina. Once Doña Susana saved up a bit of money, she and Perla began selling newspapers as walking vendors around 18 Calle. She soon graduated to her small kiosk, and as business grew, she had the capital to purchase sheets of lottery tickets from a distributor she met on the street. Perla then began to sell the lottery tickets for herself.

Newspaper vendors expose themselves to serious risks, as they usually pay up front for their papers and therefore are stuck with any copies they cannot sell. Profits range from 30–50 percent depending on the paper (a Q1.50 copy of the *Prensa Libre* costs vendors Q1; one of the smaller graphic papers retails for Q1 and costs vendors Q.65). Lottery tickets are usually given to street sellers on credit and can be returned to the distributor if unsold. Depending on the lottery, tickets retail for between Q5 and Q20, and vendors make 15 percent of the face value of the tickets they sell. Doña Susana sells tickets from her kiosk, but Perla travels all over the downtown area selling hers as a walking vendor.

Perla typically sells six to eight *cachitos,* or sheets of ten tickets, on an average day, for a total sale of Q300–Q400 and a profit of from Q45 to Q60 per day. On weekends and holidays, she can sell as many as sixteen *cachitos* and earn Q120. She begins her day early, usually by six o'clock, by working near her mother in Zone 1 and selling to the many downtown municipal office workers. Next, she will visit Zone 4 (home to the city's largest wholesale market and bus terminal) and Zones 9 and 10 (relatively upscale shopping, commerce, and tourism districts) on her daily rounds, which she concludes at about four in the afternoon. She sometimes takes Jordán with her on her sales route, but most often he is left with his grandmother in the relative safety of the kiosk, with Perla stopping by frequently to feed him, relieve her mother, deposit her money, and pick up more tickets (carrying around too many tickets indicates to thieves that the vendor is successful and likely carrying large quantities of cash).

Another lucrative aspect of lottery sales is that sellers of winning tickets often receive bonuses or tips from their clients. Winning numbers are posted in the newspaper according to which vendor sold them, and clients check their tickets and redeem smaller prizes (such as free tickets) directly through their vendor. While Perla reports that not all winning customers do give her tips, on rare occasions she has received tips as large as Q200! Such luck and the goodwill of her customers account for the occasional bonus Perla receives in her salary, but it is her charm, her hard work, and the aid of her mother that have transformed Perla from a "teen mother" to a successful street entrepreneur.

CORTEZ'S STORY

Cortez spends most of his mornings and afternoons walking around with a huge mesh rope bag that weighs as much as eighty pounds.[2] He uses his left hand to grasp the bag and his left shoulder to support it. For balance and additional support, he tucks his right hand in his belt at the small of his back. To say that he walks with his burden is a bit misleading, as the weight of the bag propels him forward at a considerable speed, his body bent in a crouch and his head bent facing the street. His locomotion is more like a rapid stumble or a jog than actual walking. Much like Sisyphus, Cortez never seems free of his burden. But instead of forcing a stone up a hill, Cortez carries a *bulto,* or a load of cargo, and he walks on level ground. He also does not share in Sisyphus's solitude, as he carries his burden through the maze of alleys, kiosks, and human traffic that make up the El Guarda market.

Cortez, along with his older brother and scores of other boys and men in El Guarda, works as a *cargador* (porter). His job is to carry *bultos* of merchandise from the trucks that deliver them on the outskirts of El Guarda to the vendors who sell on the streets of the neighborhood. The trucks mostly come from the central wholesale market known as La Terminal in Zone 4 of the capital. The majority of the cargo consists of fresh fruits and vegetables that have usually arrived that morning from small and medium-sized farms scattered throughout the Western Highlands of Guatemala. The produce arrives at La Terminal on trucks and buses in the early morning hours, at which point the wholesalers of La Terminal load it into their stalls. The vendors of El Guarda then make their purchases and have the produce delivered to pickup trucks around La Terminal, which will then transport it to El Guarda. Cortez and the other *cargadores* arrive at selected points on the outskirts of El Guarda beginning at 5:30 A.M. to unload the trucks and deliver the produce to their penultimate destination, the retail vendors. Depending on the size of the *bulto,* as well as the particular arrangement that the *cargador* has with the owner of the delivery vehicle (usually small pickup trucks known as *fletes*), *cargadores* will receive from 50 centavos to Q2 (from US$.07 to US$.30) for transporting each *bulto* from one to five blocks.

Cortez earns the majority of his income from his morning work as a *cargador* of produce and the rest by running errands for vendors, such as retrieving dry goods and the metal scaffolding of their kiosks from nearby *bodegas* and garages. He also spends his time helping his father, Don Julio, sell onions and other assorted vegetables in his small *puesto.* In the late afternoon, he will take trash from the vendors' stalls to one of the nearby dumps for Q1 a load. Cortez usually spends twelve or thirteen hours a day at El Guarda, and he takes only one day a week off, most often Mondays, when business at the market is reduced considerably.

The most obvious skills that a *cargador* must have are a penchant for hard work and a strong back. Cortez has the former in spades, and he is developing the latter. Perhaps more important for a *cargador*'s success are an intricate knowledge of the market, which allows him to deliver the *bultos* quickly and efficiently to their owners, and a good relationship with the *fleteros* (pickup owners) and the vendors in order to guarantee a steady stream of work. The *fletera* that Cortez relies on for most of his commissions is named Doña Ximena, a sixty-year-old Ladina woman who has been a fixture at El Guarda since its founding in the mid-1970s. Doña Ximena once had a small store in the interior market but soon found that competition from outside vendors made her business difficult. She decided to convert her stall into a small *bodega* and go into the *fletero* business. She used her market contacts to find vendors in need of her services and contracted with *fleteros* to do the hauling of produce between La Terminal and El Guarda. Her business prospered, and she soon bought two used pickups and enlisted family members to work as drivers. She also now employs her daughter, Doña Mónica, to help her with the running of the business, principally collecting money from the vendors and distributing it to the *cargadores*.

Cortez, like all *cargadores,* is an independent contractor. He shows up for work each day at the corner of 1a. Calle and 3a. Avenida to meet Doña Ximena's *fletes.* While he does this on a regular basis, he is free to determine if he works that day, which *fletero* he works for, and the amount of work he wishes to perform. Nevertheless, he rarely turns down work or takes a vacation or a sick day, as his reliability and efficiency are vital to his remaining in Doña Ximena's good graces and maintaining his position as one of her top workers. His payment is based on the number of small yellow slips of paper, or *papelitos,* inserted into each *bulto* that he redeems each day. On the slips are the names of the vendors to whom the goods belong. Although these paper scraps contain just a name or a nickname, each *cargador* must know the exact location of the vendor without having to ask. In fact, *cargadores* know that a *bulto* marked "Don Chema" that contains tomatoes must go to the Don Chema on 2a. Calle and 1a. Avenida, not the Don Chema who sells mangos and apples on 2a. Calle and 3a. Avenida.

Cortez knows El Guarda and its vendors so well because he literally grew up there alongside his father and older brother. Cortez's father, Don Julio, first came to the market to sell vegetables in the mid-1990s from his home in a Kaqchikel-speaking canton outside Sololá. Soon after, he brought his sons to work and live with him while his wife and two daughters stayed in their *pueblo.* Both boys are successful in their work as *cargadores* because they have used their knowledge of the area and its vendors, many of whom also speak Kaqchikel, to make contacts that favor their employment.

Once the morning deliveries are complete, Cortez will take his *papelitos* to Doña Ximena's *bodega* in the interior market and exchange them for his payment, usually 50 centavos for each of the relatively small *bultos* he is able to carry. Doña Mónica will then take the *papelitos* to the various stalls and collect payment from the vendors for the *fletero* services, usually four or five times what her mother has paid the *cargadores* (Q2–Q3 per *bulto,* depending on its size). Of all the *cargadores,* Cortez is one of the smallest and therefore can only carry smaller *bultos.* Cortez is not small for his age, but because he is only twelve years old and relatively thin, and has no hand truck or cart to aid him in his labors, he is not yet ready to handle large *bultos* that can weigh more than one hundred pounds and earn the *cargador* more money per load. Nevertheless, Cortez is a very successful *cargador;* he usually makes about Q30 a day on weekdays, and double or triple that on weekends and holidays when the market is filled. In a typical month, he brings in from Q1,000 to Q1,100. He gives virtually all of his earnings to his father, who supplies him with pocket money for snacks and visits to the *maquinitas* (arcade).

When I asked Cortez why he works as a *cargador,* and not as a walking vendor as most children of *puesto* owners do, he replied that *cargadores* make much more money. I then said that as he turns over most of his money to his father and therefore does not see much of the immediate direct benefit of his hard work, what was the advantage of working so hard? In response, he simply rolled up his sleeve and showed me his burgeoning biceps. He is proud of the muscles that he has developed. He and his friends often discuss their well-developed physiques and compare themselves to their favorite heroes of the *lucha libre,* or professional wrestling. But as one *fletero* told me, the *cargadores* are not strong because they develop muscles for sport and entertainment as the wrestlers do, but because they are "luchadores, pero por la vida" (fighters, but for their lives).

THE VARIETY OF JOBS PRACTICED BY FULL-TIME CHILD STREET LABORERS

As can be gleaned from the stories of child laborers such as Reina, Pizarro, Perla, and Cortez, in a city like Guatemala City, where an estimated 40 percent of all individuals are part of the urban informal sector, the variety of jobs available on the streets to enterprising individuals is immense. To begin to make sense of this seemingly infinite variety, I divided child street laborers into vocational categories based on a classic study of street work in the city of Cali, Colombia, by sociologist Ray Bromley (1997). Bromley devised a typology of street labor that was composed of nine distinct categories of work (ibid., 124–125). These categories were:

1. Retailing
2. Small-scale Transport
3. Personal Services
4. Security Services
5. Gambling Services
6. Recuperation
7. Prostitution
8. Begging
9. Property Crimes

During my preliminary research in El Guarda and the 18 Calle area, I witnessed children working in each of Bromley's categories as well as two others, namely, illicit drug sales and street entertaining.

Due to the limitations of my research, I was forced to eliminate children who participate in illicit activities, namely, prostitutes, thieves, and those involved in illicit drug distribution and sales. All these activities take place on the streets of Guatemala City, and all are practiced by children as well as adults, though adults do far outnumber children in each category. As stated previously, due to the dangerous and secretive nature of these jobs, the difficulty of doing intensive ethnographic research with these groups,[3] and the relatively small percentage of full-time child street laborers engaged in these occupations, I eliminated them from my research.

I also eliminated three other Bromley categories from my research, namely, gambling services, begging, and recuperation. Children who engaged in legal gambling services, such as the sale of lottery tickets and the proffering of punchboards,[4] were included in my research, but in my estimation did not merit their own category, as none participated in informal "illicit" gambling (such as a street lottery, three-card monte, or a floating card or dice game) as their primary means of support. Gambling itself, in the form of marbles and pitching pennies, was a popular pastime for younger child laborers, while older children and adolescents would bet on card games as well as national and neighborhood league soccer games. In all these activities, the gambling occurred between children and their peers, and though winnings could be substantial, no child or adolescent lived off the proceeds or considered him or herself a professional gambler.

On the streets of Guatemala City, begging was also common, but it was largely practiced by adults and virtually never by children on a full-time basis. Most full-time beggars in the area were in some way physically disabled (usually blind or suffering from severe disability due to a birth defect or serious injury). These individuals were very skilled in defending their territory against any competition and the many predators of the streets. It is doubtful that children with similar disabilities would be as capable of self-defense and therefore be able to beg consistently without falling victim to others. While many of the child street laborers I worked with did rely on the emotional manipulation of their clients in order to procure work or other vital resources (as I will detail extensively in Chapter 6), they did not rely on these skills exclusively, as beggars do, to earn their keep.

Recuperation, activities that are consistent with scavenging for food and the recycling of cans, newspapers, and other goods, was not practiced by children in the areas where I worked. When purchased, these items were most often put to secondary uses by their purchasers and rarely discarded in any condition that would make them recyclable. As a Mexican used-tire salesman in the John Sayles movie *Lone Star* pointed out, the inhabitants of the developing world "are the original recyclers" and for years have been finding secondary and tertiary uses for goods that individuals in the developed world would have long since discarded after their first use. Some individuals in especially dire circumstances did scavenge for food among the many small trash dumps in each area where I worked, but none did so regularly enough to make this a type of full-time work.[5]

The vast majority of full-time child street laborers in Guatemala City belong to the first four categories of Bromley's typology: street sales, personal services, small-scale transport, and security services. It was children engaged in these job categories who represented over 95 percent of the more than five hundred full-time child street workers and laborers I met during survey research in El Guarda and 18 Calle (see Table 3.1).

Nearly 60 percent of the children included in my initial survey, and exactly 50 percent of those children who made up my detailed sample, worked in street sales (see Table 3.2). These vendors were a diverse group, encompassing small children walking the streets selling bags of matches for fifty centavos (seven cents) to adolescents selling designer jeans from fixed sidewalk kiosks for ten to fifteen dollars. To better understand this

Occupational Category	Location		
	El Guarda	18 Calle	Totals
Street Sales	117	166	283
Porter/Delivery	42	57	99
Personal Services	52	45	97
Security Services	12	21	33
Other	6	5	11
Totals	229	294	523

category of child labor, I subdivided the street vendors into two categories: fixed vendors who sell from semipermanent stalls located on the public streets, and nomadic vendors who either carry their stock with them as they sell or sell from the sidewalk without the benefit of any type of permanent or semipermanent kiosk, but usually only have a small tarp placed on a sidewalk. This division is useful and necessary, for it distinguishes between those whose *ventas* represent an early stage of entrepreneurship, requiring little in the way of startup costs or the cultural capital necessary to control a fixed place of business, and those whose *ventas* represent a capital-intensive business that rivals a traditional retail store and requires much more knowledge of the street economy and the connections and power to control an often highly valued location for a kiosk.

For child street laborers, the category of personal services is second only to street sales in popularity. The jobs that fit this category include shoeshiners, shoe repairmen, watchmakers (*relojeros*), and street typists (Bromley 1997, 124). Of these four activities, children in Guatemala City only engage in the first two: shoeshining and shoe repair. A few street typists can be found in the 18 Calle area with their typewriters sitting upon portable desks and crates in front of the municipal services offices as they wait for customers in need of typing services for national and municipal government forms, but in this area, this job is the exclusive practice of adults. In El Guarda, one or two *relojeros* worked on the streets, usually from a semipermanent street kiosk, but again, these men were in their forties or fifties and they bemoaned the fact that they were hard-pressed to survive themselves, much less find youth interested in

TABLE 3.2. MONTHLY INCOME* OF CHILDREN ENGAGED IN THE SIX MOST COMMON STREET VOCATIONS

	Shoeshiner	Car Parker	Porter	Delivery Person	Sidewalk Vendor (Nomadic)	Sidewalk Vendor (Fixed)	Totals
Total	22	9	12	11	22	32	108
Boys	22	8	12	5	15	24	86 (80%)
Girls	0	1	0	6	7	8	22 (20%)
Self-Employed	20	6	7	0	13	15	61 (56%)
Wage Labor	2	3	5	11	9	17	47 (44%)
Mixed**	7	6	9	3	7	7	39 (38%)
6–9 Years Old	3	1	1	2	3	0	10 (9%)
10–14 Years Old	12	6	8	7	8	12	53 (49%)
15–17 Years Old	7	2	3	2	11	20	45 (42%)
Highest Income	Q1,250	Q975	Q900	Q875	Q1,375	Q2,150	Q2,050
Lowest Income	Q250	Q400	Q325	Q300	Q200	Q575	Q300
Median Income	Q675	Q650	Q637	Q550	Q750	Q1,200	Q750
Average Income	Q758	Q643	Q608	Q549	Q865	Q1,383	Q922

*Monthly income for self-employed children is based on the children's typical daily income (per author's knowledge), multiplied by twenty-five to approximate a typical month of work, in which a child would work six days a week for ten to twelve hours a day. Self-employed children usually average twenty-five workdays per month, though this figure changes significantly when migrant children return to their places of origin to either work or visit family and friends.

**"Mixed" refers to the number of children who primarily engage in this occupation but also receive more that 20 percent of their total income from another vocation.

Note: At the time of my research (1997–1999), the Guatemalan national currency (the quetzal or Q) traded at approximately Q7 to US$1. The Guatemalan minimum wage for adult worker was Q520 per month, or US$74.

practicing their seemingly anachronistic trade. The occupational category of personal services was therefore limited to shoeshining and shoe repair for the child street laborers of Guatemala City, with a few select adults practicing this trade in the streets as well.

The third of Bromley's street vocational categories that applied to the children I worked with was small-scale transportation. Bromley's description of the jobs in this category includes the transport of human cargo, but rickshaws and hansom cabs are not to be found anywhere in Guatemala City. Minibuses, pickup trucks, taxis, and the red municipal buses transport all the urban travelers and much of their cargo. While children are often to be seen working on these vehicles as ticket takers and shills to bring in business, their work largely occurs within the vehicle and hence is not truly a street occupation (see Childhope 1993 for a study of the lives of such children in Guatemala City). Where children do perform many jobs falling under the designation of small-scale transport is in the transport of foodstuffs and other dry goods within the neighborhoods where they work. These youths usually limit their transport work to what they themselves can carry, though some use handcarts, small wagons, and occasionally bicycles to help them in this process. I further subdivided this category of small-scale transport of goods into two subcategories: porter and delivery person. There are vital distinctions between the nature of each job as well as the sex-based divisions among their practitioners. Porters, or *cargadores,* are exclusively male, work as independent contractors, and carry goods usually in excess of fifty pounds. Delivery persons are of both genders and work directly for the vendor, and though they are able to carry many items at once, they rarely carry heavy loads. There are some males engaged as delivery boys, but most are young girls who serve as street waitresses, bringing food from the many *comedores* in each area to the street workers.

Security services as defined by Bromley are composed of night watchmen and car park attendants. Night watchmen and armed daytime security guards are ubiquitous throughout Guatemala City in retail stores, restaurants, warehouses, delivery trucks, and factories of all sizes. Due to the explosion of property crime that occurred throughout Guatemala in the 1990s, private security services have proliferated, but children are not sought for work in this capacity. On the other hand, many children are employed on the street and in informal garages to "guard" vehicles. This process of guarding also involves aiding motorists in finding a parking spot on the crowded streets, guiding them into that spot, washing their vehicle, and "guarding" it to ensure that no harm comes to it. While in many cases the motorists are often paying for protection from the boy himself (girls made up fewer than 5 percent of all car parkers), due to the increase of property crime and the ever-growing number of vehicles to be found on the streets of Guatemala City, children engaged in this street occupation provide a necessary service.

Finally, I did have the chance to meet and converse with child street laborers involved in jobs outside of Bromley's typology, namely, street entertainers. Street entertaining for donations is popular both on the streets of Guatemala City and on its municipal buses. During the survey phase of my research, I spoke with two fire-eaters, one magician, three mimes, and five children who sang or told jokes, all of whom practiced their craft in public plazas, parks, and sidewalks. All these children spoke of themselves as entertainers. They took pride in their various routines and the fact that they "got by" on talent and intelligence, not manual labor or criminality. Unfortunately, their schedules were extremely erratic; they worked limited hours and would visit many locations throughout the city, so I was unable to include these children in my in-depth sample research.

As is evident from my description of the variety of jobs practiced by child street laborers, most, if not all, can be considered to be peddlers or market vendors, a group that has been studied in Guatemala from the classic era of modernist ethnography (McBryde 1933; Tax 1953) to the present (Goldín 1985, 1987; Little 2004; Smith 1974, 1976; Swetnam 1975).[6] While less than one-third of the children in my sample were actually formal market vendors or working for formal market vendors (those renting space from a municipal public market or paying the municipality to occupy a fixed public space), shoeshine boys, car parkers, and *ambulantes* thrive in market areas due to large amounts of pedestrian and vehicular traffic.[7]

INCOME GENERATED BY
CHILD STREET LABORERS

It is generally assumed that all child laborers receive only a small fraction of the typical adult wage, as is indeed the case for child laborers working in manufacturing and agriculture, the traditional sectors of the economy that avail themselves of child labor. Street workers, be they adults or children, are thought to be similarly disadvantaged, as they must work in the least hospitable job sites. Both groups are thought to be living hand to mouth, day to day. When one is both a child laborer and a street worker, even social scientists tend to dismiss the possibility that such young workers laboring in the most marginal of work sites could have any hope of earning an income that would be more than token. "And indeed, it is striking to see in any Brazilian city the lines of poor children and adolescents standing guard over small trays of goods—candy, cheap soap and perfumes, watches or hardware—hoping to sell a few small items, perhaps amounting, if they are lucky, to a couple of dollars a day" (Scheper-Hughes and Hoffman 1998, 364). This quote, taken from a recent description of child street laborers by two anthropologists, reinforces the widespread belief that children engaged in street labor make little money, especially relative to adult earnings and to the number of hours these children work. In Table 3.2, I present the earnings of the full-time independent child street laborers with whom I worked. The children are divided by age, occupation, gender, and terms of employment. What stands out most here, and contradicts much of what the authors above stated, is that, based on the median income of both my total sample and each subdivision of my sample, the vast majority of all the children involved in full-time street work earn above the Guatemalan minimum wage, Q21.68 per day for nonagricultural work, or Q542 per month during the time of my research.

As is shown, the typical child street laborer earned an average income of Q917, or 170 percent of the legal minimum adult wage.[8] While this figure is somewhat skewed by the few children who earned over Q1,500 per month (all adolescents working as vendors in fixed street stalls, usually selling goods they themselves own), the median income of the child street laborers in my sample was Q750, itself 138 percent of the legal adult minimum wage. Also impressive is that the median and average incomes of each of the subdivisions of my sample (done by age, sex, and occupational category) surpass the legal minimum wage. The lone exception are children between the ages of six and nine, who typically earn about 35 percent less than the minimum wage. The reasons why the youngest child street laborers earn less than their older peers have much to do with their age and relative inexperience in street labor, but these are just two variables that account for the differences in income of the child street laborers in my sample.

KEY VARIABLES THAT AFFECT THE INCOME OF CHILD STREET LABORERS

Although children earn more than is generally supposed, not all children earn equal amounts. Indeed, child street labor is based on a hierarchy of four essential variables: age, gender, capital investment, and terms of employment. Generally, young children earn less than older ones, service workers with minimal initial capital outlay earn less than vendors, girls earn less than boys, and the self-employed earn more than those who are working for others. Yet this is just a general rule and is best understood within the context of the trajectory of the typical child laborer's career on the streets.

TABLE 3.3. KEY VARIABLES DETERMINING INCOME AMONG CHILD STREET LABORERS

Variables	Shoeshiner & Repair	Car Parker	Porter	Delivery Person	Nomadic Vendor	Fixed Vendor
Sex	100% Male	95% Male	100% Male	80% Female	70% Male	60% Male
Age	All Ages	12–17	Generally Older	All	All	Older
						60% Salaried
Social Relations of Labor	Self-Employed	Most Self-Employed	Self-Employed	Salaried Workers	70% Self-Employed	Employees
Capital* Investment						
Minimum	Q50	Q10	Q10	NA	Q15	Q150
Maximum	Q200	Q55	Q500		Q1,000	Q2,000

Young children usually enter the street as service workers involved in occupations that necessitate a minimal initial capital outlay. Shoeshine boys need from between Q50 and Q75 to purchase the necessary brushes, polishes, a foot stand, and a seat for themselves. Porters, delivery boys and girls, and children who wash and guard cars need almost no tools or money to begin their labor. Entry into these jobs is relatively easy and can be worked sporadically when the demand or opportunity is greatest. Although children may begin these jobs because of random opportunity, they soon find themselves practicing them full-time. Based on my investigations, though these trades are at the bottom of the street hierarchy, children nevertheless manage to earn from 10 to 30 percent above the minimum wage for their efforts.

Young boys dominate all these service trades. The sole service occupation practiced by girls, that of delivery person, is also the lowest paying because of a gender-based pay ethic that reasons that girls do not work as hard nor need money as much as boys. Girls such as Reina are contracted by various cafés to solicit and deliver meals to child and adult street workers at abysmally low wages, even by Guatemalan standards. As mentioned, Reina's day is full of hard work that demands many skills, all for a salary of Q400 per month plus room and board. A boy engaged as a wage laborer in a similar service capacity would usually earn more than a girl. For example, twelve-year-old Américo, who delivered gas tanks to street vendors and houses in the neighborhood, was required to carry only about thirty or forty tins a day, but he received more than double Reina's wages for doing a job that was, while a bit more physically demanding, not nearly as time consuming as Reina's.

Most of the children in my sample began their street careers in service occupations and later moved up the ladder to vending jobs. The only older children who worked in the service sector were those who had begun their street careers at a relatively late age or, in the case of a few shoeshine boys, had developed a regular clientele that made shoeshining much more profitable for them than for many of their peers.

Once children have worked for a few years in the service occupations, most move on to street vending. Street vending is notably more profitable than service work, as is evidenced by the median incomes of nomadic sidewalk vendors, who typically earn 40 percent more than the minimum wage. Those with fixed kiosks usually earn twice the minimum wage. Entry into street vending requires either capital for the purchase of stock or connections that will enable one to sell another's stock. Children generally accumulate both of these resources on the street during their service work. Once again, in the vending occupations, girls tend to make significantly less than boys do. Female child street laborers are concentrated in the sale of prepared foodstuffs, while boys traditionally work selling newspapers, cigarettes, clothing, and dry goods—work that is less difficult and more profitable. The one selling trade that offers girls a relatively high income and a comparatively light workload is the commission sale of lottery tickets; most customers report that they prefer to purchase tickets from girls because girls are "luckier."

Children typically begin their work in sales by working for others, either as a clerk in a street kiosk or as a nomadic vendor of goods owned by a distributor (in the case of newspapers or lottery tickets) or another street vendor. An adult willing to let a child sell his or her stock generally facilitates the transition from service to vending. Child laborers new to the street rarely possess such ties, but service workers are well known to the vendors with whom they share a workspace. Earnings in these cases are predictably lower than if one were the owner of the products for sale, but the experience gained in learning merchandising and the nuances of haggling, not to mention the knowledge of where the best suppliers are found, is indispensable to young apprentices in street selling.

Vital to earning a sufficient income selling goods belonging to others is the ability to haggle. Consumers in street markets are generally very informed as to what they can expect to pay for the goods they desire, but child and adult vendors nevertheless employ many different techniques in trying to maximize their profit margin on each item they sell. This part of street vending is where most of the profits lie for the employee, as he or she can often pocket the difference between what the item in question is actually sold for and the amount that he or she reports to the kiosk owner that the good sold for. One vendor told me that, in the past, employees were never paid a salary but only what they could make above a certain price that the owner demanded for his merchandise. Over time, this system was found to be disadvantageous to the absentee owners, who could not compete with "on the premises" owners who would sell their goods for less and make money on volume as opposed to profit margin. When I asked one of my informants about the key to being a good vendor of someone else's goods, he told me that the key was "balance." When I asked him what that meant, he said it meant "to take a bit from each pocket, but not too much from any one pocket so no one falls over."

Once children have received an education in the art of street selling and have gathered the necessary capital and connections that will allow them to begin their own street vending businesses, their earnings tend to surpass 200 percent of the minimum wage. Of the child street vendors with whom I worked, those who owned their own stock and sold it as nomadic vendors had a median income of over Q725 per month; those who had their own street kiosks had a median income of over Q1,150, with some earning as much as Q2,000–Q2,500 per month. Once again, earnings were directly tied to capital investment, as those children who could only afford to sell products such as glue or baseball caps nomadically earned significantly less that those who could purchase a significant stock of small electronics or clothing to sell at a temporary kiosk or table.

The economic viability of the workers described above stands in sharp contrast to the commonly held notion of child street labor being practiced by unsophisticated economic actors. Child street laborers are uniquely inventive in how they use a combination of hard work, savings, and connections to earn an income that equals and surpasses that of many of their parents and virtually all of their peers in both rural and urban settings (see Villarreal and Peralta Chapetón 1997 for estimated incomes of child laborers working off the street). Their earnings are significant, and most move up the ladder from relatively low-paying service work to more lucrative vending positions. That said, it is necessary to make clear that the lives these children lead are not easy. They work exceedingly hard, usually an average of 60–75 hours per week, and while their earnings do far surpass the minimum wage, this in no way makes them rich. I do not mean to say that a life lived on the equivalent of three to eight dollars a day is easy. But when their earnings are examined within the context of the local economy, it is clear that they are far from marginal.

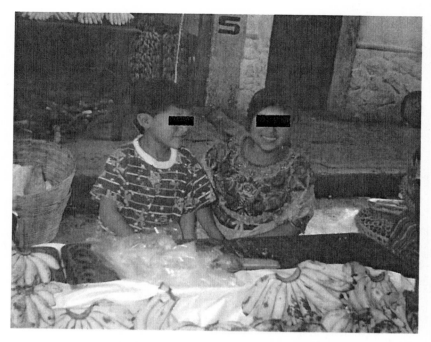

FIGURE 3.1. *Female child laborer at her street* puesto *with her younger brother,
who is a child street worker, Guatemala City.*

FIGURE 3.2. *Child street laborers, El Guarda, Guatemala City.*

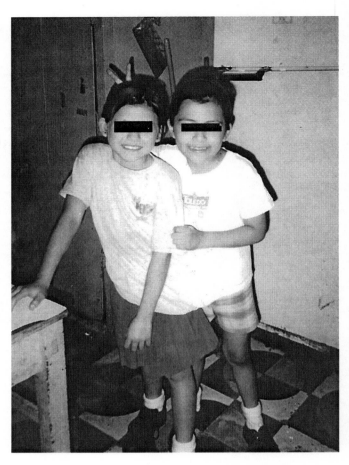

FIGURE 3.3. *Child street laborers who work as delivery girls, El Guarda,*
Guatemala City.

FIGURE 3.4. *Child street laborer (center) who works as a porter, with two child workers, Guatemala City.*

FIGURE 3.5. *Child street laborers who are all nomadic vendors, 18 Calle,*
Guatemala City.

FIGURE 3.6. *Adult street laborer with his children.*

FIGURE 3.7. *Adult street laborer with his son, a child street laborer, 18 Calle, Guatemala City.*

FIGURE 3.8. *Child street shoeshine boy, Guatemala City.*

Four # CHILD STREET LABORERS, THEIR FAMILIES, AND THE HOUSEHOLD ECONOMY

As I have shown, child street laborers are far from being marginal earners participating in marginal economic activities. Their earnings often exceed adult wages in the formal sector, and the jobs they perform are varied and vital to the everyday provisioning of the working poor, the vast majority of Guatemala's citizenry. While I believe anthropology needs to take the agency of children seriously, and ethnographically document how children take control of their lives, this does not mean that we need to see children as separate from their families. One of the primary misconceptions about child street laborers is that children working in the streets are alienated and alone, swallowed up by the violence and anonymity of the urban milieu. I believe this confusion results from a superficial treatment of child street laborers that focuses on their physical appearance and outward conditions, but fails to truly know them. While a picture of a dirty shoeshine boy or overburdened *cargador* (porter) may tell us something about that particular child, such a portrait rarely includes the many other people that that same child may be connected to, from peers to family members and benefactors. And considering that the income the children generate is vital not just to their own but also to their immediate family's present and future economic survival, an understanding of the household economic strategies of their families is necessary for a complete understanding of child street labor. Children working in the street may appear to be alone, yet appearance does not match reality, as the lives of Rey and Velásquez illustrate.

REY'S FAMILY AND SOCIAL LIFE

Up to this point I have described Rey as a very hardworking and successful child street laborer who works in the most highly traveled and trafficked urban neighborhood of the entire country of Guatemala, but this leaves our knowledge of Rey as a human being woefully inadequate. Shining shoes, selling sodas, and hawking newspapers does describe much of the quotidian reality of Rey's life, but these activities do little to define who Rey really is. To understand this complex but nevertheless central question, we must not limit our view of Rey to that of a child working alone on the streets, but must expand it to see him as a son, a brother, a young man with an extensive network of friends and kin who, through their association with him, tell us much about the true Rey.

Though Rey works the streets of Zone 1 away from his family and the town of his origin, he is in no way alone in this world. He was born in a small *cantón* (hamlet) outside of San Antonio Ilotenango, a *pueblo* (village) whose inhabitants are largely of K'iche' Maya Indian descent. San Antonio is located in the Western Highlands of Guatemala, a mere three-hour bus ride from the heart of the capital. Far from being an orphan, Rey has two older siblings and three younger ones; his parents are alive and well and living together. He is the second-oldest son in a family of three boys and three girls. His father, who himself once came to Guatemala City to sell shoes in Zone 1, is now a full-time *agricultor* (farmer), who cultivates the small subsistence land plot, or milpa, that Rey believes once belonged to his grandfather. His mother has never worked outside the home, though, according to her son, her responsibilities as an *ama de casa* (housewife) keep her busy from dawn until dusk.

Life in the *cantón* where Rey grew up was difficult, but Rey and his family were relatively fortunate to have their own piece of land to farm and a house of four rooms and a gas stove, although no running water or electricity. Education was important to Rey's parents, though his father only completed second grade and his mother never attended school. Rey and his siblings all attended primary school in San Antonio in the mornings and worked with their parents in the afternoon, a typical pattern for the children of San Antonio. His older brother and eldest sister both managed to nearly complete primary school in their *pueblo,* but Rey left school after second grade because he failed to grasp the importance of education and sought his future elsewhere. As he told me, "I didn't know what study really was when I was little, and since I had no interest in it, I said that I was not going to study but go to Guate instead."

Rey did not make this choice alone; children at the age of nine or ten, living in any society, much less a typical Maya family in the Western Highlands with a strict deference to parental authority, are seldom free to do as they wish. His father had once worked part-time in Guatemala

City, and he told Rey that if he left school, his only other option would be to work. Rey chose to go to Guatemala City to work not only because he did not like school but also because he did not relish spending all day working in the family milpa with his father. Although he had never been to the capital before, his older brother worked and lived in the city, and Rey had a place to sleep with his brother and an aunt in a small house in Zone 4 of the capital. He left San Antonio alone on a bus for Guatemala City at the age of ten. While it is often assumed that children who work away from their families do so because of abandonment or family breakdown, Rey is one of many examples that invalidate this hypothesis.

Rey may live far away from his parents, but he is intimately connected to family life. He now lives in a small rented room in Zone 9 of the capital with his older brother, who works in a food distributorship near the large La Terminal market. He sees his parents and younger siblings virtually every month when he returns to San Antonio to visit and to rest from his labors. During both planting and harvesting seasons, he will often return to his village with his brother for five to ten days to help his father with their crops, work for which he is not paid but which he nevertheless sees as his responsibility as a son to a father he admires and respects. Free agricultural labor is but one contribution to family income that he provides; without fail, he gives Q300–Q400 a month to his parents. His parents use this money to purchase many of the goods that are necessary to clothe and feed the family, as well as to provide for the school fees and supplies for his three younger siblings.

In addition to his participation in the family economy, Rey is also a regular participant in the social and religious life of San Antonio. He rarely misses any major religious holiday or family celebration such as a wedding or a *quinceañera* (fifteenth birthday celebration for girls). His family, along with many others in his village, belongs to an evangelical Christian sect that has become a social force throughout highland Guatemala (see Stoll 1982, 1990 for treatments of Protestant growth in Latin America; Garrard-Burnett 1998 for the history of the development of evangelical sects in the highlands of Guatemala; and Annis 1987 for a case study of the process in one highland village). He makes sure to time his visits home to coincide with specific religious festivals that are held throughout the department of Quiché, where *evangélicos* (evangelical Christians) come together and celebrate their beliefs, often with the aid of a guest preacher from elsewhere in Central America or even from North America. These *reuniones* not only serve to bring together the faithful from small towns to a central location, but are also viewed as a source of great fun for Rey, as he gets to visit with friends and family as well as meet girls.

Although Rey does see his *pueblo* as the focal point for his social life and his time away from work, he also has many friends and social relations in the capital. When he can, he plays soccer for a team run by the warehouse that his brother works for, as well as informally in a park near where he lives. To see the grace and skill Rey exhibits while making a dash up the wing on a soccer field is to realize that though hard work has occupied much of his youth, recreation is in no way alien to him. He has a girlfriend in the city with whom he spends much of his evening leisure time, either in her home with her family in a *colonia* on the outskirts of the city or at the church they attend near where he lives. He also has more friends in the city than it is possible to count. A snapshot of Rey may make him look alone, swallowed up by the concrete and filth of the underpass where he works, but he is in fact intimately connected to friends and family throughout the city and in his rural *pueblo*.

VELÁSQUEZ'S FAMILY AND SOCIAL LIFE

Like Rey, Velásquez is a rural-born child who spends most of his time working for a living in the city, and he is not alienated from his family, his hometown, or its culture. Unlike Rey, Velásquez still resides in the house in which he was born, located in the small Maya *cantón* of La Libertad outside San Juan Sacatepéquez, a town located on the outskirts of Guatemala City. He speaks fluent Kaqchikel, which is the language used in his home, and is fluent and literate in the Spanish language. He spent his earliest years helping an uncle of his in a small milpa near his home, and much like his peers who have never left La Libertad, when he is older, he hopes to purchase his own land and cultivate it while continuing to work as a vendor in El Guarda on the weekends. His "charismatic" church, which he and his mother and brother regularly attend on Sunday mornings, is a dominant institution in his life and that of many others in La Libertad.

Velásquez spends the majority of his life working on the streets of El Guarda. Including the time he spends in transit from his rural home, he usually is on public streets and buses about fourteen hours a day. He spends this time largely without adult supervision, save that of his employer, Doña Yoli. This would place Velásquez firmly within the group that the United Nations refers to as "children in the streets" and therefore in grave danger of becoming a true homeless street child or a member of the "children of the streets." Velásquez's mother is well aware of where her son spends his life, as she, too, sells there and once told me: "Here [the streets of El Guarda] is where my children have grown up, here is where they have earned their bread." Yet she does not have to worry about her children as much as many other mothers whose children must work on the streets of El Guarda, for her children have all had the benefit of Doña Yoli.

Doña Yoli is Velásquez's employer, a late middle-aged woman who has been selling at El Guarda since the late 1970s. But to call her just his employer is to underestimate the importance that she has in Velásquez's life and that of his family. On the surface, she looks to be just another vendor who is employing a child to help her with her labors. Doña Yoli is light-skinned and a Ladina, a member of the economically, politically, and socially dominant ethnic group in Guatemala, and does not appear to be related to the darker-skinned Velásquez, who is a Maya Indian. Yet Doña Yoli is like a wealthy relation to Velásquez and his family, though she herself is a member of the working poor as well. She employed his brother Juan for many years, until he found a better job outside the market when he turned sixteen. It was she who found the private secondary school where Juan is a night student and is only one year away from completing his junior high school, or *básico*, studies. She is also a confidante and advisor to Velásquez's mother, who sells vegetables on a nearby sidewalk and has been a single parent supporting her family since her husband abandoned her for another woman.

Velásquez's particular relationship with Doña Yoli allows him to enjoy certain advantages in his work that are not available to many other child workers. First, Doña Yoli regularly gives Velásquez two hours off each weekday to attend an informal school located nearby in the interior market of El Guarda. This school, which is run by a local NGO, offers low-cost Ministry of Education–certified primary school classes and caters to working children and those children of vendors in the area who do not have the time or resources to attend a public school. Velásquez has been attending this school ever since he went to work for Doña Yoli, and in those three years has managed to receive credit for completion of the second grade; should he manage to maintain his attendance for three more years, he will earn a primary school graduation certificate.[1]

But the time off that Velásquez receives to attend the school is benefiting not only Velásquez's educational abilities but his social ones as well.

Unlike the common view of child laborers as having lost their childhood, to observe Velásquez at the program is to see a true child who behaves exactly as one would expect a child to. The other children in the program are close friends with Velásquez, and he is one of the most well-liked and popular students in the classroom. He has good friends named Oso, Rufo, and Chino with whom he gossips, wrestles, and plays all sorts of games. He is also a member of the soccer team that has won the league championship among the informal school programs throughout the city, though he would be quick to say that soccer is not his best game. What Velásquez is most known for, besides his wide grin, is his skill at *cincos*, or shooting marbles.

One day, after the school program had concluded for the day, I came upon Velásquez playing *cincos* with three other boys in an unused corner of the interior market. The object of the game was quite simple. One boy would shoot a marble into the corner, and the other boys would attempt to hit one of their rivals' marbles with one of their own. A successful hit meant that the shooter won his opponent's marble, and a miss gave his opponent another marble that he could then target and attempt to hit and win. After a few minutes of observing, it was clear to me that Velásquez was far and away the best player, and that judging from the number of marbles in his pocket, he was cleaning up on his friends. Later that day, long after the game had dispersed and all its participants were back at work, I asked one of the boys where they bought the marbles. I then went to the stall and purchased about fifty of them and went home to hone my skills, which had deteriorated in the twenty-odd years since I had stopped shooting marbles. After a few hours of practice, my skills returned sufficiently for me to take on Velásquez. Two days later, I casually showed Velásquez my stash of marbles, made up of some of the most expensive and prized, and challenged him to a game.

After class that day, we repaired to that same corner where I had been an observer a few days before, but now I was part of the main event. As the other children gathered around, most cheering my name (Profe, Profe) and hoping that I would humble the cocky champion, I asked Velásquez if I should go first and send out the first target marble. He raised his shoulders in a shrug, smiled at me, and said, "¿Por qué no?" ("Why not?"). Velásquez then shot his marble wide of mine, and the game was on. Velásquez failed to hit my *cinco* on his first shot, but he did not miss many other shots that day. In the end, the match ended with him surrounded by his peers, slapping him on the back and eyeing the booty that he had won from me. I left the area light of marbles and friends.

I had been thoroughly beaten in a child's game by a child. And though for most hours of the day, to the casual observer, my vanquisher looked and behaved little like a true child as he carted trash, carried stacks of egg cartons, or attended to clients in Doña Yoli's stall, because of the generosity of his employer, his tight-knit group of friends, the close presence of his mother, his own considerable talents, and despite the poverty that forces him to help support himself and his family, Velásquez is a true child. And as a child, the institution that most impacts his day-to-day life is his household.

HOUSEHOLDS AND CONFLICT

Anthropology, from its earliest precursors, has always been tremendously interested in the household. Nineteenth-century social thinkers such as Lewis Henry Morgan (1877), J. J. Bachofen (1967 [orig. pub. 1861]), Henry Sumner Maine (1913 [orig. pub. 1861]), and Friedrich Engels (1969 [orig. pub. 1884]) were concerned with the evolutionary development of the family and household arrangements, and the household economy is currently the subject of numerous articles and edited volumes.[2] Much of the study of internal household dynamics has been conducted by feminist ethnographers, who have focused on male patterns of dominance and authority in the household,[3] specifically how women's work, both inside and outside the home, is consistently devalued. Be it uncompensated food preparation and domestic chores or market vending or piecework, women rarely receive power commensurate with the work they perform. This reality is an obvious result of culturally sanctioned notions of patriarchy that devalue women's labor and the contribution they make to the household. Ideology accords their labors little compensation in the form of control over household resources, and elder males enforce this ideology. Yet little research has been done to this point to fully investigate the way age works, at times in concert with gender, to create ideologies that guarantee the domestic hegemony of elders over the young.[4]

One notable exception to this has been the work of Winnie Lem (2002) on "regimes of control" in Languedoc family businesses. Lem found that senior males in the enterprises engage in either despotic or hegemonic practices in order to maintain their control over the labor of children. Hegemonic practices (from Gramsci 2000) have their base in the ethic of familism, or "what is good for the family is good for me," whereas despotic practices reward children (and women) for obedience and punish them severely for behavior seen by the elder males as disobedient or defiant. As the economics of modernity in the French countryside brings fewer opportunities for small family-run businesses in the face of rapid industrialization, and with the lure of the city being a constant pull for youth, Lem notes that elder males who once ruled their offspring via hegemony are increasingly forced to turn to despotism to dominate women and youth.[5]

Lem's work echoes an earlier formulation by David Cheal (1989). Based on the pioneering research of Sandra Wallman (1979, 1986) on households as resource systems, Cheal posits two models of resource management within households, the moral economy model and the political economy model. In the moral economy model, household resource management is "generated by shared meanings that govern the interactions between individuals occupying defined social statuses in a system of mutual aid" (Cheal 1989, 17). Much like Lem's hegemonic regime of control, family consensus and cooperation are generated by a culturally informed family unity discourse. In contrast, the political economy model assumes that interhousehold division of resources will be fraught with conflict as individuals seek to advance their own personal interests within the household power structure (Cheal 1989, 19–20). Although both of Cheal's models closely resemble the work of earlier theorists (Thompson [1966] and Becker [1976, 1991] come to mind), his work is important in that it brings these models to bear on *internal* household practices, and he emphasizes that, in the modern world, households often practice both models, depending on the resources available to the household and the social context. Before documenting the relation between Cheal's and Lem's formulations of internal household dynamics and the households of child street laborers, I must address the structure and composition of the households to which the children I worked with belong.

CHILD STREET LABORERS AND THEIR FAMILIES: HOUSEHOLD MORPHOLOGY AND THE MULTILOCALE HOUSEHOLD

Of the 108 child street laborers I worked with intensively, all but 4 were in regular contact with a member of their family. Because children must work away from their homes does not mean that they have abandoned family life or been rejected by their families; in fact, a primary reason why children work so hard and succeed at developing successful street careers has to do with their close ties with and obligations toward their families, most of which are strongly functioning units despite facing poverty and usually some degree of physical separation. Nor do child laborers come from families that would be described as pathological or broken, as only 4 percent reported never having known one of their parents, and more than 60 percent reported that their biological parents were still living together; many of the remaining 40 percent whose parents no longer live together are those who have had a parent die.[6] Of the child laborers in my sample, 30 percent were fortunate enough to currently live with one or both of their parents, and another 40 percent lived with a close relative, defined as a first cousin or closer. Of the remaining 30 percent (31 children), 17 lived with a nonrelated adult who was also their employer, and the other 14 lived with friends and/or distantly related cousins or landsmen. None of the children I worked with lived alone or were homeless.

In addition to their close ties to family members while in Guatemala City, of the 92 children who were migrants to Guatemala City, 87 percent also report having a home and at least two members of their nuclear family still living in their town of origin. This phenomenon, whereby a nuclear family is divided into some family members living in rented quarters in the capital while others stay in the original village, is very common in Guatemala and throughout Latin America (see Altamirano and Hirabayashi 1997; González 1988). While not all family members live under the same roof, one of the primary determinants of the household definition is the fact that the urban segment of the household pools resources with the rural-residing part, and that decisions regarding the production, distribution, and consumption of resources are made collectively between both groups. Thus coresidence is not a necessary condition for considering these rural and urban living units to be one integrated household. The resulting arrangement I have deemed the "multilocale" household. Unlike the case of long-distance migration by family members, which often creates two distinct households with some pooling of resources, as is common in the remittance economies of many Latin American and Caribbean nations (see Cohen 2004 and González 1988 for two examples), in a multilocale household, it is not just money that is shared; rather, all decisions regarding resource deployment and consumption for all members of both locations are made as if they were one coresident household. This type of multilocale household is itself an intermediate step in rural-to-urban migration, and theorists debate as to whether this arrangement is a temporary one that will eventually lead to the entire family migrating to the urban area or is instead an enduring strategy for the economic sustenance of the family while maintaining traditional economic and social ties to their home village (see Rizzini et al. 1994). Of the children in my final sample, only 11 who were born in the countryside later moved with their entire family to the capital, but due to the age of my informants, it is difficult to tell if these cases represent the rule or the exception. In almost all cases, these multilocale households are divided along the lines of males moving to the capital and females, along with some males, remaining in the sending community. Unlike other cases of male-only migration for employment, as most families retain a subsistence agricultural plot in the sending community, a male member of the nuclear family is usually left in the *pueblo* to work the land. As I detail later, this arrangement is vital in maintaining the traditional family structure and culture, as children who work in the capital return to their rural homes frequently to help out with agricultural labor, especially during planting and harvesting seasons.

CHILD STREET LABORERS
AND BIRTH ORDER

Multilocale households are especially common among child street laborers because their families, both rural and urban alike, are usually quite large, even by Guatemalan standards, where the fertility rate is 4.7 children per woman (UNICEF 2002), down from 5.6 in 1990, which is closer to the time when most of my informants were born. There was just one "only child" among my informants, and the fertility rate for the mothers of the children in my sample was 7.5 children per woman, nearly 3 "children" more than the current national average, and the typical nuclear family was composed of nine individuals.

As far as birth order is concerned, the children I worked with tended to be part of either the oldest or the youngest groupings of their families. Not including the singular "only child," 28 of the 107 children were the eldest in their families, of whom 17 were males and 11, females. While eldest males therefore make up 20 percent of all male child street laborers, a relatively proportional number, eldest females make up over 50 percent of all female child street laborers, indicating that when girls do perform street labor, they are far more likely than boys to be the eldest in their families. This discrepancy can also be attributed to the fact that in families who base part of their income on agriculture, the eldest son will often remain in the village working the fields with his father, grandfather, or uncle, while younger males whose labor is not as necessary will be sent to work in the capital. Eldest females are also equally prized for their domestic and child-care work while in their *pueblo,* but they can more easily be replaced by a junior sister if the father or mother needs her assistance in the city. In families with six or more children, which made up 72 percent of my total sample, children belonging to the eldest one-third of their families[7] made up half of all children, whereas children who were part of the youngest one-third made up only about 20 percent. Once again, it is the oldest children who are most likely to work for wages, on the street or elsewhere.

CHILD STREET LABORERS' ROLE IN THE HOUSEHOLD ECONOMY

While I argue that child street laborers are far more than merely shoeshiners and vendors, the work itself is in many ways essential to maintaining strong relationships between children and their families. Firstly, children gravitate toward street work because one or more close family members has experience in urban street work itself, in formal market vending, or at the very least with some form of labor in the capital city. As stated previously, 70 percent of the children I worked with were living in the city with a member of their nuclear family or a first cousin, and nearly all had found their first work in the city through the assistance of a family member. Of the children who did not report their fathers as deceased (90 of 108), 19 of them had a father who at the time of my research worked as a vendor outside the city, and 18 reported that their father was currently working as a market or street vendor in Guatemala City. Of the 103 children who reported that their mother was alive, 26 had mothers who worked as market vendors outside the city, and 16 had mothers who were either formal market or informal street vendors in the capital. The most popular vocations for the children's parents were agriculture for fathers (39 percent) and housewifery for mothers (45 percent); nevertheless, a significant number of the children relied on their parents' vocational experiences and connections to find their initial job in the street. Those who did not have a parent whose experience could help them with placement or advancement in the street economy would often rely on siblings or cousins to help them gain entry, as was the case for 28 children who lived with close cousins (but not with members of their nuclear families) who had experience in either formal or informal vending or service work in the capital.

The reason why so many children followed kinsmen into vending and street work has to do with general vocational patterns among the working poor, as documented by William Wilson (1997) for the urban poor in Chicago, Philippe Bourgois (1996) for crack dealers in Spanish Harlem, and Martha Wittig (1997) for market-working children in Honduras. As is logical, jobs are easiest to find when close relations have the experience and connections to assist one in getting in the door with employers or learning the ropes in the case of self-employment.

CHILD STREET LABOR AND HOUSE-HOLD ECONOMIC DIVERSIFICATION

Child street laborers are especially likely to go into street work related to the experience of their relations because they are often enmeshed in a nuclear family–and extended kin–based network of economic diversification. Dating back to the seminal work of Sol Tax in his book *Penny Capitalism* (1953), researchers have long noted that among the Maya of highland Guatemala, and indeed in many indigenous subsistence-farming communities, a kin-based pooling of economic resources has been essential to the maintenance of traditional highland village life based around subsistence milpa farming (see Hill 1989, 1992 for examples of this pattern as it occurred during the colonial era). Many milpas yield crops that exceed family needs and can therefore be sold for cash at local or long-distance markets, but due to the vagaries of the market or climate conditions, yields will often be insufficient to support a family, and thus a "backup" plan for survival must be in place. Backup plans traditionally involved work on coastal fincas as paid agricultural laborers or family members involved in petty commodity production, trade, and commerce, most often in a nearby city or the nation's capital.[8] With the disruption of traditional seasonal migration patterns due to the earthquake and the civil war,[9] not to mention the destruction of the material basis for subsistence throughout the highlands during the late 1980s (see Smith 1988), many families found their only reliable means of survival to be based on commerce in the nation's capital.

In the case of the children I worked with, when a multilocale household arrangement occurs, this pattern is evenly divided between fathers who move to the capital with older sons and both engage in street work, and those families in which the father stays in the sending community to maintain the family milpa while older sons migrate to the city to perform street work and live with a relation or fellow villager, usually of the same age group. When a father and son(s) migrate to the city, they are usually the primary means of income and support for the family members left behind in the countryside, and urban street work is a full-time job for both family members. When a child migrates without a parent, his or her purpose in the city is both to learn the trade of street work and to provide much-needed cash for his family left in the *pueblo*. Intermediate cases of this type also exist, whereby one child uses his time on the street as a means of establishing himself in business and another is merely earning money to temporarily aid his family. This type of arrangement was typified by the Castro family of clothing vendors I worked with in the capital.

Don Diego Castro had established a street-vending kiosk selling sporting clothes and footwear in the 18 Calle area in 1988 with help from a cousin who sold similar goods nearby. He maintains a small subsistence plot in his home village outside Momostenango, which he works on two days a week and which is tended regularly by a younger brother of his in exchange for part of the harvest. Don Diego therefore gets the benefits of cash income from his street work and is able to maintain his milpa, which provides much of his family's food. He comes to the city five days a week with his two eldest sons, fourteen-year-old Ponce and eleven-year-old Américo. When in the city, they live with Don Diego's cousin in a small rented room nearby that serves as both the *bodega* (warehouse) for their goods and rudimentary living quarters. On his weekly trips back to his village, Don Diego will take Ponce with him to help in the fields, while Américo stays in the city with his cousin. When I first asked Don Diego why he did not travel to his *pueblo* with both of his sons, he explained that his younger son, Américo, could not leave his *mercadería* (merchandise) unattended, which made little sense, as their stock was regularly placed in storage when he and Ponce were outside the city.

Upon further questioning, he explained that Ponce, though of great help to him in the city, was his assistant and did not work for pay, whereas the younger sibling, Américo, was slowly purchasing and selling his own stock of goods, working for himself as a true *comerciante* (retailer/businessman). He then pointed to a small side table attached to their kiosk that contained about forty pairs of athletic socks, emblazoned with the logos of local soccer clubs, and a similar number of tank-style undershirts.

This merchandise, amounting to perhaps Q150, or about US$20 in wholesale value, was selected, purchased, and sold by his younger son, Américo. Ponce, he explained, did not want to sell his own *mercadería* as his younger brother did, and was far more comfortable working in the milpa with his father. Don Diego also pointed out that Ponce would soon be responsible for the family plot and would live in the *pueblo* full-time, allowing Don Diego to attend to his kiosk full-time. The family land holdings would not be sufficient to support both young men and their families in the future, therefore it was more important that Américo learn the business and begin to understand the intricacies of street vending rather than his older brother, whose life would be based in their village.

ETHNICITY, BIRTHPLACE, AND RESIDENCE OF CHILD STREET LABORERS IN MY SAMPLE

Velásquez and Rey are representative of most child street laborers in the areas in which I worked: Maya children who began life in small rural *pueblos* and came to the city at a young age. Of the 108 children in my final sample, 92 (or 85 percent) were born outside of Guatemala City, most in the ethnically Maya Western Highlands of Guatemala in the departments of Quiché (37 percent) and Totonicapán (26 percent), with a few each coming from the other highland departments of Sololá (4 percent), Chimaltenango (5 percent), Sacatepéquez (3 percent), Huehuetenango (5 percent), and Quetzaltenango (1 percent). Only 4 of the children in my sample came from the Oriente, the Ladino-dominated eastern part of Guatemala, specifically the departments of Escuintla (3 percent) and Jalapa (1 percent). As is typical among all street workers in Guatemala City, those who self-identified as belonging to the Maya ethnic group outnumbered Ladinos more than four to one (82 percent to 18 percent), though the terms they used to describe their identity varied tremendously.[10] Of those children who identified as Maya, nearly 80 percent spoke the K'iche' language, with others speaking Kaqchikel (10 percent) and Q'anjob'al (8 percent). Three children who identified themselves as Maya did not speak any Mayan language, and, interestingly enough, though the Ladino children did not speak any Mayan language, most did know at least some words in one of the Mayan languages spoken by one of the larger groups, especially the slang and "dirty" words that are common currency in the street setting.

Despite their largely rural origins, all but three of the children I worked with are at least part-time residents of Guatemala City or Mixco, a satellite suburb that went from a small town to a contiguous neighborhood that is indistinguishable from the capital in a few short years. Those such as Velásquez, who do not live in Guatemala City or Mixco, lived in the bordering department of Sacatepéquez, in either small *pueblos* or the departmental capital of Antigua. Though these children were most often recent migrants to the city, this migration in no way cut them off from their families.

INCOME THAT CHILD STREET LABORERS PROVIDE THEIR HOUSEHOLDS

As a child street worker, Ponce does not contribute income to his own or his family's sustenance; he is not a breadwinner, perhaps the most vital role that all the children in my sample played. As I illustrated in Chapter 3, the income that child street laborers earn is substantial relative to typical adult wages among the working poor, and it is the child's ability to provide for him/herself as well as to make significant contributions to the family's overall sustenance that aids their family.

There are two different ways in which children contribute to their household's economic fortunes. The first and most common manner is via unpaid work in a family subsistence or business endeavor. This is child work, and it is the rule rather than the exception for a majority of Guatemala's children.[11] Although child workers are not included in my study, it is important to note that all but 3 of the 108 children in my sample of child street laborers were once child workers, 78 on a family agricultural plot and the rest helping out a parent who was a street or formal market vendor or working in a cottage manufacturing capacity such as textile manufacture or food preparation. It is also vital to mention that while all the children in my study receive income commensurate with the work they perform while on the street, many also return to the villages of their origin on a regular basis to perform work, usually of an agricultural nature. This pattern is easily noticeable on the street, as shoeshiners and child street vendors are not nearly so abundant on the streets of the capital in the late weeks of May and early weeks of August when they flock to their *pueblos* en masse to help out with either the planting or the harvesting of the traditional highland staples of corn and beans.

It is difficult to estimate the degree of a child's contribution in of these cases, as they vary from children procuring and producing tire objects for sale (such as the hats that eight-year-old Roberta manufactured) yet receiving no monetary compensation whatsoever, to small children aiding their fathers in their milpas, doing basic tasks that have as much to do with enculturating a child into what it means to be a Maya subsistence farmer as they do with helping with actual work that makes a parent's job more productive or more efficient.

The second way that child street laborers contribute to their households' economies is through direct payments out of their income. As far as actual cash contributions that child street laborers provide to their families, all but eleven of the children in my sample were true breadwinners. Thirteen children, like Velásquez and Reina, had their salaries delivered monthly directly into the hands of their parents (in the examples of Velásquez and Reina, to their mothers) from their employers. This is often the case when children work for an employer who has a relationship and regular contact with the child's guardian. Velásquez's monthly salary of Q400 provides a good percentage of his mother's income that goes directly toward providing the basic necessities such as food, clothing, and shelter for himself and his siblings. Reina's salary of Q350 also goes directly to her mother, yet Reina's basic necessities are met by her employer, with whom she lives, and she is therefore a complete economic asset to her mother, who provides her with virtually no support.[12] It is worth noting that both children do have their own money and do see some of the direct fruits of their labors, in that Velásquez gets to keep some of the funds he earns from hauling trash, which he spends on himself, and Reina receives tips from her customers, which, although infrequent, do provide her with pocket money to purchase snacks and small items such as barrettes and school supplies. Reina and Velásquez are typical of children whose employers give their salaries to their parents in that they are both relatively young for child street laborers (eleven and ten) and their basic needs are provided by an adult guardian, thus they are not responsible for themselves.

Self-employed children, such as Rey, and those who work for employers who do not have regular contact with the child's legal guardian, do not have to turn over any of their income to their families, but still nearly all do. Of the ninety-five children who receive direct payment for their labor, all but eleven report giving part of their salaries to their family guardians.[13] On average, of all children who reported contributing to their family's income (ninety-seven), children who were given food

TABLE 4.1. CHILDREN'S SELF-REPORTED CONTRIBUTION TO FAMILY INCOME*

Contribution (in quetzales)	100	150	200	250	300	350	400	450	500	550	600	Total
Independent Workers	1	5	5	6	13	2	9	3	6	0	3	53
Dependent Workers	0	0	5	3	8	3	14	2	8	0	1	44
Totals	1	5	10	9	21	5	23	5	14	0	4	97

*Children were asked to give their monthly contribution to their parents' income to the nearest 50 quetzales. Intermediate numbers (150, 250, 350, etc.) were less popular responses than the 100-quetzal intervals (100, 200, 300) due to what I believe to be the children's ease at estimating in hundreds of quetzales. Though grouping the responses into 100-quetzal intervals might have been more indicative of this reality, I chose to keep the original intervals that were included in my interviews with the children in the interest of recording their actual responses to the question.

and shelter by their employers (dependent workers), be they related or unrelated, gave 70–75 percent of their income directly to their parent(s), whereas those who were entirely responsible for their own sustenance (independent workers[14]) while in the city gave their parent(s) between 30 and 35 percent of their income.

Interestingly enough, the mean monthly amount of money given by children to their parents by both independent and dependent child street laborers was very similar (Q300 for independent workers, Q400 for dependent workers; see Table 4.1, p. 106) due to the larger incomes of independent child street laborers and the fact that dependent children were expected to contribute more of their income to family coffers, since their basic needs were met without dipping into their earnings. In both cases, the cash contributions that a child can make to his or her family are in no way insubstantial, they often provide the necessary funds for the family to survive, and, in some cases, they allow for familial economic advancement, such as the purchase of additional land or capital goods, as well as funding the continuing formal education of younger siblings, both in the *pueblo* and in the capital city.

CHILD STREET LABORERS' FAMILIES AND THE WORK ETHIC

A child's work and labor-related income may be essential to family survival, but these are not the primary reasons that most parents give for why their children work. In interview after interview, the immediate response to this question by parents was "so as not to be thieves." Even though crime is an ever-increasing problem in urban and rural Guatemala, this response does not so much indicate a fear of creating a generation of thieves as it does the fact that in the rural Maya world that most of my informants come from, hard work, for children as well as adults, is a moral as well as an economic matter. Parents who have children who do not attend school and labor on the streets as well as children who attend school are quick to point out that it is good for all of their children to work, and that it is school rather than work that is optional and up to the child's particular skills and desires.[15] Work is universally esteemed as necessary for young children and adolescents, boys and girls alike. As Don Julio, father of a twelve-year-old *achimero* told me, "If a child is not taught to work, he will become a vagrant, and you must teach them when they are very young, because if not, they will not want to work when they are older. This one [referring to his son] has friends in our neighborhood who go to school and play in the street all night. That is not right, for they do not learn anything about what it is to work . . . it is important to teach a child a job, any job, for even the *lustrador*, he goes about earning."

In other words, to be a good child, parent, community member, and Maya, one must have a strong work ethic. This work ethic was born of both the need for children's work in small agricultural endeavors[16] typified by the traditional Maya milpa, as well as an enduring cultural logic that sees child play, and ultimately child work and child labor, as integral to cultural training (see similar examples in Loucky 1988; Porter 1999; Whiting 1963).

CHILD STREET LABORERS AND HOUSEHOLD REGIMES OF CONTROL

The work ethic exhibited by the child street laborers I worked with is intrinsically related to what ethnographer Walter Little has described as the three ethnographically demonstrated constants to the ideal Maya household, namely, deference to elders, a division of labor according to gender, and the pooling of household resources (2004, 162, based on the work of Nash 1970 and Ehlers 1990).[17] A good Maya child not only works hard but also does so for her/his family, in a gender-appropriate task, at the behest of her/his elders.

The vast majority of the child street laborers that I studied did conform to the household behavioral ideal for children, and this was the case for both those who identified as Maya and those who identified as Ladino.[18] As Little mentions, though this is indeed the cultural norm, numerous studies (including Bossen 1984; Ehlers 1990; Hendrickson 1995; Warren 1989; and his own) point out that this cultural ideal is often altered in the case of actual household practice. This alteration most often occurs when traditionally subordinate groups such as women and children are able to take advantage of economic opportunities that allow them to break free of the constraints imposed on them by this typical household ideology, though increased earning power is not necessarily enough for women or children to gain greater power within the household decision-making process.[19]

For the majority of the children in my sample, increased earning power does give them greater power, yet paradoxically this does not conflict with the ideal family ideology, as noted above. Of the ninety-seven child street laborers who do make cash contributions to their families' household economy, most are completely deferential to parental control of the household budget and of all decisions regarding the income that they contribute. This is especially true of independent workers, who number fifty-three of the ninety-seven contributors.

Independent workers, who generally provide 30–35 percent of their income directly to their household, have little or no say with regard to what happens to the funds they contribute, as the following dialogue with Matador, a twelve-year-old *achimero*, illustrates:

Interviewer:	So you give your parents about two hundred and fifty quetzales a month.
Matador:	Yes, sometimes more. And one time four hundred for Christmas.
I:	What do they spend the money on?
M:	Things they need.
I:	Like what?
M:	Things they need.
I:	Things for you? Things for themselves? Things for your sisters? Food?
M:	Things they need. Food. They are building a new house, too.
I:	Do they tell you what they do with the money?
M:	No.
I:	Do they ever ask you what they should do with the money?
M:	(Laughs) My father decides.
I:	What would he do if you did not come home with money?
M:	Why? (confused)
I:	What would happen if you did not give him money?
M:	I don't know. He would be angry (*enojado*).
I:	Would he hit you?
M:	Why would he hit me?
I:	Because you did not have money for him.
M:	But why would I not have money?

Matador seemed unable to conceive of not having money and of not sharing that money with his parents. While Matador has no control over the income he provides, he dutifully returns home every fifteen or thirty days to hand it over to his father. When asked why he does not just keep the money for himself, he struggled for an answer. Matador and independent workers like him are completely enmeshed in what Lem (2002) calls a hegemonic regime or what Cheal (1989), E. P. Thompson (1971), and James Scott (1976) would call a moral economy. They behave dutifully because that is how a "good" son or daughter behaves. Failure to contribute to the family's subsistence is inconceivable for independent child laborers, for to do so would be to cease truly being a member of a family. They do not contribute to their household out of fear, though fear of either punishment or banishment may exist, but instead out of a firm cultural and moral belief that the pooling of resources and deference to elders is the logical and correct way to behave.

Independent workers also exhibit little desire to exclude their families from the proceeds of their labors for another reason, namely, that they do control a significant part of their incomes, the 65 or 70 percent that they do not turn over to their families. These funds, which are spent largely on day-to-day survival, allow these children to control a percentage of their incomes. This allows them to act in their own interests, as is described in Cheal's political economy model (1989, echoing Becker's [1976, 1991] formulation of entire household behavior), without engendering the interfamilial struggle that often occurs when all resources are pooled. Part of their personal surplus (money not given to a parent or spent on basic personal survival) is usually invested in small consumer goods (clothing, electronics, grooming products) and entertainment that allow the children to, as Mills (1999) describes for adolescent Thai female factory workers, both reap the rewards of their labor and participate as consumers in the urban milieu, a hallmark of modernity. The remaining amount is available for the child to invest in his or her own business, be it for new supplies, additional stock for sale, or long-term savings for future needs. Independent child street laborers remain such strong participants in the household economy of their families because the nature of their livelihoods allows them to pool resources with their natal household (the moral economy/familial hegemony model) while maintaining some degree of economic self-interest and self-determination.

Unlike their independent counterparts, dependent child laborers are less likely to directly control the proceeds of their labor. This is the case with children such as Reina and Velásquez, as some (Velásquez) or all (Reina) of the proceeds of their labors are given directly to their parent by their employer. This is especially true among girls, who make up just 18 percent of my overall sample of child laborers, yet except for rare cases (such as Perla), are all dependent workers whose entire earnings are taken by their parents. This situation is one in which the child laborer is more likely to describe their contributions to their family's household economy as being unjust, leading to a household regime of control (Lem 2002) based on coercion. Coercion, in the form of verbal abuse and threats of physical abuse, is an effective means by which elders assert control over children within the household. The victims of this abuse are usually girls suffering at the hands of their female and, at times, male elders.

Yet children involved in household regimes that may be described as despotic do utilize other means to assert their autonomy and resist their domination. In the cases of those working for nonrelated adults, this resistance is usually directed at their employer, as with thirteen-year-old Emiliana, whose employer, Doña Josefina, told me the following, "Oh, Profe, how this one steals. She is pretty, and she knows that they [the customers she delivers food to, largely adolescent boys and men] will help her get away with things. I have to watch her every minute, or she will rob me."

Ironically, Emiliana told me that though she did at times take "a few centavos" for herself, she complained that her mother received her salary directly from Doña Josefina and did not give her money for clothes, and as Doña Josefina only supplied her with dirty secondhand clothing, she was entitled to money for clothing, considering how hard she worked. Those dependent workers who labored for related adults also frequently used the types of techniques mentioned by Scott in his work on "everyday" peasant resistance in Malaysia (1986), such as feigning ignorance, stretching the truth, or simply underperforming their duties in order to protest their treatment. This resistance is often met with complaints from employers, who pressure the parents to control their offspring better. This is a continuing tension that exists in the lives of many dependent child street laborers, a tension that can mount to the point that the child or the parent finds coercion insufficient for the domestic unit to remain economically viable.

WHEN HEGEMONY AND DESPOTISM FAIL: CHILD STREET LABORERS WHO DO NOT CONTRIBUTE TO FAMILY INCOME

Of the eleven children I worked with who did not contribute at all to their families' economic fortunes, two types of children emerged. The first are the "abandoned/abandoning" children most often detailed in work on true homeless street children (Aptekar 1988; Hecht 1998). These children were either abandoned by their immediate families or themselves chose to leave due to a lack of emotional and material support provided by their parents. They represent the breakdown of household regimes of control, both hegemonic and despotic. While some of these children become homeless "niños de la calle," some manage to find other adults who will take them in, and they pay for this support via street labor. These children also form friendships with other child laborers and may end up sharing living quarters without any formal adult supervision, much like homeless street children of the *galladas* (gangs) of Colombia (Aptekar 1988). The second type of child street laborer who does not contribute to family income is the truly independent child street laborer, such as Perla, who, though still technically a child (under the age of eighteen, according to most national and international legislation governing child labor; see appendix), is in the process of establishing her own household and therefore is not expected to contribute to the maintenance of anyone else's. These children see themselves as adults and are viewed by their families in a similar manner, regardless of their age.

Roberto and his sister Roberta are typical of the abandoned situation. They lived with their mother in the eastern Guatemala city of Escuintla until Roberto was ten and Roberta, eight. At that time, their mother remarried, and her new husband had no desire to take on another man's children, so Roberto and Roberta were put on a bus to Guatemala City and told to live with their grandmother and aunt, who were street vendors on the outskirts of El Guarda in front of the driveway to the Hospital Roosevelt, the second-largest public hospital in Guatemala City. Though unprepared for their arrival, their relatives reluctantly agreed to take them in and use them as workers in their street-vending operation.

Roberto's aunt took full advantage of his labor, as he was recognized as being both very smart (*listo*) and a good vendor, with a skill akin to street hustling in his ability to bring clients to the kiosk and close the sale at a good price, and he was routinely praised by her at the same time that she would insult his sister for being stupid and lazy. He resented his aunt for this treatment of his sister and for her constant reminders to him that his mother had thrown them away and she had "rescued them." Nevertheless, Roberto was a success, and his kiosk was bringing in more than three thousand quetzales in profit per month, with Roberto in complete control of everything except the vast majority of his earnings.[20]

Though Roberto was independent and successful, his sister Roberta was not so lucky. Due to her young age (she was eleven when I worked with her) as well as her sex, she was forced to work as an unpaid child street worker with their aunt after Roberto took over his kiosk on his own. Her aunt and her grandmother were routinely verbally abusive to her, especially when Roberto was not there to defend her. She abruptly stopped coming to El Guarda to sell with them in February of 1999, and when I inquired about her whereabouts, her aunt told me that she was sick at home, as she had been raped by a cab driver whom she knew well, as he was routinely stationed at the entrance to the hospital. They also indicated that they believed that she may have become pregnant as well, and that her grandmother would no longer allow her to come to sell and that she was working in the house performing domestic chores. When I asked if they had reported the incident to the police, they replied that they believed that Roberta had teased and flirted with the cab driver and was likely responsible for her own fate. I never again saw Roberta at El Guarda.

As noted, Perla, who now has her own child and household to care for, is a strong example of those children who have become independent adults with their families' consent despite their relative youth. Perla's income goes toward her own, her husband's, and her child's needs, and not to her mother, Doña Susana, who nevertheless provides Perla and her son with multiple services such as child care and food without any compensation. This is especially vital to Perla's success as a street vendor, for if she were forced to carry her son throughout her daily rounds selling lottery tickets, she would be far more physically taxed and vulnerable to thieves, not to mention less attractive to many of her customers who enjoy flirting with her.

Sebastián is similar to Perla in that he is only seventeen yet is a completely independent adult. He is still in contact with his mother and siblings in the small *aldea* in Quiché where he was born, but due to extreme poverty (he reported that no member of his family had land for a milpa, his father was deceased, and most of his siblings were either coastal finca workers or mendicants), he came to the city in search of work and goes to his *pueblo* only once or twice a year. He shines shoes for a living and plans to save money so that he can purchase and sell *fantasía* (costume jewelry) in a small local market near the room he shares with three others in the outskirts of the city. He told me that he loves his family and hometown and wishes to marry a girl who speaks K'iche' and dresses in *traje* (traditional handwoven skirt and top), but he realizes that his future is in the city and that he needs to save all of his funds for his own sustenance and so he can become a fixed market vendor, therefore he cannot give money to his mother or siblings. When I asked him if this did not cause strain between him and his mother, he replied that more money would make things easier for both of them, but that she would always be his mother and he would always feel a strong affection for her.

Most of the children who labor on the streets of Guatemala City are more fortunate than Sebastián in that they maintain close ties with their families and still participate in family economic and social networks that keep them tied to their town of origin while allowing them to take advantage of economic opportunities elsewhere. Just because they live in a different town from their parents and work on the streets of Guatemala City, they do not cease to be beloved sons, daughters, brothers, or sisters, nor do they have to renounce their ethnic identity and affiliation. They are not alone, though at times they may appear to be. Their reasons for leaving their towns of origin have to do with economic opportunity, but also with the many skills and connections they gain by working on the streets of their nation's capital.

Five

THE SOCIAL NATURE
OF ECONOMIC SUCCESS

Children enter into street labor because they and their families need money. But the *necesidad* (need) that brings children to work on the streets and the income that street labor provides do not entirely account for why some children choose to remain as street laborers or for what makes certain children successes on the street while others soon leave the street for other jobs and job sites. As I show below, public streets, by their very nature, are an especially social environment, and vocational success as a street vendor, porter, or shoeshine boy has as much to do with a child's social skills as it does with the more traditional determinants of professional success, such as the quality and price of the goods they sell or their speed and dexterity while buffing a boot or delivering lunches. But developed social skills are not merely a necessary aspect of success as a street worker; they are also one of the primary products and major benefits of working in such a public location, where socializing among workers, between workers and their customers, and between workers and other street regulars such as police and NGO workers is constant. Social skills and the relationships they foster are also essential for children in combating the dangers that physically immature children encounter while working in such a public place. The physical survival and ultimate economic success of any child street laborer is a social process.

ISABELA'S STORY

Isabela has an indomitable spirit, a quality that has served her especially well in her fifteen years. She was born in Puerto Barrios on the southeast coast of Guatemala. When she was two, her parents' relationship dissolved and she moved with her mother to Quiché in the Western Highlands, where she lived and worked with her grandmother, weaving hats that a relative sold at the tourist market in Chichicaste-nango. Once Isabela became proficient at the weaving, she was forced to devote ten to twelve hours a day in the family cottage industry. During this time, she never attended school and was more often than not the primary caregiver for her younger sister. Her grandmother never paid her and frequently denied her food or physically abused her when she made mistakes at her work. Frustrated by her treatment, at the age of nine, Isabela appealed to her mother for help, but her mother was living with another man, who had no desire to take her in.

Isabela's mother did help her find work as a live-in domestic servant for an unrelated family nearby, where she was responsible for minding two young children from dawn until dusk and for cleaning the entire house. She received food, shelter, two inexpensive blouses, and frequent blows with a stick in exchange for over one-year's labor. She ran away from this home and returned to her grandmother's, but was soon kicked out of her grandmother's house for accidentally smothering a few chicks by keeping them as pets in an old cowboy boot. Again she appealed to her mother for help, and her mother advised her to leave Quiché and find work in the nation's capital.

At the age of eleven, she went with a thirteen-year-old friend to Gua-temala City to find work. The two young girls arrived at the Zone 4 bus terminal at eleven o'clock in the morning and found full-time work and housing by three that same afternoon. The girls worked as domestic ser-vants for a family of eight who also sold food from the house to nearby street vendors in Zone 1.[1] She was the youngest of three girls working and living with the family, and she made Q200 a month in addition to her room and board. She left this job after about six months, due to low pay and her employer's penchant for charging the girls for any dishes they broke while cleaning. She was also quite proud of the fact that she would challenge the arbitrary punishments of her boss, daring to talk back to her while the other girls remained silent.

Over the next two years, she lived with various families, working as a domestic, a dishwasher, and finally alongside an older woman who sold tortillas on the street corner in front of a popular fast-food res-taurant. Although she made only Q250 per month, Isabela was quite happy working this final job and would have remained with her *patrona* (boss) indefinitely had the older woman not become ill and been unable to provide work for the child. Isabela then walked from street stall to street stall in the area where she had sold tortillas in search of a job with a clothing vendor. As she was known in the area, she once again found work quickly, with Doña Sami, as an *ambulante* vendor selling girl's dresses. Isabela was paid with a free room and a small commission based on the number of dresses she sold. As she told me, "When I first started selling, I was no good and had no money for food. Sometimes I would be so hungry and sad I would get on a bus to try to go to another place I had heard of to sell, but I got lost and scared and would stay on the bus all day." Isabela was a fast learner though, and she soon became a proficient vendor, understanding both how and where to sell and how to get the maximum price for the clothing she did sell in order to pocket the maximum commission.

As Isabela became more and more successful, she came to work with Doña Eileen, Doña Sami's mother, and has been working for her for over eighteen months. Doña Eileen has four street kiosks around 18 Calle and Sexta Avenida where she and her employees sell athletic clothing and fashions that cater to young adults. Isabela is in charge of one of the *puestos*, though Doña Eileen closely supervises her. She works from eight in the morning to eight in the evening, six days a week. For her efforts, she receives food, housing, and Q400 a month. She is able to earn a few more quetzales by pocketing the proceeds from sales where she manages to obtain a price above what Doña Eileen expects for her products, but these occasions are rare, as Doña Eileen is usually close enough to Isabela to take the proceeds from all sales once they are completed.

During Isabela's fifteen years, she has lived in three very different parts of the country, in at least ten different homes with scores of family members and virtual strangers, and has performed four different jobs for seven different employers, not to mention her uncompensated work in childcare and family endeavors. For a girl who has lived her life like a pinball, bouncing between towns, people, and jobs, it would seem that she is the ultimate victim of poverty and exploitation, a helpless child devoid of a stable support system and the skills to allow her to find regular employment. Isabela is a victim of poverty, in some of her jobs she has been exploited, and she lacks a family with sufficient means or desire to care for her, but to characterize her as unskilled would be a gross error. She possesses many skills, such as being able to sew, cook, wash dishes, clean house, and care for young children, skills she shares with most young girls with similar socioeconomic backgrounds. She also has the particular skill of selling, gained over nearly four years as a walking and kiosk vendor of food and clothing in the heart of Zone 1. Isabela also has a variety of skills that are less visible to the eye but are, nevertheless, essential to her success, both personal and professional. Like most successful child street laborers, she is a brilliant actor. Her stage is the street. Her audience consists of her employers, her customers, her working peers, and anybody else she deals with on a daily basis. Her role is constant—as Isabela the child clothing vendor—yet her script and the particular attributes of her character are undergoing constant change and modification according to the dictates of the situation and the effect she wishes to have upon the audience member who is opposite her at any given time.

ERVING GOFFMAN AND THE SOCIAL NATURE OF CHILD STREET LABOR

To be human is to perform, like an actor, before audiences whom we con into accepting us as being what we try to appear to be. Our humanity is the costume we wear, the stage on which we perform, and the way we read whatever script we are handed. (Cuzzort and King 2002, 155)

As the above commentary on the work of sociologist Erving Goffman illustrates, Isabela is not alone in her ability to perform, to become the persona she needs to be in order to be successful in the multiple interactions that make up her daily routine. According to Goffman, the ability to perform is a human characteristic, and we are all, to a large extent, "con artists," intent upon manipulating our personae to make others perceive us in a way that we deem appropriate to the audience and the situation. Goffman's life's work, the study of how the self is constructed and made manifest in social interactions, is developed most fully in his classic work, *The Presentation of Self in Everyday Life* (1959), in which he proposed what has come to be known as the "dramaturgical model" of social interaction.

As its name implies, the dramaturgical model depicts social life as a dramatic performance, whereby actors utilize a stage, props, and their self-presentation (dress, posture, gestures, and the style and content of their orations) to convince an audience of their authenticity or, in Goffman's terminology, to present a legitimate performance. Legitimacy in this case has little to do with whether or not the performer is representing herself in a truthful or accurate manner—a judgment that is often impossible to make, considering the brevity and variety of interactions individuals engage in—and more to do with whether the performance strikes the audience as being genuine. The result of a legitimate performance is that the audience accepts the performer as she appears to be, providing her with a satisfactory outcome whereby she gains some sort of benefit, be it social approval or something more concrete, such as the aid or the patronage of the audience.

While legitimate performances have little to do with the objective truth, Goffman did not believe that the use of contrivances in the performance of self implied that the individual actors were in essence liars. Instead, he located the need for deception in systematic contradictions. It is the cultural or institutional ideal that the individual must conform to that often conflicts with other ideals or the basic needs of the individual, and this conflict is resolved via the deception that so often occurs in everyday interactions. A classic illustration along these lines is presented in his book *Asylums* (1961). Workers in a mental institution involved in direct care of patients must maintain order, but they may not physically mistreat their charges. As subordinates within an institution with these defined rules or norms, workers often find that it is impossible to maintain the order demanded by their superiors without resorting to brute physical force, much of which would be labeled mistreatment. They therefore developed techniques such as "necking," that is, gaining control of an unruly patient by wrapping a wet towel around the patient's neck and choking them, a technique that, while brutal, does allow for the rapid subduing of an unruly patient and leaves no telltale marks of the harm done. Society would likely label the patient attendant guilty of abuse and assault, but Goffman believes that such a judgment would be overly simplistic, as it falls on the worker to resolve two institutional guidelines that ultimately conflict with one another. The fault lies not with the attendant but with the institution (ibid., 118).

The reason why the presentation of self, and social skills in general, is so vital to a child street laborer's vocational success has much to do with contradictions similar to those facing the asylum caregiver. In the case of the latter, the contradiction lies in two seemingly impossible objectives (maintenance of order and the prohibition of mistreatment of the patients), given the low staffing of the institution. For child street laborers, the need for continuous manipulation of their self-presentation and outright deception lies not with the children, who, like the asylum caregivers, are on the front lines and therefore forced to manage such contradictions, but with the institution, namely, Guatemalan and indeed international society.

According to the Guatemalan government, the International Labour Organization, and most citizens of the capital city, children belong in school and not working full-time. They belong with family and socially approved caregivers (teachers) in controlled environments where they can be supervised, not among strangers in the street. It is incumbent upon a child's parents to guarantee his or her safety and healthy development, and if they are unfit or unwilling to do the job, the community, the state, or a private caregiver (NGOs, the Church) should ensure that parents and children receive the assistance they need in order to do so. This is a cultural ideal, one that is advocated by virtually every Guatemalan and indeed every inhabitant of the world. Unfortunately, the resources needed to ensure such ideal conditions are not allocated in sufficient measure to make them possible. Debt of developing nations is not forgiven, national governments do not invest adequately in social service programs, multinational firms and the private for-profit sector do not wish to pay living wages to employees, and private charitable organizations simply do not have the resources to get the job done. As a result, communities and families are forced to do the best they can. To survive and to provide for themselves and their families, children must work for pay.

Parents of child street workers and laborers almost uniformly believe in the value of education for their children, and they bemoan the fact that they are not in a position to provide for their children to attend school. They, too, subscribe to the ideal of childhood as a time for learning and playing, and those whose children work directly for them and receive no compensation (child workers) often refer to their children as helping, not working, as they are too young to be of any serious benefit to the family enterprise. Those whose children are child street laborers often expressed feelings of guilt that their children must work, though more often than not they assigned to their children the ultimate agency when they decided to abandon schooling.[2] They reported that they allowed their children to work as a result of them having abandoned school, though, as I have emphasized, since most child street laborers give a great deal of their incomes to their families and are closely enmeshed in family social networks, with the father or an uncle holding great power and influence, many of the children do not seem to be independent in many other respects except in their power to decide whether or not to attend school.

Those who employ nonrelated children are also involved in many contradictions. Many have children themselves who do not work, yet they are willing to employ other children. They hire children because they can be paid less and are more malleable employees than adults. Children also often live with their employers and therefore can be expected both to work longer hours, sometimes sixteen to eighteen hours a day, and to perform domestic as well as vocational work. Yet those who employ others' children do not see themselves as Fagin-like characters profiting from their helpless charges, but as benefactors. These employers, who provide food, shelter, care, and a cash wage to their workers, contrast themselves to the children's parents, who are unable or unwilling to provide these same services. Isabela's boss, Doña Eileen, who herself has a child in school full-time, yet employs and lives with three child street laborers, told me that the children she employs were more of an economic liability than an asset, explaining that she hires them for other reasons: "Believe me, hiring an adult would be far less costly, as they would not make errors, play games, get sick all the time, and disappear to their *pueblos,* but taking care of these children is my labor, what God wants me to do." She sees herself as a caregiver and a surrogate parent first, an employer of children second.

Those who patronize child street laborers are also forced to face many contradictions. Children provide services for a price that an adult could not, therefore patronizing a twelve-year-old shoeshine boy or street cobbler makes economic sense for most of Guatemala City's inhabitants, who themselves have little margin for luxury. Although they, too, believe in the ideal that it is not right for children to work, by patronizing the children, they play a part in keeping children on the street and attracting others to these occupations. When confronted with this contradiction, many clients of child street laborers report feeling as Doña Eileen does, that they are in a sense the children's benefactors, providing for their survival first, and consuming their goods and services only as a means of doing so. Others are less idealistic about what they provide the children who carry their burdens, deliver their goods, or sell them their clothing, saying that they patronize child street laborers because if they do not, the children will join the ranks of thieves and muggers who prey upon law-abiding citizens. In either case, they avail themselves of the cheapest labor available and betray their stated ideals concerning what activities children should perform.

Once again, what is most important here is that for a vast majority of those who are the parents, employers, or clients of child street laborers, the fact that children must labor full-time on city streets and not attend school is unfortunate, and contrary to cherished ideals concerning childhood. Nevertheless, for reasons having largely to do with economics, specifically the poverty of a nation, very few of these same individuals forbid their children to work, abstain from hiring them, or refuse to patronize them. While they all believe children are less competent than adults are, they depend on their abilities to provide income, extra hands, and low-cost goods and services. Consequently, children are placed in many difficult situations, caught between adults who either condemn or grudgingly accept their participation in the workplace, and the abundant forces that encourage them to work and make this work profitable. Their limited age, size, and experience make them less competent than adults, yet these same adults are still eager to employ and patronize them. Finally, while all of these adults are willing to concede that it is dire poverty and deprivation that force these children into the streets to work, few want to hire, patronize, or feel responsible for a child who fully portrays his or her hardship. It is therefore incumbent upon child street laborers to present to adults—their parents, employers, clients, and benefactors—the face and attitude of the child they wish to see (namely, that of a happy, resourceful child with a resilient spirit), which then frees the adult from the onerous burden of being an exploiter of children. The contradictions were fashioned by society, but it is the child who must resolve them, and doing so involves the type of "presentation of self" that Goffman's research described.

Goffman gave birth to the dramaturgical method of study, but many others have built on his foundation. The recent field of performance studies has come to encompass a variety of distinct disciplines, most notably theater arts and anthropology, and in the United States, schools such as New York University and Northwestern University have developed entire departments devoted to performance studies. Scholars such as Judith Butler (1990) and Peggy Phelan (1997), with their studies of the performative aspects of gender, and Barbara Kirschenblatt-Gimblett, with her work on performance in cultural domains such as storytelling (1975) and cooking (1999), have further developed Goffman's[3] work and have provided theoretical perspectives upon which many anthropologists have elaborated (see Castañeda 1996 and Little 2004 for studies on the performance or Maya ethnicity). For my purposes here, particularly the study of how child street laborers use self-presentation to meet their economic ends, I rely primarily on Goffman's insights on dramatic performance, not because they are the only available tools, but because I find them to be the most appropriate and generative of insight.

METHODOLOGY

Goffman's research methods for studying the presentation of self largely involved participant observation, with a special emphasis on observation. His research primarily took place in institutions (hospitals) and in relatively isolated rural communities (the Scottish Hebrides), thus he was able to observe specific interactions involving small groups with little distraction or interference. Research on busy urban streets, where the sidewalks are congested with vendors and pedestrians and the noise of traffic is omnipresent, necessitated a more formal approach. Much of the analysis that follows is based on pure observation, but I was able to augment observation by conducting interviews with the child street laborers who made up my sample on how they presented themselves to their customers, their bosses, and their peers. I also conducted interviews that touched on similar themes with the children's bosses, peers, and advocacy workers.

To gain a true appreciation for how the children were perceived by perhaps their most important audience, their customers, I conducted hundreds of very brief interviews with customers who had purchased goods and services from the children with whom I worked. These interviews involved only five questions: (1) Why did you buy from this particular vendor? (2) How would you describe this vendor (age, origin, etc.)? (3)What makes a good vendor/service person? (4) Why do you think this vendor works in the street? (5) Do you think children should work? Answers to all these questions were hastily written on a small pad once the interview was completed. While interviewees were in no way selected in a random scientific manner, and indeed many individuals declined to be interviewed or simply ignored the request, the information they provided did give a great deal of data concerning what customers believed the vendors to be, compared to my own intimate knowledge of the vendor's self. I was also able to record a few occasions of the specific dialogue in interactions between a few of the children I worked with and their audiences, either via direct transcription or a microcassette recorder, and these linguistic data were also of great use in understanding the techniques that children and their multiple audiences utilize in their self-presentation.

ASPECTS OF THE DRAMATIC PERFORMANCE

In his writings on the dramaturgical model, Goffman identified three vital aspects of the performance: the script, the audience, and the front. Two of these aspects, the script, or the linguistic content of the interaction, and the audience, or those with whom the performer interacts either directly or indirectly, are relatively self-explanatory and shall be explored as they relate to child street laborers within an analysis of the front. The front, a larger and slightly more ambiguous concept, involves the setting, the actor's manner, and the interaction between the two. In the case of child street laborers, the front consists of the city streets and the manner a child must adopt to work them successfully and safely.

The Front: The Street Setting

Goffman defines the front as "that part of an individual's performance which regularly functions in a general and fixed fashion to define the situation for those who observe the performance" and as "the expressive equipment of a standard kind intentionally or unwittingly employed by the individual during the performance" (1959, 22). The front is the agglomeration of tools that the performer utilizes to frame the interaction and to provide context for the audience about who the performer is and what type of interaction is about to occur. It is the front that therefore gives the audience vital clues about who the performer is, and what he will try to convince them of. Goffman divides the front into both the physical setting, such as the stage and set decor in a dramatic production, and the "personal front," or the appearance and manner of the individual actor.

In general, the street was the setting for the vast majority of the interactions that the children I studied were involved in. In the street, the child performer has much less control over his or her setting than other performers, such as actors, bureaucrats, or teachers. These latter performers all work in semipublic places where access is restricted physically and by social convention. The teacher works within the confines of *her* classroom, just as the bureaucrat works within the confines of *her* office, and the stage, while not the actor's alone, is usually physically separated from the audience, who are prohibited from intruding upon it. The street, however, is entirely public. The absence of walls and control over those who have access to the setting means that children must find alternate means of establishing proprietorship.

The complete accessibility of the public street, while presenting its workers with various obstacles also carries with it certain advantages as a setting for commerce. It is assumed by virtually all who utilize the street as a shopping bazaar that the street, due to the virtual absence of traditional overhead,[4] is a place where everyday goods and services can be acquired at the lowest price. Therefore, as a dramatic stage, the street carries with it the impression that it offers the maximum economy for those who choose to avail themselves of its products. In addition, the street, partly due to its complete accessibility, is considered a marginal work environment, and its workers are thought to be sufficiently in need that they will accept such a work environment and lesser profit margins. The street also has a cachet of providing illicit goods, both contraband and stolen goods, that are either not available elsewhere or are available on the street at greatly reduced prices. Although this does impact some street vendors negatively, as some individuals believe that all vendors are criminals selling inferior or stolen goods, the vast majority dismiss these concerns in exchange for saving precious quetzales. This, as well as the obvious advantage of high customer traffic and visibility, is what makes the street setting a viable location for sales and services rendered by both children and adults.

Much as the street is an effective stage for consumers who seek the lowest possible prices, children are perceived as the most attractive salespeople and service workers. Children are cheap. Due to their youth and their limited capital and experience, it is assumed either that they will accept less or that they need less than their adult peers. The child selling caps as an *ambulante,* hawking sweets from a wooden stall, or shining shoes on the corner is assumed to be in even more dire circumstances than her adult peers and therefore willing to accept even less profit for the goods she sells or lower compensation for the services she offers. Conversely, a child working in the street is also assumed to have some primary form of sustenance (food, clothing, shelter) provided by a parent or guardian and therefore is only contributing to her sustenance or perhaps earning money for amusement only. Interviews conducted with the children's customers revealed that the latter often resolve these contradictory beliefs using the following logic: while the customers are pleased to patronize the children because they believe they are receiving the lowest prices available, they also believe themselves to be the children's generous benefactors, providing for individuals who, though in need, are generally cared for by others. The children with whom I worked appear to be cognizant of the contradictory perceptions held by their audiences, and this awareness affects both the scripts used by the children and their personal front.

The Personal Front: Physical Props

Beyond the stage of the street, it is the personal front of the child laborer that sends out the most information about who the child is and what his or her reasons are for being in the street. Goffman divided the stimuli that make up the personal front into "appearance" and "manner," according to the function performed by the information that these stimuli convey (1958, 24). Central to the child's appearance are the many props child street laborers use to further convey information to their audiences. These props come in the form of such obvious material goods as work-related tools, clothing, and merchandise, as well as innate characteristics such as age, sex, and race.

Every child street laborer is sure to keep some sign of his chosen job as nearby as possible, thereby distinguishing him from other children on the street whose reasons for being so are less accepted, such as children in gangs or homeless street children. These props serve purposes similar to those served by the teacher's classroom and the bureaucrat's office: they convey marginal proprietorship and even limit access. In the early stages of my research, when I asked one shoeshine boy if he ever hung out with the many street children in the area, he replied that the groups rarely mixed, and that the *malandros* (literally "bad ones," used in reference to street children and gang children) were easy to distinguish from shoeshiners because shoeshiners always had their *bancas* (stools), a combination footstool for customers and container for shine rags and *pasta* (shoe polish), or *cajas* (shine boxes) with them, whereas street children always carried their plastic bags or small bottles of *pegamento* (glue) with them, and thieves and gang members would have nothing in their hands, ready to grab a purse or jewelry from passersby. In a rather ironic note, he distinguished the good working children from the bad ones by simply stating that "nosotros tenemos nuestra capital, y ellos no tienen nada" (we have our capital goods, and they have nothing).

A shoeshine boy, usually wearing a dirty T-shirt with a North American design and heavily soiled pants, both likely purchased from a *paca*, or bulk dealer of imported secondhand clothing, will always have his dual-purpose *banca* within close proximity. When taking time off for recreation or errands, shoeshiners will either carry their *bancas* with them, or, if a game of street-corner soccer breaks out in the small public parks, they will place them in an orderly pile along with those of their peers. Even while utilizing the streets for leisure or recreation, as many *capitaleños* do, a child street laborer must always have his *banca* nearby as a sign of his right to occupy the street.

Cargadores and delivery girls, both of whom engage in physical labor that keeps them dirty and in clothing similar to gang and street children, also utilize material culture to distinguish themselves from the *malandros*. Very successful *cargadores* will usually have a hand truck or homemade wheelbarrow with them while working on the street, and those with less will possess a belt for back support and a few net bags with a tumpline for attaching to their forehead to mark their chosen profession and their status as workers and not idlers or thieves. Girls who deliver food for *comedores* will wear their aprons, either a full-length one for those who regularly cook or just a waist-high version for holding money and utensils. These aprons are worn at all times to mark them as "good girls" and not idlers or something worse. Aprons also serve to somewhat insulate female child street laborers from sexual predators, as they are a sign that the child is known in the area and looked after by someone, therefore not an easy mark for those who prey on young girls. Just as the apron worn by the young delivery girl alters her audience by marking her as a girl at work who is watched over by other market employees, it also allows her to change her script. Delivery girls can allow themselves to be much friendlier to their customers who work within the market and are unlikely to take advantage of them than salesgirls who must haggle over prices and deal with a larger audience of customers.

Of all child street laborers, street vendors, both *ambulantes* and kiosk vendors, make the most extensive use of props, namely, their merchandise. Vendors of dry goods tend to look and dress similarly to their clientele, such as an *achimero* wearing de rigueur sunglasses with a Walkman around his neck, enticing customers and offering a template of young urban style for his young working-class clientele. Clothing vendors virtually always wear the goods they sell, be they fancy shoes, athletic T-shirts with the names of local and international soccer clubs on them, or dress pants and shirts bearing designer labels. One vendor of dress clothes told me he never would wear soiled clothing, like so many other child street laborers, as customers would only buy expensive things from "one who is as clean as they are." Second to chatting up their peers and potential customers, street clothing vendors spend much of their time brushing and dusting their merchandise so as to keep it clean and fresh looking in the heavily polluted streets. Street vendors also stay close to their merchandise both to advertise and sell their products and to protect their goods from thieves.

Girls selling vegetables and foodstuffs will wear dresses and clean aprons, and in the case of produce vendors, most of whom are Maya, they wear *traje* typical of the village or region they come from. This use of Maya *traje* is not only a marker of ethnicity, but proof of the connection between the vendor and her produce, assuring the customer of the quality and authenticity of the produce as being sold by a typical rural subsistence farmer, in the case of Guatemala, a Maya Indian.

In each of these circumstances, child street laborers use the material means at their disposal to distinguish themselves from those whom society sees as idlers or potential threats. Even in a place like Guatemala City, a child on the street must indicate to all others—peers, adults, and authority figures—that they are unaccompanied in the street so they can earn money to survive, not because of irresponsibility or laziness. A good child, one worthy of patronage, has a front that includes props to indicate his or her status as just another member of the working poor.

One final prop that also distinguishes a laboring child from all other children in the street is money. Having sufficient cash on hand is essential to many basic business tasks, such as making change for customers and purchasing supplies needed for the day's labor, but also for the purchase of food and drink.[5] What is unique about this final prop is that children work hard to keep their capital hidden, but make very public use of it when necessary. On one particularly rainy day, a twelve-year-old boy named Maradona, who shined shoes by the parking lot of the large municipal office complex known as the Muni, was sitting underneath a tarpaulin he had pulled over himself and was looking quite ill. I knew him quite well as a boisterous boy, but today he was unusually quiet. After he told me that he thought he had the flu but still needed to come to work, I immediately went to a pharmacy across the street to buy some medication for him. Pills such as Tylenol Fever are sold individually in Guatemala, and I picked them up for Q7, a relatively small sum, even for a shoeshine boy. When I raced back to Maradona, thinking myself something of a hero, he was standing off in a corner making change of a large bill for a nearby umbrella vendor, reaching into his shoe for a thick wad of bills totaling at least Q200. A few days later, when I jokingly asked him about his long face when telling me of his illness and need to come to work despite the stash he had in his shoe, he told me he always kept all his money with him in his shoe and often had more than the amount I had seen him with.

As we talked more, I learned that Maradona had many reasons for carrying his money with him and keeping it out of sight. Security was an obvious concern, as the apartment he shared with his brother and five friends was not safe, and flashing around his stash was not a particularly wise thing to do while on the public streets where muggers and pickpockets abound. But beyond the practical level, he said that he did not want his customers to see that he had a lot of money, as it was important for them to think that he was very poor, and that by coming to him for a shine they were providing for his daily tortillas. As a child street laborer, he was shining shoes for his daily tortillas, but the fact that he had any capital at all, any savings that did not go to immediate survival, would damage his clients' perception of him. To be an "authentic" shoeshine boy, Maradona would have to be practically broke and eking out survival on a moment-to-moment basis.

The Personal Front: Immutable Props

Essential to this authenticity of being a true child street laborer, one who is honest and worthy of patronage as well as available for a lower cost than a similar adult, are the immutable props that make up a child street laborer's personal front, namely, their sex, age, and racial classification. Children are immediately recognizable in the street and anywhere else for their diminutive stature and lack of the outward signs of sexual maturity. Those under the age of thirteen or fourteen, before the onset of adolescence, are easy to pick out, but once adolescence hits, it is more difficult to tell the difference between a fourteen-year-old child, who by Guatemalan law needs special governmental permission to work, and a sixteen-year-old who is entitled to work, free of any legal restrictions. Therefore, for youth to be an advantageous prop as part of the personal front for a child street laborer, the children must either be pre-adolescent or appear to be, whether by natural (late onset of adolescence or especially small stature) or artificial means (dressing or behaving in a way that makes them seem younger than they are).

Youth has its advantages and its disadvantages. First and foremost, especially for young males, the younger the boy, the less he is perceived as a potential threat by his customers on the street. This is not an issue for those who have many obvious material props that indicate why they are in the street, such as kiosk vendors and *ambulantes* with a large volume of merchandise, but for shoeshine boys, porters, and car parkers, many of whom dress and appear similar to their more feared peers, street children and gang youth, youthful appearance is a definite asset that affects both the scripts they can use and their various audiences' perceptions of them. A preadolescent boy soliciting passersby, no matter how he is dressed, does not inspire fear in adults, and can be either more aggressive or more playful in his solicitation. Conversely, a postadolescent will often be ignored or avoided for fear of robbery or assault. Younger children are also more likely to play upon the sympathies of their customers, and customers are more likely to buy from a younger child who seems more desperate and therefore more "worthy" than older peers.

A preadolescent-appearing child has a greater likelihood of attracting customers than his older-looking peers, and children are aware of this. Therefore, it is incumbent upon older children to go out of their way to compensate for this via recourse to other tools of the personal front, for example, by making sure that the material indicators of their profession are readily apparent (their *bancas* or *cajas*, weight belts, and carts, or water buckets and rags). In addition, they must alter the script they use to avoid frightening or offending their audience. The older male street laborer often behaves in an obsequious or deferential manner to minimize being viewed as threatening. Older children will also use younger children as a front, positioning them in the most visible locations, such as street corners and intersections, and having them lure customers to their kiosks or service sites a few steps away.

Youth can also be a distinct disadvantage for child street laborers, as they appear less competent than their older peers in service occupations demanding a degree of physical strength (porter), dexterity (shoeshining), or street smarts (car parking and guarding). They compensate for this by either offering their services at a lower price or allying with older laborers as a means of getting some work and income, as well as the benefits of the comradeship and the experience that older children offer. Alliance with older peers also provides the younger children with protection from the dangers of the streets, namely thieves, sexual predators, and police and youth authorities. This protection is especially vital for young girls, who rarely if ever are away from their adult employers or others who look after them.

Female child street laborers also experience some distinct disadvantages that their male peers do not face, disadvantages that may greatly affect the girls' success and enjoyment in their jobs, yet are nevertheless common to all women in Guatemala and many parts of the world.

First, the jobs available to female child street laborers are limited to those of vendor and delivery girl, since regardless of their strength, skills, or inclination, porters, shoeshiners, or car parkers are seen as male-only preserves. I never met a girl engaged in any of these occupations, yet, ironically, women are often called upon to do much heavy lifting as well as "security" work for themselves or their families, though never in a full-time paid capacity.

The immutable prop of biological sex also alters the script or the interactions a female child street laborer can have with both her audience and her peers. Girls are more limited in the behaviors they may engage in on the street, as any sign of goofing off, gambling, or associating with undesirables is seen as a sign of moral and therefore vocational laxity, whereas boys are entitled to such behaviors and not seen as unworthy by their employers or customers. Although the female delivery girl wearing her apron can be friendly to customers, she must restrict this sweet discourse to customers, and if she is even approaching adolescence, she must ensure that these friendlier scripts are not perceived as flirtatious. Girls also must closely watch their patterns of dress for fear of being seen as too sexually advanced for their age or promiscuous, once again a sign of moral and therefore vocational laxity, as well as to avoid possible confusion with prostitutes or female gang members. These strictures are faced by many women throughout the world, but they are especially important for a young girl working in the streets, as the predators are many. As previously mentioned, eleven-year-old Roberta was raped and impregnated by an adult cab driver. Her peers and family relations later blamed her for wearing seductive clothes and therefore playing a part in seducing the cab driver, whose stand was some twenty feet from where the girl regularly sold beverages from a small cooler.

Gender stereotypes also damage a girl's front in that they are assumed to be less in need than their male counterparts. While boys in the street are seen as providers for their families and in need of money to do so, girls are most often judged as just "helping" in a family enterprise and thus in less need of cash. When I informally questioned the girls' clients, specifically those who patronized child delivery girls and vendors, virtually everyone not intimately associated with the girl and her employer (or "regulars") assumed that the female child laborer in question was working with her mother, grandmother, or other family relation, and was not a paid employee of a nonrelated boss. They are therefore paid less by employers than their male peers and are less likely to receive "tips" from customers than boys engaged in similar work. Other dominant popular conceptions of the character of girls, from their supposed lack of serious-ness to their inability to perform any other tasks than those related to domestic life, also limit girls' options when it comes to presenting their personal fronts. The sole advantage of being a female child street laborer involves lottery sales; many customers believe that girls, especially at-tractive ones, are "luckier" than their male counterparts. This innate luck is part of a girl's front in that she will highlight it to her clients, but again this luck is limited to the sale of one specific good that is not usu-ally sold by children in Guatemala City.

The final permanent prop that makes up a child street laborer's per-sonal front is ethnicity.[6] In Guatemala, the population is virtually split between those who identify as Ladino and those who identify as Maya. From physical indicators, it is often impossible to distinguish between the two groups. In addition, most men and boys dress as their ethnic counterparts do, while many Maya women wear the distinctive dress of a *huipil* and *corte*. Yet many ethnic markers do exist, the most impor-tant being that most of those who identify as Maya speak one of the two dominant Mayan languages in Guatemala City, K'iche' and Kaqchikel.

Among street laborers, based on my own population research in El Guarda and the study of street vendors on Sexta Avenida by Porres Castejón (1995), Mayas outnumber Ladinos more than two to one, and when it comes to full-time child street laborers, the ratio approaches four to one. As previously noted in Chapter 2, the reasons why Mayas domi-nate street sales and services have to do with poverty, the country's in-ternal violence, and custom. But among the particular children I worked with, Maya ethnicity has a multitude of distinct advantages that are vital to a child street laborer's success and safety. Of the five types of jobs per-formed by the children with whom I worked, all were dominated by eth-nic Mayas except for delivery girl. Virtually all the delivery girls worked for local *comedores*, usually owned by Ladina women who preferred to hire neighborhood Ladina girls for delivery work. All the other jobs are based around the concept of individual and small-group entrepreneur-ship, and in these tasks Mayas have established social networks that have taken over sectors of the street economy. As I heard time and time again from experienced vendors in both areas of my research, street vendors, porters, and shoeshiners were once almost all Ladino, but a few ethnic Mayas slowly entered the field and soon brought along family members and paisanos from their hometowns to work with them. The Mayas' abil-ity to establish and use social networks for self-defense and communal interest, from physically defending their turf to buying collectively from wholesalers, soon forced their Ladino competitors to the economic and geographical margins.

Being identified as Maya on the street by customers and passersby does provide child street vendors with some inherent advantages. As mentioned above, the produce and flowers, or indeed any product with a seemingly rural origin, sold by a Maya vendor is perceived by customers as being fresher, less tainted by chemicals, and more "authentic" than the goods of Ladino vendors, despite the fact that most customers are Ladino. Ironically enough, most of the vendors with whom I worked buy these products not from their rural home but from wholesalers in La Terminal wholesale market, most of whom are Ladino. Maya children are also seen as more benign than Ladino children on the street, as most customers I interviewed said the *malandros de la calle* (bad children of the street) were almost always urban-born Ladinos who belonged to gangs, and that children they identified as Maya rarely posed a threat.

The primary disadvantages of being identified by others as Maya have to do with age-old prejudices in Guatemala concerning the hygiene and trustworthiness of the Maya. Street vendors of prepared foods identified as Maya were singled out by customers as being "dirtier" than their Ladino peers, and customers frequently mentioned that they were unsure if Maya vendors of dry goods were giving them fair prices, as they all seemed to work together and were frequently speaking "behind the backs" of their customers by communicating with other vendors in Mayan languages. As one middle-aged Ladina mother of three who was shopping for school uniforms for her children told me, "All you need to do is tell one of them [the Maya street vendors of clothing] what you want, and they call out to their *tíos* [uncles, kinsmen] and they all come running with whatever you need, each saying his goods are the best and the cheapest."

When I asked my informants if there were any advantages to being Maya in street work, many could not think of one, though they were quick to say that there are no advantages to being Ladino either. Virtually all said things were initially more difficult for them in learning their way around the city and mastering the Spanish of the street, but these deficits were generally credited to lack of experience and youth as opposed to ethnicity. Maya ethnic identity is utilized by these same children in many subtle ways integral to their personal fronts, even if they do so without conscious recognition of this. When asked what separates them from all the other children on the street, one informant simply said that "we understand the importance of hard work, and they do not." When

I asked him who "they" were, he said, "the schoolchildren and thieves." When I asked him if they were *de pueblo* like him,[7] he responded "no." This opposition between thieves/idlers and workers was central to the children's identity, and all worked hard to present the image of the honest, hardworking Maya child to their customers and others on the street.

The Personal Front: Manner

The final aspect of the personal front in Goffman's dramaturgical model, manner, is inextricably bound to script and audience. According to Goffman, "Manner may be taken to refer to those stimuli which function at the time to warn us of the interaction role the performer will expect to play in the oncoming situation. Thus a haughty, aggressive manner may give the impression that the performer expects to be the one who will initiate the verbal interaction and direct its course. A meek, apologetic manner may give the impression that the performer expects to follow the lead of others, or at least that he can be led to do so" (1958, 24). One vital aspect of manner is its relation to appearance. Manner must be consistent with appearance, and both must match the expectations of the audience, especially as regards the different social statuses of the participants. In most interactions, appearance and manner should also be consistent with the setting, as in the case of a neighborhood beat cop who walks the streets in his uniform and weapons, indicating his authority, and a manner that indicates confidence and control as befits an individual charged by the municipality with maintaining order.

For child street laborers, manner, as well as its consistency with both appearance and setting, is highly variable. Isabela presents an interesting example of this chimeral self-presentation as regards to manner. First and foremost, she must appear both industrious and deferential, as must all child street laborers, to convey their right to belong in the street and not be seen as idlers or potential threats. An industrious and deferential manner also conveys to her boss and her customers that she feels fortunate to serve them, as she is below them in social status as a "poor" (hence needing to work in the street) "child" (therefore below them in an age-based hierarchy concerning respect) "of Maya descent" (catering to shoppers who are largely Ladino). This manner is also necessary for dealing with other adults she regularly comes into contact with, such as police, who realize that she likely has no legal right to work at all, much less in the public streets, and NGO workers (including myself), who offer her services (informal schooling, recreation opportunities) free of charge. As a female child street laborer, Isabela's serious and deferential manner must conform to her social status, as indicated by her setting and appearance, in order for her to keep her job, be a successful vendor, gain the benefit of education, and keep out of trouble.

Yet, as previously mentioned, Isabela is far from a pushover, and in times when she has felt others have treated her unfairly, she has repeatedly behaved in a manner and used a script incongruent with her status, as when she talked back to her employer when she was charged for broken dishes and eventually changed jobs. Her current boss, Doña Eileen, with whom she also lives, revealed to me that of all her workers, Isabela was the best worker, but also the smartest: "This one, she seems so obedient to you, Profe. Let me tell you, she gives it to me all the time. The others might run off home [to their rural homes of origin], or run off for an hour or two, but when I can see them, they do what I say. She is different; she has a smart tongue and will give it to me any time for anything. Don't let her fool you."

Modifications in script and manner are often determined by changes in audience. Indeed, while Isabela often told me of how she challenged Doña Eileen, a behavior that I had witnessed while they attended the kiosk together, she was never anything less than deferential toward me. I had assumed that this deference was related to embarrassment she appeared to feel; Isabela was virtually illiterate, and we worked together frequently on her written Spanish. But when I asked her why she never talked back to me, she said, "Profe Tomas, you don't want anything from one [me]; you just try to help." Isabela did not think of me as a saint; she was aware of my research and had heard me joke with others who worked near her. But she felt that I had nothing to gain by taking advantage of her, and therefore she never had cause to present to me any other manner. The "resources" I offered (interest in her, friendship, help in learning how to read and write) were best garnered through typical "sweet" behavior. When it came to Doña Eileen, though, Isabela felt that she had to alter her script and manner in order to avoid exploitation.

Virtually all the children with whom I worked utilized multiple scripts and manners to be successful on the street, and learning how to vary their style of presentation and adopt different scripts and manners for diverse audiences was an essential part of their street education. Ronaldo is a very successful shoeshine boy who was the unofficial leader of a group of five shoeshine boys, all of whom came from the same village in

Quiché and worked the same block of Sexta Avenida. He explained the process as follows:

> When I first came here [to Guatemala City], I was scared. My cousin [who brought him to the city to shine shoes] and his friends used to laugh at me, because I didn't really know how to shine, and I didn't know how to get customers. I used to shout *"lustre,"* but I would turn to the wall when I did it, because I didn't want them to hear me and to come. But after I learned, I went after it, like you see. I grab their pants, block their way, sometimes even put their foot on my stool if they are just standing and waiting. That's why I get the most. These others here, they're just learning.

In the classic Goffman sense, Ronaldo's manner and his script went from meek, due to his fear and relative inexperience, almost forcing customers to take the lead in seeking out his services, to assertive to the point of excess in physically maneuvering customers onto his stool. As I observed, Ronaldo, like the best shoeshiners, completely takes control of the situation once he has a customer, moving and prodding the customer's feet so that the customer, whether reading a paper, engaged in conversation with someone else, or window-shopping, need not even take notice of the shine process. Ronaldo is a master at making his rags pop and bringing a brilliant luster to the shoes he works on, and his command of his job and the quality of his work bring him much repeat business. One aspect of Ronaldo's manner that has little to do with his appearance is the fact that he was born with a noticeably deformed hand, something that would tend to either elicit sympathy or aversion in potential customers, but his manner while at work is so boisterous and commanding that he completely negates his physical stigma and is a very successful shoeshiner.

Ronaldo's commanding manner and expansive script are not limited to one audience or his behavior with customers, for amongst his peers he has the reputation of being a "master of the street." He is one of the best soccer players I have met, dominating informal street games of "papi-football (*papi-fútbol*)"[8] as well as the soccer league established by PEN-NAT for child street workers and laborers. He seems to know everyone, from shopkeepers to other street vendors and even homeless street children, a group that most child street laborers rarely mix with. He is an adept street conversationalist, a master of double entendre, quick retorts, and humorous one-liners and anecdotes that are highly regarded in street socialization. Though a boy, he behaves in the manner of a seasoned street veteran, and this has earned him the friendship and respect of virtually all who know him.

There is one audience of customers for whom Ronaldo has altered his script and manner. His skills in self-presentation have earned him other job opportunities on the street, and he works occasionally selling prepared fruits from a cart in Zone 1. Through his work as a shiner, he befriended the young man who regularly tends the cart, and the man recognized that Ronaldo has *"pilas"* (literally "batteries," meaning intelligence and energy) and allows him to handle the cart on days when he is unable to. The income Ronaldo makes while working the cart is similar to his earnings from shining shoes, but the work is much cleaner and clearly a step-up in the hierarchy of street work. He explained that his manner shifts when he is selling fruits, and that many of the techniques and scripts he uses to attract shoeshine customers are not applicable to selling fruits:

> Look, the fruit sells itself. People see it and are hungry. I just stay here and collect money and cut fruit. One must have chile and salt [two condiments customers often desire on fresh-cut fruit], but all you have to do is keep cutting it. The only secret is to keep cutting it all day, so that people see it is fresh, and it does not get "tired looking" in the bags, and so you don't cut too much that you don't sell.

The aggressive and confident Ronaldo is decidedly laid-back while selling fruit, letting the fruit bring the customers and only occasionally shouting *"frutas"* or moving the cart a bit in search of more customers. He spends his time visiting with friends and chopping the fruit, often ignoring the customers until they literally wave the bags of fruit in front of him and hand him their payment.

Unfortunately, Ronaldo's manner and scripts can and have worked against him. His boisterous, confident street-smart manner, combined with his typical shoeshiner appearance (T-shirts and pants from a *paca,* usually encrusted with dirt from his work shining shoes and sitting on a congested city sidewalk), can cause certain audiences to mistake him for a homeless street child or a thief. Ronaldo was the only child street laborer I knew who had actually spent time as a homeless street child, addicted to inhalants and scavenging and stealing in order to survive. I believe he was only living this way for about two months, until an older cousin from his village was sent to the city to find him and bring him back to Quiché. I know very little about the details of his life during this period, as Ronaldo turned quiet and evasive each time I asked him about it. His younger cousins were the ones who told me of his experience, and their information and Ronaldo's reticence indicated to me that he was not only ashamed of his loss of control and betrayal of his cultural values as a young Maya boy from Quiché, but had also suffered serious trauma during his time living in the street. According to a friend of his, his descent began when he was "shaken down" one night and robbed by two private security guards in the area who believed him to be a homeless street child and a thief.

While all child street laborers are vulnerable to this type of exploitation, Ronaldo was particularly vulnerable because of his street-smart manner, his appearance, the scripts he uses, and the audiences he entertains. As noted earlier, Ronaldo is the only shoeshiner I encountered who talks with street children. What works so well for him as a shoeshiner also puts him in danger, a danger that he currently does a great deal to mitigate by altering his manner to a more meek and deferential one should he encounter audiences he perceives as dangerous, such as unknown adults and the police. He says he takes great care with his appearance and dress when he is not shining shoes and thus is easily identifiable as a "good" working child.

One final example of the importance of the interaction between manner, script, and audience for the vocational success of child street laborers has to do with two relatively young laborers named Sapo and Chino.⁹ Like Ronaldo, Sapo was a shoeshiner, but he worked a few streets away, usually near an older friend named Jorge who also shined shoes. Sapo was nine years old when I met him, but his slight build and stature made him appear even younger. He also had very big eyes relative to his face (hence his nickname: Frog), which contributed to his helpless appearance. Though he was well liked and good at his work, his appearance and his penchant for working alone made him look like a poster child for a scared, hungry child swallowed up by the impersonal, unforgiving streets. When I first met him, he was having lunch with Jorge and a family of street kiosk vendors; he could not stop clowning and telling jokes long enough to eat his food. His distinctive style of telling jokes, as well as his awkward appearance and use of gestures, had the group in stitches.

The next day, I ran into him again, but this time he was alone, kneeling on his shine box looking out at passersby with a passivity that seemed to indicate depression and despair. He immediately brightened up when

I saw him and said hello, but when I asked him how he was, he explained that he couldn't find any customers and was both hungry and badly in need of more shoe polish. I found myself unable to ignore his sadness, and breaking one of my first rules of not handing out money indiscriminately to children unless they were in an emergency situation, I immediately went and bought him a *torta* (sandwich) from a nearby vendor. When I ran into Jorge nearby, I told him what Sapo had said, thinking he could help Sapo get more customers and share his *pasta* with him. Jorge just smiled and put his arm around me, and as if explaining the ways of the world to a small child, he said, "That's Sapo, Profe, he does good, but he looks sad so people feel sorry for him and help him." Indeed, when I later came to know Sapo well, I learned that he had developed a manner that worked well for him, as it matched his appearance perfectly and distinguished him from the many other shoeshiners. He prided himself on his ability to look sad and to receive two or three quetzales for a shine, whereas others were likely to find customers willing to pay only one quetzal. When his audience shifted and he was with peers, Sapo's manner and script were that of a child with loads of personality and pluck.

Like Sapo, Chino was relatively young for a child street laborer, only ten years old when I met him, and he was known as a jokester. Chino stood about four feet tall, but with a thick build that made him seem more like a short adult than a big child. He was a favorite of all who knew him, as he provided nonstop entertainment all day. A rare and fortunate full-time child street laborer, Chino had his parents nearby, his mother selling *licuados* (fruit smoothies), *batidos* (shakes), and candy from a kiosk bordering Sexta Avenida and his father selling socks and underwear in the Mercado Sur 2. Chino's primary job was selling candy as an *ambulante*. His mother made some of the candy, but most was prepackaged hard candy that he purchased from a *bodega*. But what Chino really sold was his personality, and therefore much of his work came from a combination of street entertaining and vending. Before I knew him, he would have a friend paint him in clown face and then he would do the majority of his selling on public buses, either traveling with city buses for a few stops or selling to customers waiting for the departure of long-distance buses.[10] While on the buses, he would tell jokes and funny anecdotes that he had learned from his time on the street and that usually involved an old priest and young women. While telling these jokes, he would place a few pieces of hard candy on the lap of each passenger. At the conclusion of his routine, he would then go through the bus picking up either 25 centavos for his candies or the candies themselves. This routine, which combined entertaining and selling, was a very successful endeavor for him, netting as much as Q40 a day in profit until his father got wind of it and made him stop, displeased that his son would put on ridiculous makeup and tell dirty jokes. He has nevertheless incorporated his joke telling into his regular candy sales and works hard to have a new one to tell every day. The success of Chino's amusing scripts and manner is in part due to the audiences he selects. Chino tells his jokes only to the street vendors and to the other customers he sees every day, individuals who know him as a working child with parents close by. The candies that Chino sells are ubiquitous on the streets, but his ability to cash in on his comical manner, scripts, and stature makes him a very successful vendor at a very young age.

From Ronaldo the aggressive to Isabela the obedient, Sapo the sad, and Chino the joyful, manner and script are vital aspects of self-presentation. When variations of script and manner are used skillfully with fluctuating audiences, child street laborers are able to distinguish themselves from the many others who work their same trades on the streets. It is the combination of social skills that make up the self-presentation that leads to economic success, but once again, social skills are not just vital to success as a street worker; they also provide some of the benefits.

TIME-ALLOCATION STUDIES

To better understand both the social and physical components of street work for children, I also performed time-allocation studies on the child street laborers from my 18 Calle sample. Time-allocation studies, as the name suggests, are designed to provide a relative accounting of the amount of time individuals spend engaged in specific activities. In cultural anthropology, they have been most notably utilized in the study of nomadic foraging groups to determine how much time is actually spent engaged in subsistence activities (see the rather basic techniques used by Lewis [1951] and Lee and DeVore [1968] and the famous commentary made by Sahlins [1972], as well as the more developed methodological uses of the time-allocation studies done by Bock [2002], Johnson [1975], and Scaglion [1986]), but others (Szalai 1972) have applied this technique to urban and suburban populations. An excellent study of time allocation among rural Maya children in Guatemala (Loucky 1988) also exists, and served as both a model and a comparative case for my own research.

To gather evidence on time allocation, I relied on the particular technique of random-interval instantaneous sampling (Bernard 1994, 319), also known as spot observation. This entails a description of the child's activities the instant before he or she became aware of my presence. This technique is often problematic in rural settings where the approach of the ethnographer is easily evident, but it was particularly appropriate for the urban streets where the constant pace of activity usually allows for the observer to approach the subject with some stealth. Most anthropologists have only noted the primary physical activity taking place at the time of observation (i.e., hunting, food preparation, nursing), yet in the context of street work, where interacting with potential customers is omnipresent, I found it important to note both the physical activity the child was engaged in as well as any social interaction they were participating in. For my purposes, social interaction was defined as either speaking to or listening to another individual or group of individuals.

My observations were conducted over a three-month period while working in the 18 Calle neighborhood and were limited to the daytime hours (seven in the morning until five in the afternoon) when my subjects were at work. I divided my time into five two-hour blocks (7–9, 9–11, 11–1, 1–3, and 3–5) and attempted to observe each of my subjects once a day and each day in a different block of time per week, providing for a total of up to seventy observations of each child over the three-month period (fourteen weeks).[11] I did not observe on Mondays, as these were the slowest days of the week, and many of the children I worked with took Mondays off. I also randomly chose one day a week that I did not observe so I could perform other personal or research-related tasks that would not allow me to make my appointed rounds. While some of the children in my sample did work a few hours after five in the afternoon, the relatively few children who actually did so (usually only kiosk vendors and car guarders) and the difficulty and safety risks involved made nighttime observation untenable.

My research sample includes all the children with whom I worked intensively in the 18 Calle neighborhood and is presented below in Table 5.1, divided by occupation. While variables such as a child's age and sex are relevant for the time-allocation studies performed by Loucky (1988, chap. 5), where his subjects varied significantly in the time they spent performing certain activities according to their sex and age, this was not the case among the children I worked with. Besides nomadic and fixed vending, child street labor is highly segregated by sex, with boys accounting for nearly all porters, shoeshiners, and car parkers/guarders, and girls accounting for nearly all prepared-food delivery positions, therefore division by sex would have been redundant to the vocational divisions.

	Shoe-shiner	Car Parker	Porter	Delivery Person	Sidewalk Vendor, Nomadic	Sidewalk Vendor, Fixed	Totals
Self-Employed	15	5	5	0	10	11	46
Hired Laborer	0	0	0	7	2	9	18
Totals	15	5	5	7	12	20	64

Where boys and girls perform the same jobs, they are called upon to perform identical functions, and therefore do not differ significantly as far as physical activity is concerned. Age was not a vital distinction for similar reasons, as a shoeshiner or vendor, regardless of age, was called upon to perform identical tasks, and if they were not suited to these, they would soon find another occupation. Terms of employment were recorded because, based on my socialization-activity typology (see below), only children working for someone else would interact with their boss.

To best group the spot-observation data that I gathered, I developed a typology of both physical activities and social interactions. I developed my own basic typology of social interactions (see the list below titled "Social Interaction Categories"), as I found nothing comparable available in the existing research. I also developed my own typology of physical activities, presented below in the list titled "Physical Activity Categories," yet this typology owes much to a typology of children's activities performed in two rural Guatemalan Maya *pueblos* created by James Loucky (1988).

Social Interaction Categories

1. Working Peers—includes other street laborers, street-working family members
2. Nonworking peers—includes street friends or family not engaged in work at the time of the interaction
3. Potential or Actual Customers
4. Boss—in the case of non-self-employed children
5. Street Educators or Advocates
6. Police
7. Other
8. No Social Interaction

Physical Activity Categories

1. Eating and Personal Hygiene—includes food preparation, purchase, and consumption; washing; grooming; waste elimination

2. Recreation—includes playing physical sports (street soccer), recreational table games (*cincos*, cards), gambling, non-school-related reading

3. Education Related—includes all activities related to formal or informal education programs

4. Work-related Tasks

    For Shoeshiners—includes shining, preparation of supplies, maintenance of supplies, purchase of supplies, doing business accounting, travel in search of clients, soliciting clients

    For Car Parkers—includes guiding cars into spots, soliciting funds for services, car washing, soliciting clients, business accounting

    For Porters—includes loading and delivery of goods, negotiation of price/payment, business accounting, travel in search of clients

    For Delivery Persons—includes delivery of goods, receipt of payment, making change, soliciting clients and orders, travel to and from clients, shopping/food preparation, café-related tasks such as cooking and cleaning

    For Nomadic and Fixed Vendors—includes merchandise/kiosk set up, merchandise maintenance/cleaning/repair, wholesale purchase of merchandise, business accounting, solicitation and servicing of clients

5. Inactive/Resting—no physical activity whatsoever

RESULTS

The most important finding from my spot observations of child street laborers' social interactions is that child street laborers spent a tremendous amount of their time engaged with others, or, put another way, child street labor is a tremendously social endeavor (see Table 5.2 below). Contrary to the reality of child laborers who work in factories or fields and are forced into a repetitive and taxing monotony, child street laborers spend only 11 percent of their time alone, without any sort of conversation or social interaction. This finding also contradicts the general idea that children are swallowed up by the city streets, resulting in the production of anomie-filled delinquents who are forever alone and at the mercy of exploitative adults.

This generalization is further contradicted by the finding that a full 41 percent of the time children spend while working on the streets is spent interacting with their working peers, most often other child street laborers. As opposed to being isolated from other children, caught up in an adult-centered world, they spend much of their time interacting with others their own age. The other prominent group that the children interact with is their customers, largely adults, as is necessary in order to earn their incomes. This is especially true for shoeshiners and nomadic vendors, who need to expend extra effort to advertise their goods and services, and applies to *comedor* delivery girls, who usually interact with each of their customers four times a day while taking and delivering food orders and collecting payment.

Child street laborers also interact with street educators/advocates and police. In the case of street educators, this interaction occurs on a fairly regular basis but usually at the same time of day and only for a short duration. Police are rarely encountered except among those whose jobs are sufficiently mobile and subject to disrepute and confusion with vice (shoeshiners, car parkers, and nomadic vendors), but this is still very infrequent.

As far as particular jobs are concerned, it is important to note that shoeshiners, car parkers, and nomadic vendors all spend nearly half of their days in conversation with their peers. In each case, safety and protection from theft or other street workers usurping their turf demands group cohesion, an added benefit of which is frequent socialization with peers and kinsmen. The added time car parkers spend with their peers results from the fact that they have the ability to control only a limited area for parking and guarding, therefore they need not solicit customers as frequently as shoeshiners or nomadic vendors.

Porters, all of whom are male, spend the greatest amount of time alone and the least with peers, due to the demands of their job. They frequently carry their goods to a street kiosk without the companionship of others, and they tend to go out in search of additional customers alone, as most jobs frequently require only one person. In contrast, *comedor* delivery girls, who seem to be similar to porters in the work they perform, most often work in pairs for safety (they frequently carry

	Shoe-shiners N = 15	Car Parkers N = 5	Porters N = 5	Delivery Persons N = 7	Side-walk Vendors, Nomadic N = 12	Side-walk Vendors, Fixed N = 20	Total N = 64
Working Peers	44%	67%	39%	27%	31%	46%	41%
Nonworking Peers	3%	9%	5%	4%	3%	3%	4%
Customers	38%	8%	30%	39%	47%	32%	35%
Street Educators/ Advocates	4%	1%	2%	1%	5%	2%	3%
Boss	0%	0%	0%	18%	3%	8%	6%
Police	1%	1%	0	0	1%	0	<1%
None	9%	15%	24%	10%	11%	9%	11%
Totals	99%	101%	100%	99%	101%	100%	100%

cash) and therefore spend more time with peers. Also, as they are all salaried employees, they spend significant time in the *comedor* interacting with their boss. Salaried fixed and nomadic kiosk vendors also spend significant time interacting with their bosses, though in most cases their interactions are fewer than would be perceived, as the children and their employers rarely work side by side because bosses usually will supervise multiple kiosks or nomadic sellers and do not stay in a fixed location all day with a particular seller.

Considering the vast amount of time most child street laborers engage in peer socialization, it would be amiss to believe that while they are interacting with their friends they are ignoring their labor. As is evident from Table 5.3, virtually all child street laborers spend from 50 to 90 percent of their time at work engaged in work-related physical activity. At one extreme, delivery girls like Reina rarely are not actively engaged in shopping, food delivery, or food pickup in the streets, or cooking and sweeping back at the *comedor*. Only 2 percent of their working lives are spent idling in the streets or at rest in the *comedor*. Pure recreation and study are virtually unknown to these young girls, who find themselves constantly on the go to get meals out of the *comedor* and to their street

	Shoe-shiners N = 15	Car Parkers N = 5	Porters N = 5	Delivery Persons N = 7	Sidewalk Vendors, Nomadic N = 12	Sidewalk Vendors, Fixed N = 20	Totals N = 64
Eating/Hygiene	7%	6%	7%	4%	7%	13%	8%
Recreation	17%	9%	21%	3%	7%	17%	14%
Education	4%	0%	<1%	1%	1%	3%	2%
Work-Related	68%	43%	60%	90%	75%	52%	65%
Inactive	5%	42%	11%	2%	10%	15%	12%
Totals	101%	100%	99%	100%	100%	100%	101%

customers on time, and all dirty plates and cash back to the *comedor*, where they are quickly relieved of the latter and made to confront the former before their day is done. The unfortunate irony of their work lives is that they are seen by their employers as the least able and hardworking group of the child street laborers I worked with, and are therefore subject to the strictest supervision and the lowest wages. As previously noted, their low pay and status has much to do with a street logic that sees girls as less responsible and less serious than their male counterparts, and less in need of income, as they are not perceived to be as vital to family incomes.

It is in the male-dominated professions of porter, car parker, and shoeshine boy where the least time is spent performing work-related activities. In the case of car parkers, the only group in my sample who spend less than 50 percent of their time engaged in physical work, this has to do with the nature of their job. Two or three children can control the parking activity on a single city block, direct and oversee the movement of cars in and out, perform perfunctory window and body washing, and look out for car thieves and vandals with little difficulty, yet they must rarely stray from their appointed block. Taking on two blocks would be virtually impossible because the demands of constantly being on the spot to exhibit domain over the area, thus staking their claim so as to be worthy of payment, and of protecting their turf against other car parkers demands some vigilance. Therefore, though these children spend relatively little of their time actually guiding their customers into spots, cleaning windows, and collecting from customers, they must always be on-site, so spend much of their time in idle conversation, card playing, and horseplay.

Porters must perform very physically strenuous labor, carrying awkward and heavy bundles a few hundred yards, but the time it actually takes to deliver goods from trucks or *bodegas* to street stalls is relatively minimal. They therefore spend the most amount of time sitting or lying down on *bodega* storage boxes, recovering from their exertions and whiling away time. They also have ample opportunities for recreation such as semiorganized street and league-organized field soccer games, since much of the middle of their day is spent idle because setup and disassembly of kiosks as well as delivery of goods occur in the early morning and late afternoons. Porters also had the additional advantage of having ample access to *bodegas* to store their few tools, such as bags and tumplines and the occasional wheelbarrow or hand truck. They therefore could spend their free time unencumbered by goods needing protection, unlike most vendors. Because they had such large portions of their day unfettered, porters were also frequent targets of street educators, but the macho ethos of the porters prevented most from participating in educational activities, seen as child's play by those who worked in such a "manly" profession.

Shoeshine boys live up to the "work hard, play hard" maxim. When at work, shoeshiners are always physically active—shining shoes, pitching customers verbally and physically (tugging on pants and skirts being a preferred technique), cleaning rags, refilling supplies, washing their polish-covered arms, and writing up their accounts in the paper notebooks they keep in their shine boxes. Most shoeshiners have a fixed location where they spend most of their day, but they also make the rounds of less occupied streets and office buildings in search of more clients during the day's slower times. Yet because they congregate in the largest groups, usually with peers from their same village or family, recreation in the form of a pickup game of *papi-fútbol* or a visit to the *maquinitas* is always just a moment away. They can also easily transport their shine boxes to anywhere they want to be, and it is a common sight to see a bunch of children kicking a soccer or tennis ball around with a stack of shine boxes nearby. Shiners also spend the most time of all child street laborers engaged in street education, which is explained by a variety of factors. First, they are younger than many of their street-working peers and are therefore particular targets of street educators, as they seem the most deprived of education and in need of basic training. Second, they are the most visible of child street laborers, since they must work in full public view in order to procure the most customers. Finally, as shoeshiners work in packs of boys, usually related, from eight to eighteen and beyond, street educators will often direct their appeals to the oldest and most respected individual, and he in turn will direct the younger ones to participate in the program, and due to his superior stature, he is rarely challenged.

Nomadic street vendors, selling *gorras* (baseball hats), T-shirts, or toothbrushes and toothpaste, do not have nearly the freedom that shoeshiners possess. They cannot simply lay down their goods under a park bench and play games. To engage in recreation while at work is to either stash their goods in a *bodega* or with a friendly fixed-kiosk vendor, which makes the transition from work to play not so easy. They spend little of their day engaged in actual recreation (7 percent) and are either walking with their goods, showing them to pedestrians, or vigilantly guarding them as they are laid out exposed on a tarpaulin on a sidewalk, unprotected and within easy reach and visibility of their customers and thieves alike.

Fixed vendors who sell their goods out of kiosks share many advantages with their less secure street-working peers, in that they spend a good deal of their time seated in the shade, with ample rest and plenty of opportunity for recreation. Fixed vendors rarely are not surrounded by another fixed vendor abutting either side of their kiosk, and quite often the adjacent vendor is very well known to them, either a kinsman, a landsman, or a fellow employee of the same owner of the goods. They can therefore call upon their peers to mind their kiosk should they wish to go play soccer or visit a café. Theft of goods by the peer is virtually unknown, as ample opportunities for revenge would present themselves, and the "guest" vendor also dutifully waits on his peer's clients, as any commission from the sale goes directly into the pocket of the "guest." Fixed vendors also spend a great deal of time logging their inventories and sales into account books and straightening and dusting their stock (due to the ever-present smog and dirt in the city). They are also frequent participants in street education programs, as they are a fixed target for educators, spend a lot of time seated and relatively idle, and since they pay such attention to their account books, are likely to desire more training in basic literacy and mathematics. Another fact that stands out with fixed vendors is that they tend to spend a disproportionate amount of time eating. I am somewhat unsure of the exact explanation for this, for although fixed vendors are generally the most prosperous of child street laborers, it is not as if they consume more food or that the other child street laborers go hungry. My best guess is that because they are the sole group with a protected and secure place for their food at their work-place, and frequent idle time, they simply prolong their meals, unlike most child street laborers, who must either eat on the street or lose time away from their work to eat elsewhere.

In summation, time-allocation studies are vital for a complete understanding of the extremely social nature of street work as well as the physical demands placed on street workers. When compared to the depictions of child laborers engaged in maquiladora factory work (Goldín 2001; Peterson 1996), domestic service (Bossen 1988), manufacturing of *bidis* (clove cigarettes; ILO 2002), or plantation work (UNICEF 2000, 4; 2002, 2), the workplace discipline and physical demands of child street labor are far more favorable for the children than other forms of child labor. This is not to say that child street laborers have it easy or are not really working as adults do, but that relative to the variety of labor available to children, child street laborers are far better off than their non-street-working peers. With opportunities for education, recreation, and time spent interacting with their peers, child street laborers do indeed experience many of the aspects of what is considered a more appropriate "childhood."

SOCIAL MEANS OF KEEPING THE STREETS SAFE

In the popular writings and advocacy literature on child street labor, perhaps the most detrimental aspect of street work for children is the relative defenselessness of children vis-à-vis older individuals on the street. Street labor is considered especially dangerous for children, whose exposure to exploitation and violence on the streets is heightened by their small size and relative lack of strength. Self-defense is considered impossible, as it is viewed largely as a physical process that individual children must master, not a social one (Meyers 1988, 128):

> In their work in the streets they were widely exploited and robbed by both peers and adults, and were without recourse to resist beyond their own wits, lacking the physical strength to resist.

Nevertheless, children not only work together to form their own soccer teams but collectively protect their turf and effectively unite to deal with thieves, police, and other potential threats. Of the 108 children I worked with, only 16 mentioned having been the victim of an assault or robbery, and only four of these crimes occurred while they were working. More frequently, the children's rooms or homes were robbed when they or their families were at work, or the children themselves were assaulted, usually by other children, when alone and waiting in the central bus terminal/Terminal market to catch a bus to their homes of origin.

Unlike homeless street children, whose scars and wounds are typical badges of honor and experience (Connolly 1990), child street laborers have few permanent physical reminders of the dangers of their workplace. Perhaps the most significant threat to their safety comes from automobiles and public buses, which routinely strike pedestrians, old and young alike. Two children I worked with were hit by buses during the period of my research; one thirteen-year-old female nomadic vendor was badly hurt and required repeated surgeries and hospitalizations, and another boy suffered a broken leg. While the streets do present dangers to the children who work on them, the children use social means to minimize them and to make the streets a profitable, enjoyable, and safer place for their labors.

Child street laborers use systems of whistles and catcalls to alert one another to the potential dangers of the street. To the uninitiated, these sounds quickly blend in with the general noise of the street, but any seasoned street worker immediately picks up on them. Through collective action on the part of both adults and children, robberies and assaults during the daylight hours when most noncriminal street workers are working are few and far between. Over the course of my investigations, I witnessed more violence directed toward thieves by street laborers than I did the reverse, for as one older child told me, copying the informal slogan adopted by one Guatemala City market vendors' committee, "Ladrón visto, ladrón muerto" (A caught thief is a dead thief).

I personally witnessed two thieves beaten to death by crowds of vendors and pedestrians, and numerous others stripped of their clothing and beaten publicly.[12] One of the most startling moments in my fieldwork was similar to Clifford Geertz's famous cockfight story (1973). As I was chatting with an adult vendor of girls' dresses, who sold from a fixed kiosk in the interior El Guarda market, we heard two women scream "Ladrón" (Thief), and soon a young boy was running down a narrow passageway directly toward us. I was standing in the passageway and therefore had an opportunity to attempt to tackle the young man, but I lamely let him run by me. While shock and perhaps cowardice led me to inaction, I also believe that I did not want to be responsible for what I was sure would be the savage beating or perhaps death of this young boy. Luckily, my inaction was witnessed only by my friend, yet had it been witnessed by more vendors, my credibility in the market as an advocate of the vendors would have been severely damaged. Unlike Geertz, I let my opportunity to truly "become" like a vendor pass by me, though I have never regretted this, as the consequences would have been far more dire for the boy in question, who was luckily caught soon after by the police and rushed into a police car before the angry crowd had a chance to get at him.

While the horror stories of the abuse of homeless street children at the hands of the police are common throughout Central America, most recently in Honduras where over twenty murders of street children by the police have been reported in a three-year period (Casa Alianza 2006), in post–peace accords Guatemala, the police present little threat to child or adult street laborers. I witnessed repeated small fender benders and disputes between vendors and/or pedestrians in the street where the police were on the defensive. Once a crowd had gathered, police frequently became a scapegoat for their own and their government's corruption and inability to protect its citizenry, and more often than not they fled the scene, with or without any arrests. Any attempt to hassle a child street laborer for not having a *cédula* or a work permit or perhaps for selling contraband would be met with such rapid action by street workers and pedestrians that the police would be lucky to escape unscathed. No child I worked with had any trouble with the police during the time of my research, and only two older males had ever been arrested or sent to a youth detention facility previous to my tenure on the street.

While peer networks are essential to safety and success on the streets, child street laborers also benefit from significant family relationships, whether or not their families work on the streets or even live in the capital city. As I illustrated in Chapter 4, the idea that child street laborers are all Oliver Twists, living in families constructed only of other youths or street dwellers and without significant ties or obligation to their natal group, is also a result of a partial view of the street-working child that sees only his or her immediate context, not the reality of their lives.

Six   CHILD STREET LABORERS
       AND EDUCATION

Street labor does provide ample opportunities for an education in vending and impression management, not to mention the chance to socialize with peers and adults while at work. Yet the most damning critique of all child labor is that it denies children the opportunity for education and socialization in their most appropriate environment, namely, the formal educational system. Schools, not streets, are the appropriate venue for a child's preparation for adult life. Virtually all of the national and international legislation meant to protect child laborers (see appendix for a summary of this legislation) specifically states that children belong in school, and that any work that interferes with their schooling should be discontinued. School should not be an option for children, and the state has the responsibility to make it compulsory and accessible to all. While formal education for all children is indeed a worthwhile dream, the needs of poor families and the reality of public education in Guatemala make formal schooling an unavailable or unlikely option for its poor children, as the cases of Salazar and Bartolomé illustrate.

BARTOLOMÉ

Bartolomé goes to school. He pays an inscription fee, as all students in Guatemala do; he shares his classroom with other classmates; he takes home his textbooks; and he gets chided by his teachers if he fails to bring in his *deberes* (homework). He is a stellar performer in his classroom, regarded by his teachers and peers as very smart, especially when it comes to mathematics. He is quick to raise his hand when a question is asked of the students, and his answers are usually correct. He is also very eloquent and a natural leader, and he seems destined for high academic achievement. He is a child who truly seems "in his element" when he is at school.

Yet Bartolomé is thirteen years old and in third grade. He likely will never finish elementary school, much less earn a high school diploma or attend university. He only goes to his school two days a week, about forty minutes per session, and his classroom is a somber room where one window and an open door provide minimal lighting, with a few rickety benches to sit on and trash strewn about the floor. His "school" is the unused *bodega* located inside a public elementary school in Zone 1. His classroom is actually an informal street education program run by a local nongovernmental organization called PENNAT (Programa Educativo del Niño, Niña y Adolescente Trabajador, or Educational Program for Child and Adolescent Workers), and his teachers are a Guatemalan university student pursuing a degree in physical education and a gringo graduate student in anthropology.

Bartolomé values education, and he is the first and only member of his family to have been enrolled in any educational program, informal or otherwise. His older sister is fourteen and works as a domestic, and his three younger siblings all go with his mother to help her sell at a market in Zone 5, near their home. When I first asked him why he never attended public school (before he began working as a bicycle delivery boy), he said that it was too expensive for his family. But Bartolomé does not live with his parents; he stays with a Ladino family in Zone 5 who own a propane distributorship. When Bartolomé is not in school, he is delivering *tambos* (cylinders) of propane gas to clients throughout Zones 1 and 5. He's been working for two years, and he usually works six days a week, twelve hours a day, and often a half day on Sundays. He got the job because he had a friend who got sick and needed a replacement, and after seeing Bartolomé work for fifteen days, the owners of the business offered him a full-time job and a place in their home. Like his boss, Bartolomé wants to own his own business when he is older, and like his boss's wife, he values education as a means to get the skills that he will need in running a business (the owners' two children are both graduates of the University of San Carlos). It was his bosses who encouraged him to enroll in the PENNAT program and who ensure that he has the roughly two hours weekly to attend classes and time at home to do his homework. But the time and resources that Bartolomé can devote to his studies are minimal, as his family depends on the Q400 a month he earns delivering gas, which he gives to them. Bartolomé himself does see the benefits of his labor, as he gets to retain the estimated Q300 a month he receives in *propinas* (tips) for delivering and connecting the gas, as well as taking the old *tambo* back to the warehouse, though he will share this with his family if they are in special need. When I asked Bartolomé if he thought it good that many children like him worked instead of studied, he quickly replied "No." He said that he studied because he liked it, and because "when I am big, I don't want to keep doing this, working and not earning a lot . . . [I study because] I want to get ahead."

SALAZAR

Unlike Bartolomé, Salazar has attended public schooling, both in the *pueblo* where he was born and in Guatemala City where he now lives. He is the youngest boy in a family of six children, and all of his siblings have attended formal schooling at some point, though none are currently enrolled in a formal program. When Salazar was six, he started in the public elementary school in his *pueblo* in Quiché and lasted two years there until he abandoned school in the second grade and moved with his father to the town of Mixco, adjacent to Guatemala City. Due to difficulties with the paperwork required to enroll in school in the capital, Salazar did not reenroll in school until he was ten years old. He was placed in second grade, and after having attended school regularly for two months, an emergency back in his *pueblo* forced him to return there once more for three weeks, after which he returned to the capital with his father and never darkened the door of his neighborhood school again.

Both Salazar and his father, Don Julio, are strong advocates of education. As Don Julio told me:

Interviewer: Did you go to school when you were a child?
Don Julio: My father died when I was three, and I had to defend [fend] for myself when I was young, though my uncles gave me advice. I never had the chance to go to school, so I make sure that my children go to school. . . . They (children) have the right to learn to read and write, and it serves one well throughout life.

And in a separate instance, Salazar, too, told me that education was a right, something that all children deserved. Yet Salazar, like many children, abandoned school by his own choice, though with his father's consent. He said that school was simply boring, that it was difficult to make friends, and that the friends he did make his father did not approve of. He also said that, for him, selling was a "más alegre" (more fun/enjoyable) course for him, and that he learns more by running his own business as an *achimero,* selling alongside his father. Salazar firmly believes every child should work, indeed must work, or else, in his words, "They will become thieves."

Salazar shows his dedication to his work by never leaving his *puesto,* from seven in the morning until nine at night (very late for a street vendor in Zone 1[1]). This dedication he learned from his father. His and his father's belief in the value of education and work is evidenced by the fact that Salazar is also enrolled in PENNAT, though he receives his instruction not in a classroom but while sitting on a small bench in front of his *puesto.* Salazar is visited by PENNAT educators twice a week, for twenty minutes a visit, at which time his previous homework is reviewed, he is given a lesson for the day, and his new homework is assigned. It is obviously very difficult to replicate a week's worth of educational instruction in forty minutes or one hour, but with Salazar's diligence and his desire to succeed (and his father's strict vigilance), he has advanced further in his informal studies in PENNAT than he ever did in the formal educational system. While this is undoubtedly due to the hard work of the PENNAT educators, it also says a great deal about the limitations of the Guatemalan public educational system.

THE REALITY OF PUBLIC EDUCATION IN GUATEMALA

The reality of public schooling in Guatemala is atrocious.[2] Guatemala currently invests 1.6 percent of its Gross National Product in education, the second-lowest figure in the hemisphere after Haiti (Rodríguez 2000b), and less than half of the average national spending for all Latin America. Illiteracy is also an overwhelming national problem; Guatemala again ranks only second to Haiti in the region, with an estimated 39 percent of the population unable to read or write. National educational enrollment figures provided by the government indicate that gross primary school enrollment is at 86 percent, but the same figure falls to 60 percent for gross secondary school enrollment, and UNESCO estimates indicate that only half of all primary school students reach grade five, and only one out of four even enters secondary school *(básico),* much less completes it (UNICEF 2000).

At the public school where I worked in the heart of the downtown area, teachers estimated that less than 20 percent of the children initially enrolled would complete primary school. Entering first-grade classes regularly had forty or fifty students, all the responsibility of one teacher, yet fifth- and sixth-grade classes had only sixteen and fourteen students enrolled. According to the school's principal, upper-level classes (fourth through sixth grades) had an average attendance rate of only slightly above 50 percent during my tenure at the school, and this statistic was heavily influenced by five or six students in each class who did not miss a day. With an entry-level salary only 30–40 percent above the minimum wage, teachers were so underpaid that they were nearly impossible to obtain. Teachers that the school did retain averaged a high absentee rate, with no funds provided for substitutes.

Teacher absenteeism was just the beginning of the problems that the school faced. The bathrooms worked only sporadically, textbooks were in short supply, and sharing of books among three students was customary. Basic teaching implements such as chalk and erasers were often purchased by the teachers themselves because the general supply was depleted. My school was considered one of the lucky ones because it did have a full complement of teachers, which is a rarity in Guatemala (Rodríguez 2000b). Other schools have experienced such difficulties as classrooms without roofs (Rodríguez 2000b), insufficient quantities of the free breakfast that all students are supposed to receive (Rodríguez 2000c), and school principals who are overcharging parents for the enrollment fee (Rodríguez 2000a).

THE MYTH OF FREE PUBLIC SCHOOLING

The enrollment fee for the compulsory education provided by the Guatemalan government was Q2 (US$.35) at the time of my research, yet that was just the beginning of the actual costs of sending a child to school, especially in Guatemala City. Schoolchildren in the city were required to purchase uniforms,[3] which, depending on the size of the child, cost anywhere from Q28–Q50 for boys to Q40–Q75 for girls. This amount purchased only one uniform of a white shirt and blue pants or jumper; it did not include sweaters that were necessary on cold mornings. Children were also required to purchase all their own school supplies for the year, which, depending on their grade level, averaged between Q22 and Q45. Students are regularly charged for the cost of student ID's, special events, field trips, and nongovernment-supplied classroom aids such as maps and classroom posters. Based on my research, the cost of "free" public schooling for students at the school where I worked was typically Q300 or more per school year, more than half the minimum adult wage for a month. If parents were to have more than two children in school at the same time, the costs of schooling could easily become economically unfeasible. The opportunity cost to school a child, based on these figures and the typical wage of Q750 for a child street laborer of primary school age (7–14 years old), makes school attendance an even more unrealistic option for those whom the "free" public educational system is intended to help.

EDUCATIONAL EXPERIENCES
OF CHILD STREET LABORERS

Of the children with whom I worked, virtually all had at one time or another attended public schools and abandoned them. As can be seen from the summary "Educational Histories of Child Street Laborers," though 88 percent of the full-time child laborers with whom I worked had attended the public schools, only 6.25 percent of this group

TABLE 6.1. EDUCATIONAL HISTORIES OF CHILD STREET LABORERS (NUMBER OF CHILDREN IN SAMPLE = 108)

Had attended public primary school	96
Currently enrolled in primary school	00
Graduated from primary school	06
Currently enrolled in básico (junior high school)	03
Currently enrolled in alternative education program	78
Had completed a grade in alternative schooling in past three years	21
Had attended at least two different primary schools	33
Had migrated to Guatemala City	87
Of migrants, those who had attended public school in their towns of origin	81
Of migrants, those who had attended public school in the capital	16

had managed to complete their primary school studies, with fewer than half of the *primaria* graduates continuing to the next level.

When the children were asked why they had abandoned their schooling, almost all mentioned the need to make money for their families as a primary reason for leaving school. More than half said that their family could not afford to send them to public school. Another mitigating factor in school attendance was that many migrant children who moved to the capital never continued their formal schooling upon arrival. Of the migrant children who made up over 80 percent of my sample, more than nine out of ten had attended school in their town of origin, yet fewer than one in five of these children continued their formal schooling in the capital.

Child Street Laborers' Five Most Common Responses to the Question "Why did you stop going to school?"* (Number of children in sample = 93)

1.	Had to work	72
2.	Did not like it	50
3.	Too expensive	44
4.	Moved	22
5.	Parents would not let me	16

*The question was an open-ended one, and as the children could mention as many factors as they chose, many mentioned more than one.

In addition to the difficulty of moving from the countryside to the city and enrolling in a new school, many of the children felt that city schools were not comfortable places for them. Children from rural areas said that the students in the city made fun of them for their country ways. When rural children came from ethnically Maya areas of the countryside to the Ladino-dominated city, they encountered myriad difficulties: the inability to speak proper Spanish, for which they were ridiculed by classmates and teachers alike; differences in clothing and dress, especially pronounced for girls who could not afford school uniforms and wore their everyday *traje* to class;[4] and attitudes and customs that were mocked by their Ladino classmates. Although the school where I worked had many Maya children in the lower grades, the pejorative term *indio* was regularly used by non-Maya students to connote someone who was ignorant in the ways of Ladino urban life. Even for ethnically Ladino children born in the city, outward markers of extreme poverty, such as dirty or damaged clothing obviously purchased from the *pacas* (discount bulk sellers of used, usually North American, clothing), few school supplies, or no pocket change with which to purchase treats at the attached *comedor,* were regularly met with scorn by classmates, making school attendance a depressing reminder of what they lacked. Faced with such challenges, most poor children seemed to "take the hint" that is given to them by their peers, their teachers, and even their government: that school was no place for them.

Informal schools, such as the PENNAT program that both Salazar and Bartolomé participate in, are a popular option for those child street laborers who wish to further their education in a style and setting that is more conducive to their needs.[5] Though abandoning school is very common for child street laborers, many do find ways to continue learning despite their arduous work schedules. As is shown in Table 6.1, of the 108 children in my sample, 78 were currently studying in one or more alternative school programs that were financed by local and international nongovernmental organizations. Programs such as PENNAT provide a flexible curriculum, approved by the Guatemalan Ministry of Education, that allows child laborers to receive instruction while at work or in a nearby classroom for just a few minutes a week. PENNAT's curriculum, heavily influenced by the pedagogical philosophy of Paulo Freire (1970, 1983), aims to give the students the basic skills they would obtain in formal schooling (grammar, mathematics, natural and social scientific knowledge) in a format that is relevant to their personal experience and to the sociopolitical climate of modern Guatemala. PENNAT students receive low-cost (usually Q10 for the semester) folios (stapled-together folders of readings and exercises) that guide them through the learning process, and these folios allow students to advance at their own pace according to the time they have to dedicate to study. The folios are also specifically tailored to the life experiences of a child laborer. Examples draw from the students' immediate experience, such as a mathematics sheet that teaches advanced multiplication and division using as an example a woman who must decide whether to sell more tomatoes or onions in her market kiosk. Other elements of the curriculum speak to the children's cultural experience, such as a unit on environmentalism that explains the logic of milpa farming while teaching children about geology, animal husbandry, and the historical relationship of peasants to the land. Even human evolution is given a "local" angle, contrasting the generally accepted land bridge theory of the population of the Western Hemisphere via Asian migration through the Bering Strait with the hypothesis of independent evolution of *Homo sapiens* in South America.

Though the success rates of these programs varied as far as managing to get the children promoted from year to year, they nevertheless did provide working children the opportunity for learning in an environment that was far less hostile and more amenable to their work routines.

Child Street Laborers' Five Most Common Responses to the Question "Why do you study in an alternative school?* (Number of children in sample = 78)

1.	To learn more/it's good/important to learn	71
2.	Need to graduate *primaria* to get a good job	40
3.	Parent makes me	15
4.	To learn English	9
5.	Because I like the teacher	9

*The question was an open-ended one, and as the children could mention as many factors as they chose, many mentioned more than one.

They also provide child street laborers with basic literacy skills, a chance to earn a governmentally recognized elementary school diploma, and content that does much to stimulate pride in their national and cultural heritage. Considering the number of children in my sample who have left school and are now working full-time, and that most of them make some time for alternative study programs, it seems that the formal schools are failing children and not the other way around. Poor children and their families decide that, given the expense, opportunity cost, quality, social environment, and likelihood of success that Guatemalan public schools offer, the streets and the income they provide are the superior alternative.

Seven

THE FUTURES OF
CHILD STREET LABORERS

Child street laborers abandon school because of the low quality and the high cost of public schooling, and they work because they and their families need the money. National and international legislation that aims to remedy this situation misses its mark because those who draft these laws fail to consider the quality and the conditions of local schools and the dire need of these children and their families. Yet these are not the only reasons why children abandon school and go to work in the streets. The streets provide an invaluable education of their own that affords children the skills and the opportunities needed for advancement both in the street economy of Guatemala City and beyond. Children and their families believe that this street education will provide the children with opportunities that are severely lacking in their rural hometowns or the shantytowns that ring the capital. They also feel that of the options available to them, this type of informal education holds the greatest promise for the children's future success. It is not lost on these children or their parents that they are living in a world where the forces that draw them onto the streets are not just local but national and international. The local economic realities that are the most obvious cause of child street labor are embedded in the larger global economy. An understanding of the part these larger economic forces play in the lives of these children holds the key to comprehending the causes of child street labor and may also lead to the formulation of solutions that will enable future generations of children to have a more diverse set of opportunities.

AN EDUCATION ON AND OF THE STREETS

Street labor is generally seen by academics, social workers, legislators, and most of the developed world as a dead-end job. Like most other forms of child labor in which work comes at the expense of school attendance, street labor is believed to doom the child to an adult life mired in poverty. Based on the research I conducted, this is not an accurate representation of the child street laborers in Guatemala City. Instead, the streets provide an invaluable education of their own that gives children the skills and the opportunities needed for advancement in the street and beyond. Obviously, this street education is not a substitute for a traditional education. That children are deprived of a formal education is criminal, and yet, at the same time, a street education does prepare them for lives in which they have the chance to overcome the limits of the crippling poverty that brought them to the streets in the first place.

Rather than a homogeneous collection of dead-end jobs, street labor offers the enterprising worker a hierarchy of increasingly lucrative positions. Child street laborers seek to move from service work, the least capital-intensive, lowest-paying and lowest-ranking of the street occupations, to the acquisition of their own retail street kiosks. Of my sample of 108 child street laborers, 19 had moved from service or wage labor jobs to the acquisition of their own street vending businesses, all before their eighteenth birthdays. Street labor therefore can be seen as entailing its own logical educational plan, as Hernando, a thirteen-year-old Maya street vendor told me in the following interview:

Interviewer: What job do you want to have in ten years?
Hernando: I want to sell the same things that I sell now, but better.
I: Do you know anyone who currently has that job?
H: Yes, a man from my town has a store and two stalls right nearby here.
I: Do you need more education to get this type of job?
H: Yes, of course, but to study, no, no; one has to be there, with them, in order to see real well how they do it; only there can they teach one.

What Hernando is talking about is essentially an education in capitalism. This education can take the form of self-study, or the child can seek the guidance of an adult employer or, in some cases, a benefactor with whom the child becomes acquainted on the street. Children working for adults, such as many of the boys and girls in clothing retail, and the girls in street *comedores,* often use their work time as an apprenticeship in running a street business. During this apprenticeship, the children learn what items sell, and they forge connections with the best suppliers.

As my research on the income available to child street vendors suggests, both children and adults who own and run their own street businesses can earn enough money to provide quite well for their futures.

Hernando went on to say that he admired this man from his town a great deal and hoped to get a part-time job working for him in the future in order to learn more about the art of street retailing. He said that unlike his family, the man had a large house in their hometown of San Jerónimo, Quiché. Whereas most of the children from San Jerónimo worked rather than attending school, the man's children all completed primary school before they went to work for him in the city. Hernando's family was very poor, even by local standards, therefore Hernando had only had the opportunity to study for two years before he was sent out into the fields full-time to work with his family members on their milpa. Two years later, at the age of nine, he came to Guatemala City to shine shoes with other boys from San Jerónimo who came from families similar to his.

Like most rural migrants, Hernando came to the city in search of economic opportunity that could help him provide for his own and his family's support in the present and in the future. Although Hernando would say that he came to the city in search of work and adventure, as a shoeshine boy, he also accumulated something almost as important as quetzales. While laboring in the city, Hernando acquired an impressive store of cultural capital (Bourdieu 1980), including his mastery of the Spanish language, his knowledge of the city, the connections he forged with nonrelated adults who could aid his cause, and his ability to create a living for himself with little assistance from others. In a few short years, Hernando, a member of a large family enmeshed in a typical peasant subsistence economy, developed the skills and resources to become an independent merchant selling largely Mexican and Korean products and working on the streets of a city of over 2 million people. Although Hernando still spent significant time with his family, provided them with vital financial aid, and was proud of his Maya ethnic identity, in a few years as a street laborer, he had gone from a rural peasant to a street-wise member of the global capitalist economy.

Hernando is now a member of this new global economy, but as a child street vendor in Guatemala City, he occupies one of the lowest rungs in this global order. At fourteen years old, Hernando is well aware of this, and like so many of his peers in Guatemala and throughout the developing world, he plans to take the next step up the ladder by migrating to the North. Many young men in Guatemala have close family members who have already managed to make it to the United States, but Hernando is not one of them (see Arriola 1996 for an example of these relations in Chuj- and Q'anjob'al-speaking Maya towns, and studies of the Maya in the United States, including Burns 1993, Hagan 1994, Hamilton and Stoltz-Chinchilla 2001, and Loucky and Moors 2000). Currently, he and his family do not possess the connections or money to get him to the United States, but through his work on the street, Hernando hopes to acquire this additional cultural capital. He already knows many coyotes who use the busy downtown streets of the capital to recruit their customers, and he has learned a good deal about life in the United States from the many adults and the odd gringo, myself included, who have spent time in the States but now work the streets with him. When I asked Hernando what he planned to do when he arrived in the United States, he said that he hoped to find work in a factory, as many of the other people he had met had done. When I told him that these jobs were not always so easy to get and asked him what would he do until he found such a job, he said that he would work in the street and survive.

As illustrated in the responses below, Hernando's desire to migrate to the United States is common among the child street laborers with whom I worked. Most do not, however, envision staying in the United States. Instead, like Hernando, they hope ultimately to return to the Guatemala City street economy with the capital and the expertise needed to run larger and more successful businesses. The contradictions inherent in their plans, in their paradoxical desires both to go abroad in search of opportunity and to seek success at home, may reflect the larger difficulties they face in negotiating their place in the global economic order. Most of these children seek to maintain integration with their familial economy and traditional culture, as well as to improve their economic standing in the global economy. Many manage to do both by reconceptualizing the United States as a place where one goes to work hard and send money home that will provide for the present and the future. The United States is therefore seen as a bank where one deposits years of hard work in exchange for the capital necessary to move up the economic ladder at home. In the eyes of many children working on the streets, migration to El Norte is a necessary step, but not the final one. While their aspirations may seem unrealistic, research on the migration patterns typical of most Guatemalans, especially Mayas, shows that many do hold on to this dream, returning home and establishing businesses in Guatemala City or in their hometowns (see Arriola 1996 and Loucky and Moors 2000 for examples).

*Five most common responses to the question "Where would you like
to live in ten years?"*

1. Guatemala City	40
2. United States	34
3. My town	17
4. Los Angeles	5
5. Mexico	5

*Five most common responses to the question "What job would you like
to have in ten years?"*

1. Street work	47
2. Factory work	16
3. Own an off-street store	13
4. Construction	8
5. Restaurant work	6

While the majority of my informants seek to migrate to the United
States,[1] many reported that they would prefer to stay in Guatemala and
follow one of three possible strategies. Some of these children plan to
use the streets of Guatemala City to gain the skills, the money, and the
connections that will enable them to acquire more stable, if not more
lucrative, off-street employment. Others plan to return to their homes of
origin and utilize their skills and funds to make a better living for themselves there. Finally, many children seek only to elevate their position in
the street economy, a dream that nineteen have already realized despite
their young age.

LOCAL RESPONSES TO NATIONAL
AND GLOBAL PHENOMENA

Regardless of whether child street laborers envision their
futures in the United States, Guatemala City, or the highland *pueblo* of
their birth, they and their families are well aware that it was economic
necessity that brought them to the streets in the first place. Most often,

when rural-born children or their parents were asked why they left their *pueblo* and came to live and work in Guatemala City, the answer was either "no hay oportunidad" (there is no opportunity) there or "no hay tierra" ("there is no land," signifying the necessary material base to survive). Such responses seem reductionistic in their simplicity, yet they are nevertheless true. In a country where 60 percent of the population lives below the poverty line (CIA 2002), and where the percentage of the population under fifteen years of age (42%) nearly equals half of the nation's 13 million inhabitants (CIA 2002), the present looks bleak and the future looks even worse. In Guatemala, the inequitable distribution of income is striking: 10 percent of the population accounts for 50 percent of all income, and the top 20 percent accounts for more than two-thirds of all income (CIA 2002). The distribution of land is no more equitable: 2 percent of the country's landowners own two-thirds of all productive land (Franko 1999). As a result of the inequitable distribution of both income and land, the majority of Guatemalans must find the means for economic advancement and even survival outside small agricultural hamlets, the homes of origin for most child street laborers and their families.

The practice of child labor is certainly not going to help alter these structural economic problems. In fact, child labor is tremendously beneficial to those who control the land and indeed the economy of Guatemala. Beginning with Karl Marx (1967), political economists have repeatedly demonstrated that the primary benefit of child labor to the capitalist class is the lowering of wages and of the cost of production. If families must rely on their children to provide some income, then children swell the ranks of the labor pool. This labor surplus allows the owners of the means of production to keep wages low, ensuring maximum profits. Of course, if wages get too low, the workers are unable to feed and clothe their children, endangering the labor force for the next generation. The employment of children allows poor families to meet the cost of reproduction without burdening the state or capitalist producers. In a country like Guatemala, where the state has traditionally refrained from developing social welfare programs and the capitalist elite is reluctant to forego huge profit margins, child labor is a necessary aspect of daily survival.

While all child labor in Guatemala is a response to the aforementioned national economic reality, there are also three major aspects of the current global economic integration that indicate that the forces that drive children to work will only increase in the future. First, the continued emphasis on export-led growth (ILO 1998) will draw many more children into export-based industries, as has been evident in the proliferation of *maquiladoras* in Guatemala (Goldín 2001; Peterson 1992). Within export-based production, there has been a growing trend that involves the use of child labor in an "informal manner." Factories keep costs down by relying on children who work as "informal" suppliers of labor-intensive segments of production, usually working in informal subcontracting operations that provide formal-sector industry with raw materials or home-based assembly. Unlike the child street laborers I have studied, who work in the true informal sector, these "informal" factory workers are not able to work independently and acquire cultural capital. Unlike the child laborers who work in the *maquiladoras,* these children do not reap the benefits in wages and legal protection that formal-sector workers enjoy. Finally, reliance on export-led growth will direct more children into Guatemala's export agriculture industry, where child labor has traditionally been the norm and where abuse of child laborers is notorious (see Villarreal and Peralta Chapetón 1997 for numerous examples).

The second feature of the current global economic integration that may result in an increase in child labor involves the International Monetary Fund (IMF). The IMF mandated structural adjustment programs that have impoverished millions in Mexico and Argentina. These programs were mandated in Guatemala as part of the international donors' backing of the 1996 peace accords. Central to these programs are the privatization of public utilities and the removal of subsidies for them, the removal of obstacles to all foreign investment, and the reduction in public-sector spending (ILO 1998). As a result of these externally designed policies, there have been massive cuts in national health care budgets and education budgets, leaving public health and public education in Guatemala further diminished and government regulation even less adequate. It seems reasonable to assume that these changes will hit the poorest segments of the population the hardest, resulting in an even heavier reliance on child labor.

Third and finally, economic globalization and the emphasis on free markets and export-based growth has further forced Guatemala to rely on an unequal trading relationship with its primary trading partner, the United States. Fifty-seven percent of Guatemala's export revenue comes from the United States (virtually all from agricultural goods and apparel), and 35 percent of all imports are from the United States, most in the form of industrial, transportation, and military machinery (CIA 2002). Yet perhaps Guatemala's most common export to the United States is labor, in the form of illegal immigrants who may number more than five hundred thousand (Loucky and Moors 2000). They leave Guatemala for economic and political reasons, and they come to the United States because opportunity abounds here, especially in the form of jobs paying low wages that American workers will not accept.

But in order to get to the United States, a migrant needs the assistance of a coyote, whose services, according to the children with whom I worked, cost between five and seven thousand dollars. This sum of money is virtually unattainable for most poor Guatemalans. Usually, the migrant's relatives in the United States must pay for the coyote's services, in exchange for repayment with interest once the new migrant has found work in the United States. For those without family members in the States, gathering such a sum of money requires tremendous effort and foresight. As most migrants are young men, they must begin saving early by working for pay as child laborers.

The streets of their nation's capital, Guatemala City, afford the children with the best place to earn the money and obtain the skills needed for their arduous journey to the United States. In December 2002, I learned that of the 108 children with whom I worked intensively between 1997 and 1999, 11 are currently living in the United States; I have had the opportunity to meet with 3 of these migrants. Of the mountain of capital that goes from Guatemala to the United States, the most vital to the economic survival of both countries is human capital, much of it in the form of children who once labored on the streets of Guatemala City.

WHY CHILD STREET LABOR WORKS

Hernando was not among those eleven children who migrated north. Regardless of whether Hernando manages to make it to the United States and find the factory job he seeks, the time he has spent working on the streets of Guatemala City has provided him and his fellow child laborers with many advantages: a wage that is above what many of their adult countrymen receive and that provides for their own support and aids their families greatly; working conditions that have permitted them relative freedom from the exploitation that is typical in so many nonstreet settings; an education in selling that they can utilize in the present and the future, wherever they live; and knowledge about and access to the global capitalist economy, albeit from one of the lowest points. Becoming an undocumented worker in a foreign country or a successful street vendor of maquiladora pants with fake labels is a difficult life, especially for a child. However, it is one of the best means available of responding to their unjust reality.

During the course of their labors, Hernando and those children like him who work on the streets of Guatemala City have made a life for themselves, and have done so on the basis of their own hard work. Children must labor long hours and be doggedly determined to evade the hazards of the streets that do claim many of their peers. Their lives are far from easy, and their perseverance is nothing short of heroic. The questions nevertheless remain: Would it have been better if Hernando had never come to the streets of Guatemala City to work? Would he and those children like him be better off if they had attended school through high school and college? Is it unjust that children must work like adults to ensure their families' basic survival? The answer to all of these questions is undoubtedly yes. However, the conditions that would have to be in place for these children to abstain from work are a distant dream, one that grows more distant each day as the global capitalist economy gains strength. In lieu of this dream coming true, children in the developing world—and in the developed world—will continue to work, and the city streets will continue to be a beneficial workplace where they can earn above "marginal" wages and advance into careers that surpass the expectations of most Guatemalans.

Appendix SUMMARY OF GUATEMALAN
AND INTERNATIONAL
LEGISLATIVE RESPONSES
TO CHILD LABOR

Governments and private organizations throughout the world have at varying times and to varying degrees attempted to eradicate child labor through the use of legislation. The most recent efforts toward this end have come from the International Labour Organization (ILO). The ILO, a United Nations agency, was created in the aftermath of World War I to devise and support international labor standards. The first international conventions created by the ILO and concerned with child labor were targeted at specific industries and practices, such as the conventions banning forced labor and underground work by children (ILO Conventions 105 and 123 respectively). Their most recent efforts have been far more general, namely, ILO Convention 138, or the Minimum Age Convention of 1973, and ILO Convention 182, or the Worst Forms of Child Labor Convention of 1999.

ILO Convention 138 is the first international convention that as a condition of its signing commits the member nation to "pursue a national policy designed to ensure the effective abolition of child labor" (ILO 1973, art. 1, par. 1). Convention 138 also demands that signatory countries "specify, in a declaration appended to its ratification, a minimum age for admission to employment or work . . . [*and*] no one under that age shall be admitted to employment or work in any occupation" (ILO 1973, art. 2). Later in the convention, the age of fifteen years or "less than the age of compulsory schooling" (ILO 1973, art. 1, par. 3) is offered as the ideal starting point for an introductory national law on minimum age of work, though nations whose "economy and educational facilities are insufficiently developed may . . . initially specify a minimum age of fourteen years" (ILO 1973, art. 2, par. 4). The ideal minimum age for employment of fifteen or fourteen is further lowered to twelve years in the case of "light work," which is:

(a) Not likely to be harmful to their [children's] health or development; and
(b) Not such as to prejudice their attendance at school . . . or their capacity to benefit from the instruction received. (ILO 1973, art. 7, par. 1)

In addition, Article 6 of Convention 138 notes that work such as school-based vocational training by those over fourteen is exempt from the minimum-age provisions, as is "a programme of guidance or orientation designed to facilitate the choice of an occupation or of a line of training" (ILO 1973, art. 6, par. 1). This last provision seems to include any adult-supervised work undertaken by a child of any age that bears some relation to a vocation that the child could practice as an adult.

Unfortunately, the convention's standards suffer even further erosion concerning the actual jobs and industries that the convention covers, of which only the following jobs must be included:

> mining and quarrying; manufacturing; construction; electricity, gas and water; transport storage and communication; and plantations and other agricultural undertakings mainly producing for commercial purposes . . . (ILO 1973, art. 5, par. 3)

Excluded here are the children working in family agricultural endeavors and children working in the urban informal sector, two groups that, in my opinion, make up the majority of child laborers. Convention 138 claims to seek to establish laws to protect all child laborers, yet it in fact only guarantees protection for those working in the formal-sector industrial trades.

Realizing the limitations of this approach, the ILO later undertook to construct a convention that would protect the most invisible of child laborers and those in the most dangerous and exploitative occupations, with the result being ILO Convention 182: Worst Forms of Child Labor Convention, 1999. Convention 182 takes a much firmer stand toward work that is considered most damaging to children and calls for the immediate elimination of these forms of child labor:

> Each member which ratifies this convention shall take immediate and effective measures to secure the prohibition and elimination of the worst forms of child labor as a matter of urgency. (ILO 1999a, art. 1)

Unlike Convention 138, age minimums are not equivocated or modified in consideration of the signatory nation's economic or educational deficits: "For the purposes of this convention, the term *child* shall apply to all persons under the age of 18" (ILO 1999a, art. 2). Children covered by Convention 182 are engaged in the following occupations:

> (a) all forms of slavery or practices similar to slavery, such as the sale and trafficking of children, debt bondage and serfdom and

forced or compulsory labour, including forced or compulsory recruitment of children for use in armed conflict;

(b) the use, procuring or offering of a child for prostitution, for the production of pornography or for pornographic performances;

(c) the use, procuring or offering of a child for illicit activities, in particular for the production and trafficking of drugs as defined in the relevant international treaties;

(d) work which, by its nature or the circumstances in which it is carried out, is likely to harm the health, safety or morals of children. (ILO 1999a, art. 3)

In addition to the elimination of child labor in the aforementioned occupations, signatory states are also obligated by the treaty to ensure that the children from these professions receive rehabilitation and training that will guarantee their reintegration into the society at large. Though the language and provisions of Convention 182 are indeed more rigid than those of 138, by their very focus on only the most extreme forms of child workplace exploitation, the convention fails to address the vast majority of the 250 million child laborers who are not exposed to the worst forms of child labor. What is novel about Convention 182 is its realization that "child labor is to a great extent caused by poverty and that the long-term solution lies in sustained economic growth leading to social progress . . ." (ILO 1999a, Preamble). However, this theme is never further developed in the body of the convention.

The ILO's parent organization, the United Nations, created the most ambitious legislative document that applies to all the world's children, working and nonworking alike: the United Nations Convention on the Rights of the Child (CRC), 1989. The CRC promotes a multitude of measures to protect children's rights in all areas, from the freedom of expression to food and shelter. It also sets the definition of the term "child" to refer to anyone under the age of eighteen. As far as child labor is concerned, the most important legislation is contained in Article 32:

1.   State parties recognize the right of the child to be protected from economic exploitation and from performing any work that is likely to be hazardous or to interfere with the child's education, or to be harmful to the child's health or physical, mental, spiritual, moral or social development.

2.   State parties shall take legislative, administrative, social and educational measures to insure the implementation of the present article. To this end, and having regard to the relevant provisions of other international instruments, state parties shall in particular:

(a) Provide for a minimum age or minimum ages for admission to employment

(b) Provide for appropriate regulation of the hours and conditions of employment

(c) Provide for appropriate penalties or other sanctions to insure the effective enforcement of the present article. (United Nations 2007, art. 32)

The CRC also contains provisions that seek to prohibit the employment of children in the most dangerous and exploitative forms of work such as prostitution and pornography (art. 34) and soldiers, for those under fifteen years old (art. 38). In addition to these provisions, the CRC also insists that children have access to free compulsory primary education and that secondary education, vocational training, and higher education be accessible to all on the basis of capacity.

As far as child labor is concerned, the CRC serves the same purposes of ILO Conventions 138 and 182: the establishment of a minimum-age provision, the elimination of child participation in the worst forms of labor, and the obligation of the state to provide free compulsory primary education—these elements are present in both group's conventions. The CRC does, however, offer a stricter definition of what constitutes a child: anyone under the age of eighteen, a lofty goal that the admittedly more realistic ILO Convention 138 does not aspire to.

The CRC and ILO Convention 138 were both ratified by Guatemala in 1990. ILO Convention 182 was ratified by Guatemala in 2001.

THE GUATEMALAN LEGISLATIVE RESPONSE TO CHILD LABOR

Children in Guatemala can count on the protection of the aforementioned international documents concerning child labor, but provisions also exist in the Guatemalan Constitution, the Guatemalan Labor Code, and the Child and Youth Code that apply to them as well. The Guatemalan Constitution, by far the most general of the documents, contains general and specific provisions that relate to child labor. The first, Article 50, states that "the State shall protect the physical, mental and moral health of minors and older persons. It shall guarantee their right to food, health, education, social welfare and security" (Guatemalan Constitution of 1985, revised 1993, translation from US-DLBILA 1998). Minimum educational standards for all children are addressed in Article 74, which states that both *primaria* and *básico* (grades 1–9 in U.S. terminology) should be compulsory and free for all children. Article 102 Part L of the constitution states:

Minors under 14 years of age cannot be employed in any type of work, with exceptions established by law. It is forbidden to employ minors in work incompatible with their physical capacity or which endangers their moral formation. (ibid.)

These provisions are very general, yet the fact that they appear in the Constitution of the Republic does indicate that the welfare of children and the reality of child labor are not lost on the national government. The specifics of the general minimum-age provision of Article 102 Part L and the entirety of child labor are elaborated and given much more scrutiny in a series of articles from the Guatemalan Labor Code:

Article 147: Work of women and minors must be tailored specifically to their age, physical condition, and intellectual and moral development.
    Article 148: The following are prohibited:
(a) work by women and minors in unhealthy and dangerous places
(b) [suppressed]
(c) night work and overtime work for minors
(d) daytime work of minors in bars and other similar establishments where alcoholic beverages for immediate consumption are served
(e) work of children below 14 years
Article 149: The daytime workday for minors as established in Article 116, paragraph 1 (maximum 8 hours a day, six days a week), must be reduced by an hour a day and six hours a week for those over 14 years and by two hours a day, 12 hours a week for those who are 14 and younger as long as their work is authorized in accordance with Article 150.
    Article 150: The General Inspectorate of Work can give, in exceptional cases, written authorization to permit normal daytime work by minors under 14 years of age, to decrease or eliminate the reductions stated in Article 149. Parties interested in having the necessary authorizations granted must prove:
(a) that the minor will work as an apprentice or that he/she needs to contribute to the family income, due to the extreme poverty of his/her parents or guardian;
(b) that the work is light in duration and intensity, compatible with the physical, mental, and moral health of the minor;
(c) that in some way the obligation of school attendance is met.
Each written authorization must clearly state the minimal conditions under which minors may work. (Ministro de Trabajo, 1996, 51, translation in USDLBILA 1998)

The final document that concerns the plight of Guatemalan child laborers specifically is the Child and Youth Code. This code was passed into law by the Guatemalan National Congress in 1996 but was never put into practice. The Child Code was scheduled to become law in March of 2000, but it was buried by the passing of a new law that annulled the passage of the original code. The Child Code was only enacted formally in 2003, after a bitter political fight, and as of 2007, many of the initiatives that the code demands are underfunded or simply ignored.

The Child Code represents an attempt to enact national legislation that is far more directed and pointed than the international legislation that inspired it (CALDH 1999). It contains over 221 articles, and over 20 have direct bearing on the lives of child laborers. For the purposes here, only the most important will be mentioned:

> Article 53: Children and youth have the right to be protected from economic exploitation, work that may be hazardous to their physical and mental health, or that impedes their access to education . . .
>
> Article 62: Working youth (ages 14–17) are those who directly participate in an activity that generates income on a formal, informal, or family basis. The work must be fairly remunerated and undertaken in conditions suited to their age, capacity, and physical and intellectual development, as well as their moral and cultural values, and must not interfere with school attendance.
>
> Article 63: Working youth in the formal sector are defined as those older than 14 years of age, who have an individual or juridical employer, or who work for an enterprise according to the norms of the Commercial Code, in a relationship of subordination and dependence, with a set work schedule, and subject to an individual work contract.
>
> Article 64: Working youth in the informal sector are defined as those older than 14 who undertake work activities on their own for an employer who is commercially active but does not comply with the tax and commercial legislation of the country.
>
> Article 65: Youth below 14 years of age are prohibited from working, except as set forth in Article 150, with properly regulated and prior authorization from the Protecting Unit for Working Youth.
>
> Article 66: Working youth shall be protected not only by the norms contained in this Code, but also those in the Political Constitution, the Labor Code, and the International Conventions on this matter that have been ratified by Guatemala. (USDLBILA 1998)

In addition to these articles, the Child Code also calls for the creation of a national Child Labor Commission (arts. 101–106; CIPRODENI 1998, 16, in USDLBILA 1998) that will both ensure that the extant laws on child labor are being adhered to and continue to study the phenomena to develop further means of ensuring the rights of all child laborers and the eventual eradication of all child labor in Guatemala.

Although the work of child street laborers is rarely addressed specifically in the national and international legislation designed to protect child laborers, most of the legislation is applicable to this population. In principle, all of the aforementioned international legislation applies to the children in my sample, at least those under fourteen years of age. As all of the children do not attend formal government schooling and are working full-time, they are in violation of ILO Convention 138 if it is applied to all forms of child labor and not the minimum of formal-sector industrial work. They are in violation of the CRC because, once again, their labor interferes with their education, and the CRC makes no distinctions as to the type of work covered by the convention. If, in addition, the exposure that child street laborers get to the city streets can be considered a threat to their health, safety, and morals, then all child street laborers below the age of eighteen would be covered under Convention 182 and the two ILO conventions as well. Threats to the children's health and safety may be considered to be the pollution, crime, and traffic threats that are a daily part of a child street laborer's work environment, as well as the moral vices such as violence, prostitution, and drug use that are a regular part of life where the children work.

As regards the Guatemalan legislation that protects child laborers, all of the child street workers in my sample below the age of fifteen are working illegally. According to the Guatemalan Constitution, both *primaria* and *básico* education is compulsory, therefore all children in my sample below the age of fifteen (the customary end of *básico* study) are in violation of the mandatory school attendance law. This constitutional provision is contradicted by the Guatemalan Labor Code, which allows children fourteen and over to work, at maximum, seven hours a day, six days a week, and this loophole provides children with an incentive to abandon school for work before the mandated age of termination. The Labor Code also takes the step of allowing a child under fourteen to apply for a work permit if his/her family faces extreme poverty, if the work is compatible with the child's physical abilities, and if the obligation of school attendance is met. Children given this permit are only allowed to work six hours a day for at most six days a week. Although this law is part of the Labor Code, none of the children in my sample had attempted to obtain such a permit, and all worked far longer than the maximum thirty-six-hour workweek. It is unclear whether their participation in informal schools would satisfy the additional requisite of school attendance that a minor's work permit makes necessary. Should the Child and Youth Code be enacted, it would make the work done by all the children in my sample illegal, because the new compulsory schooling age would now last until the age of seventeen, and only work that does not interfere with school attendance would be permissible.

Inherent in all the laws aiming to protect child laborers is the belief that school, and not work, is the place for children. What is rarely acknowledged in any of the international and Guatemalan national legislation on child labor is any reason why children would not want to go to school and would rather work instead (such as class and racial discrimination). Schools are thought to be the panacea to child labor, as is reflected in a recent U.S. Department of Labor publication on child labor:

> Universal primary education is widely recognized as one of the most effective instruments for combating child labor. It is believed that no country can successfully eliminate child labor without first enacting and implementing compulsory education legislation. Schooling removes children from the workforce and provides them with an alternative use of their time. (USDLBILA 1998, 55)

What is missing in this view is any understanding of the factors that make compulsory education infeasible or unattractive to child laborers and their families (see Chapter 6); nor is the role of poverty in driving children to work acknowledged. While schooling does remove children from the workforce, the alternative use of their time that is provided does nothing to help them and their families survive the immediate poverty that they are currently faced with. No existing international legislation, save a brief mention in the preamble to ILO Convention 182, states that children work because of poverty, nor is any consideration given to the loss of income that children and their families would face if compulsory schooling was enforced. Guatemalan law does allow for children whose families are in extreme poverty to work, but the law mandates some form of schooling as well as the obtaining of a work permit and therefore makes even this regulation difficult to comply with. As is detailed in Chapter 6, what is behind the advocacy of schools above work is the belief that child labor does not significantly aid the child or his family, that schooling is virtually "free," and that schools provide a means for advancement for the child that requires little or no substantial loss of income for the family. The legislation that aims to protect child laborers shows no understanding of the circumstances that bring them to work in the first place. As my research has shown, both of these beliefs are erroneous with respect to child street labor.

NOTES

CHAPTER 1

1. "Rey" is Spanish for "king." This is a pseudonym, as are all other names in this book, used to protect the privacy of my informants.

2. At the time of my research (1997–1999), the exchange rate between the Guatemalan quetzal and the U.S. dollar fluctuated from seven to eight quetzales for one dollar.

3. Excellent recent research on homeless street children in Guatemala City includes Godoy 1999, Karabanow 2003, and Tierney 1997.

4. I first heard the term *fresas*, or "strawberries," used to describe a group of young Guatemalan university students who worked with me in El Guarda as part of a course on anthropological research methods. These students had worked with me for weeks and were well known throughout the neighborhood and were, in my opinion and theirs, relatively difficult to distinguish from the other youths of El Guarda, as they spoke similar street lingo and dressed similarly as befitting the nature of their research. On a fiesta day, a group of them were invited by a vendor to enjoy a snack as part of the festivities, and as they socialized, the vendor informed them that it was well known that they were different from the typical market youth, or "Se nota que ustedes no son como nosotros, no son tan corrientes." This seemingly obvious realization came as quite a surprise to my students.

5. The involvement of children in gang activity and drug sales is a relatively new phenomenon in Guatemala, though it currently is a major social issue in the capital and the nation. Journalistic descriptions of this phenomenon are plentiful (e.g., Tierney 1997), and social-scientific analyses have also begun to appear (see AVANCSO 1996; Camus 2005; Winton 2007). Child prostitution in Guatemala has a longer history and has been well documented in Tumax and Morales 1998 and Caballeros 1993, as well as by the excellent work of Riccardo Lucchini (1994) on this topic throughout Latin America.

6. This child, as do all child street laborers and many others, participated in a long-utilized practice of appropriating public space for activities unfore-

seen by the architects and policymakers who designed them (see Chapter 2 for the story of this process in El Guarda and the 18 Calle area). Setha Low (2000) has written the definitive work on this practice as it occurs in plazas in Costa Rica; also of note is the work of Miles Richardson (1982) for plazas throughout Spanish America. On a more general note, the discussion of the cultural use of space is covered exceptionally by Low and Denise Lawrence-Zúñiga (2003), and excellent case studies can be found in the recent ethnography by Daniel Goldstein (2004) on Bolivian barrio residents appropriating public streets for performance. Also see the work of Quetzil Castañeda (1996, 1997) on vendors appropriating space at the archaeological site of Chichén Itzá and that of Walter Little (2004) on a similar process in Antigua Guatemala.

7. Street-based research is a common practice among ethnographers, from the Chicago school to recent work on prostitutes (Sterk 2000), crack dealers (Bourgois 1996), and homeless street children (Hecht 1998).

8. The topic of the fear of child abduction and organ thievery has been well documented by Abigail Adams (1998) and Diane Nelson (1999) for Guatemala and by Nancy Scheper-Hughes and Loic Wacquant (2003) internationally.

9. It should be noted that attending school and working full-time, while seemingly possible, virtually never occurs among child street laborers due to the difficulty of attending either morning or afternoon classes and maintaining a full workday, usually considered to be ten to twelve hours for most Guatemalans in a street occupation. I did meet young adults in their early twenties who worked on the street and attended evening classes at the high school level, but their situation was indeed exceptional, as elementary and junior high classes are not available at night, and most child street laborers had abandoned formal schooling long before graduating primary school.

10. The critique of photography as an objective medium for conveying reality has been taken up by such brilliant social critics as Roland Barthes (1981), John Berger (1977), and Susan Sontag (1977). Critiques of the photography from *National Geographic*, perhaps the most prominent purveyor of ethnographic photos, have been done by Lutz and Collins (1993) as well as Castañeda (1997) and Hervik (1998).

11. As pointed out to me by linguist Judith Maxwell, another explanation for the children's solemn expressions has to do with the formal nature of portraiture among the Maya.

12. I in no way mean to indicate that UNICEF is responsible for the misrepresentation of this photo. I have personally been witness to the many excellent programs that UNICEF has designed and implemented in Guatemala that have aided poor children immensely. The error that I point out was the result of a caption that was written by a well-meaning individual who was unaware of the true goings-on depicted in the photo.

13. Walter Little has made the topic of situated identities in relation to economics the focus of his excellent 2004 study of Maya *típica* vendors in Antigua Guatemala.

CHAPTER 2

1. The official minimum wage was just under Q20 per day for agricultural work and Q21.68 for nonagricultural work, but it is vital to note that many workers, especially in the agricultural sector, do not receive the minimum wage. Government enforcement of the minimum wage in the formal sector is "minimal" at best.

2. The work of the research team of Santiago Bastos and Manuela Camus has provided much of the information concerning Maya migration to Guatemala City (Bastos and Camus 1990, 1995, 1998; Camus 2002). There also exists a large body of scholarly research on this rural-to-urban migration throughout Latin America (Altamirano and Hirabayashi 1997; Hirabayashi 1993; Kearney 1986; Kemper 1977; Smith 1989, to name a few).

3. My historical description of the development of Zone 1 of Guatemala City and the accompanying history of street vending is largely drawn from Gisela Gellert's *Ciudad de Guatemala* (1995) and Gustavo Porres Castejón's *Déjennos trabajar* (1995).

4. The largest market in Guatemala City is La Terminal, located in Zone 4. It combines retail and wholesale activity; hence El Guarda is regarded by the municipality as the largest retail market in the city. Zone 1 is the most popular location for street work in the entire capital.

5. The literature on child work, indeed all childhood activity, as socialization is vast, and while I shall not delve deeply into the topic, seminal works from earlier periods include those of Jean Piaget (1926), which greatly influenced the work of Bronislaw Malinowski (1955), A. R. Radcliffe-Brown (1964), and Meyer Fortes (1945, 1949), and Sigmund Freud (1920), which was the inspiration behind multiple works of the North American Culture and Personality school (Benedict 1934, 1946; Dubois 1944; Kardiner 1939, 1946; Mead 1928; Mead and Wolfenstein 1955; and Whiting 1963, to mention a few).

6. The view of child labor as a process of social marginalization has also been a major perspective, both from the point of view of the negative experiences of minority and working-class children with schooling (see Thompson 1966 and subsequent work done by the Birmingham Center for Contemporary Cultural Studies, such as CCCS Education Group 1981; Hall and Jefferson 1975; Hebdige 1979; and Willis 1977, with Bourgois 1996 as a recent North American variant) and the crippling effects of urban poverty that bring children to the workforce, from the Chicago School: Cressey 1969; Thrasher 1963; Wirth 1938; Zorbaugh 1929, to Oscar Lewis's famous "culture of poverty" research (1959, 1965, 1974). Although the culture of poverty concept has been largely destroyed for reducing poverty to familial psychopathology while ignoring its political-economic structural causes (see Bourgois 1996; Leacock 1971; Valentine 1968), the belief that children who work, especially urban child laborers, are exclusively victims of pathological or short-sighted families still lives on in recent

work by Vittachi (1990), Tierney (1997), and even a recent op-ed piece by Nobel Prize–winning economist Gary Becker ("Bribe Third World Parents to Keep Their Kids in School," *Business Week,* November 22, 1999).

7. For the past two hundred years, all child work and child labor in the West has been viewed as exploitation, for both humanitarian (see Fyfe 1989; Walvin 1982) and practical (Nardinelli 1990) reasons, as school was seen as the only proper domain for children. With the United Nations Year of the Child in 1979 and its stated goals of the elimination of all child labor and the provision of universal schooling for all children around the globe (Black 1996), this view was applied by the developed West to children throughout the globe. The Year of the Child also made "street children" in the developing world a topic for global attention, encouraging a spate of academic research (see Aptekar 1988; Cogsgrove 1990; Connolly 1990; Fall 1986; Felsman 1981; Goode 1987; Oliveira, Baizerman, and Pellet 1992; Wright, Kaminsky, and Wittig 1993a and 1993b) and popular notice in films such as *Pixote: Law of the Weakest* (Babenco 1981), all of which combined to pathologize all children on city streets in the developing world, and made street children far more important a topic for research than urban child labor, with the former coming to dominate what Joel Best (1990) has called the "social problems marketplace."

CHAPTER 3

1. During the course of my research, the Guatemalan National Telephone Company (GUATEL) was sold to an international private firm. One of the first official acts of this firm was to convert all coin-operated public telephones into phone-card-only telephones. As a result, whereas once one only needed a coin of 25 centavos (US$.03) to make a brief local call, now phone cards costing Q20 ($2.85) at a minimum were necessary for local calls. Once the cards were issued, they became a hot commodity for street vendors.

2. Walter Little's *Mayas in the Marketplace* (2004) also provides a fine profile of the lives of *cargadores* in the Antigua market region.

3. While ethnographic fieldwork among those engaged in criminal activities is indeed difficult, many fine examples of ethnographies of this genre do exist, including ones on street thieves (Fleisher 1995), drug users and dealers (Agar 1973; Bourgois 1996), and prostitutes (Sterk 2000), just to name a few. It was impossible for me to work both with children involved in street crime and with child street laborers. The two groups, often erroneously grouped as one under the title of street children or children in especially difficult circumstances (CEDC), rarely interacted, and maintaining confidence with both groups of children (those engaged in legal work and those in illegal work) would have been impossible.

4. Punchboards, once common in the bars and cafés of Depression-era United States, are cardboard displays where, for a price, individuals may select a spot on the board and punch out the cover to win what is designated underneath. Punchboards may offer money or other prizes as the reward for luck and a small investment. In my research, many child vendors had punchboards that offered temporary tattoos at twenty-five centavos per punch, but this was the only case of such gambling that the children I worked with purveyed, and all did this in combination with sales of other goods such as clothing or personal goods.

5. There are children and adults in Guatemala City who do scavenge and recycle for a living, particularly in the massive garbage dump located in Zone 13 of the city. These individuals and families often live within the confines of the dump and work in very dangerous conditions. Their poverty and suffering are some of the most shocking I have observed in Guatemala.

6. Market vendors have been studied extensively throughout the globe, and the literature is vast. Exemplars of research on markets in Latin America include Florence Babb's (1989) research on marketwomen in Peru and John Cross's (1998) study of street vendors as political actors in Mexico City. Also of importance is Stuart Plattner's edited volume (1985) that significantly developed the theory behind the study of markets for anthropology.

7. My particular research has little to add to this literature on markets; therefore, I restrict my discussion of these topics to the general points noted above and the importance I place upon the social nature of economic success as vendors that child street laborers exemplify, as described extensively in Chapter 5.

8. It should be noted that the minimum adult wage for agricultural work during my research was just under Q20 per day, and that relative to this figure, child street workers earned nearly double the legal adult minimum wage.

CHAPTER 4

1. The informal school has a curriculum that is divided into three levels, each corresponding to two years of primary school. At the time of my research, Velásquez had completed Level 1 (first and second grade), and was in the middle of Level 2. Ideally, a child in this program can receive a primary school education in three years, though this is rarely the case. My hope that Velásquez will graduate in three years is merely an estimation—an optimistic one at that.

2. Although the term "household," referring to the household economy, was rarely present in anthropological monographs or edited volumes previous to 1980, it has become relatively commonplace since then (a few examples being MacLachlan 1987; Netting, Wilk, and Arnould 1984; Selby, Murphy, and Lorenzen 1990; Small and Tannenbaum 1999; Wilk 1989, 1997; Wolf 1994).

3. This important body of research is vast. Exemplars of work along these lines include Delphy 1984, Finch 1985, and Wallman 1984 for the developed North, and Babb 1989, Borque and Warren 1981, Clark 2003, Kyomuhendo 1999, and Nash and Safa 1976 for the South.

4. David Oldham (1994) makes the excellent point that while it has been shown how patriarchy serves the interests of the capitalist class, we can also see that children as a class are exploited by adults as a class, in effect creating a generational mode of production. One body of excellent research that has investigated the work of adolescent girls as it relates to the household economy includes works by Margery Wolf (1972), Diane Wolf (1994), and Mary Beth Mills (1999) on adolescent girls, adult women, and factory work in Asia, detailing various cases where strict obedience to elders (M. Wolf on Taiwan), desire for personal freedom (D. Wolf on Java), or desire for consumer goods (Mills on Thailand) determines the degree of struggle that defines the relations between the young female factory worker and her household.

5. Sylvia Yanagisako's (2002) excellent research on family firms in the Italian silk industry makes a similar point.

6. It is very difficult to document exactly the number of children who have a deceased parent, as children whose parents do not live together usually reported that one of their parents, most often their father, had died. Upon further questioning on this topic (Do you remember when they died? How old were you when they died? How did they die?), many children responded that they did not know, or that one parent had simply told them the other had died. In three cases, adults who knew the children told me that the child's father had abandoned their mother or taken up with another woman. Unable to separate truth from hearsay in this matter, I grouped together those children whose parents were separated with those who claimed to have lost a parent.

7. Due to the difficulty of "lumping" data on birth order in large families beyond youngest and oldest child, this one-third figure was determined by including only the two eldest children in families where there were six to eight children, and the three eldest children in families where there were nine or more children. The youngest one-third was calculated in the same manner.

8. As noted, economic diversification is a long-standing practice among "peasants" in Mesoamerica. The work of Michael Chibnik (2003) on wood carvers of Oaxaca continues this emphasis on diversified household strategies for economic survival, emphasizing how petty commodity production combined with traditional milpa farming takes advantage of work inputs of the children and the elderly that might otherwise go underutilized. This study echoes earlier work done by Sheldon Annis in San Antonio Aguas Calientes, Guatemala (1987, 34), reiterating the point that household economic diversification provides a useful counterstrategy for familial economic development that does not involve the high-cost and high-risk (though ultimately high-reward) strategies of migration or education. Many of the contributors to the landmark *Crafts in the*

World Market volume (Nash 1993) indicate that craft production, like informal-sector vending, does allow traditionally peasant households to retain a degree of economic independence in the face of the pressures of proletarianization that occur when capitalism penetrates rural areas.

9. I do not mean to imply that seasonal migration to the coast would have continued unabated even without the disruptions of the earthquake and the war. Of my 108 informants, only one had ever been part of such a migration, and only 8 reported that their parents had at one time worked on fincas. Most associated the practice only with their grandparents.

10. Whereas the anthropologist would classify these children as Maya, as far as terminology was concerned, the children themselves had only a hazy sense of ethnic identity beyond the term *indígena* (Indian). While a few did mention that they were Maya, most used a variety of terms to describe their ethnic affiliation, especially *campesino* (peasant farmer), *de pueblo* (from a small rural town), *natural* (of nature or indigenous), or the name that identifies them as originating in their village or department (*quichelenses,* etc.). In contrast, Ladino children were universally aware of their identity and were quick to identify themselves as Ladinos, some even bristling at the question, as if a possible confusion with the Maya was an insult to them. Only one child failed to identify firmly in either group, calling himself a *chapín* (slang term for "Guatemalan") and rejecting the Ladino/Maya dichotomy, telling me that *"todos somos mezclados"* (we're all mixed).

11. Excellent research on the contributions of child workers to Maya households has been done by Ronald Lee and Karen Kramer (2002) on children's economic roles among Yucatecan Maya families. Though they focused almost exclusively on child work in a rural setting (time-allocation studies did not mention any wage labor for children under fourteen years of age, and only a mean of 2.6 hours of wage labor for children fifteen to twenty; Lee and Kramer 2002, 480), their research challenges the accepted view that in many developing world contexts, adolescent children produce as much as or more than they consume. Using a very innovative methodology that looked at consumption by measuring the labor cost of the food that children consumed (as did Cain [1977]), they included the often-neglected time that goes into food processing and preparation as well as the labor time needed for the manufacture or procurement of clothing. In so doing, Lee and Kramer found that while child work is vital in rural family economic survival, Yucatecan children only produced more than they consumed after the age of thirty (Lee and Kramer 2002, 486), long after the termination of childhood. Most relevant for my research, they also found that older children's most vital role in the household economy is that of subsidizing the consumption of their younger siblings, allowing parents to support more children who will ultimately aid with household production, especially when the parents are older and unable to produce at the levels that they consume.

12. Reina did report that her mother would give her some of her salary if she was in need of special clothes for church or a fiesta, but that her employer purchased her everyday work and play clothing.

13. I was unable to visit the parents of the children in my sample who did not regularly come to either of the two neighborhoods where the children worked, which was the majority of those in my sample. Therefore, reports of how much children contribute to their families are based on the children's self-reporting, with confirmation from their parents when available. I did ask children to account for their salaries; therefore, if they overreported their family contributions, this would usually show up in their spending exceeding their income, at which point I would question them further on their contributions to their families. Nevertheless, I was unable to confirm directly that many children gave their families the exact amounts they said they did, though I am confident that my findings are generally reflective of the amounts children do contribute to their families.

14. Many independent child street laborers do receive breakfast and lunch from their employer, as is common in many formal and informal occupations in Guatemala. While this food is a form of compensation and does form a part of the child's earnings, it does not, in my opinion, make them dependent workers, such as a child who lives with and takes all meals with his employer.

15. The right to abandon school is one freedom that children are granted in families where strict deference to parental authority is the norm. The theme of parents' and children's explanations for why child street laborers do not attend school is taken up in far more detail in Chapter 6.

16. The need for children's work on family farms has been noted as early as 1925 in Chayanov's famous theory of peasant economy (see Chayanov 1966) and more recently in Minge-Kalman 1984 and Reynolds 1991. A detailed analysis of all the uncompensated work that Maya children living in rural towns provide their families is available in Loucky 1988 as well as in recent work by Ronald Lee and Karen Kramer (2002) on children's economic contributions among Yucatecan Maya households.

17. Research on the household economy in Guatemala includes the aforementioned research on child work by James Loucky (1988), as well as several other exceptional works, such as (1) Sheldon Annis's (1987) influential study of evangelical and Catholic families in San Antonio, in which he found that the "protestant" ethic that prevailed among newly evangelical families led to household savings and diversification and thus to better prospects for the future generations; (2) Carol Smith's (1984, 1990) excellent detailed research on households engaged in artisanal production in Totonicapán; (3) Tracy Ehlers's (1990) study of women's economic autonomy in female-headed weaving businesses in the face of economic development and change that is limiting their autonomy as their household economic prospects may be improving (this is the generally recognized pattern throughout Latin America, as illustrated by numerous articles in edited volumes by Nash and Safa [1976] and Nash and Fernández-Kelly [1983]);

(4) Laurel Bossen's (1984) related work on how economic development affects the economic lives of women throughout Guatemala, from a highland Maya village to the urban Ladina middle class; and (5) Walter Little's discussion of Kaqchikel Maya vendors' households in his book *Mayas in the Marketplace* (2004).

18. As noted in Chapter 2, of my key informants, over 80 percent identified as Maya, with 18 percent identifying as Ladina/o. Regardless of ethnicity, virtually all the children agreed with the three precepts of Maya household organization, even those who, detailed below, behaved in a manner that evidenced a different set of beliefs. This point has been forcefully driven home in Hecht's (1998) study of homeless street children in Brazil, where mother love and child obedience are spoken of by the children as their most closely held beliefs, though their personal experiences rarely conform to these norms.

19. Little's work emphasizes the autonomy that many Maya women *típica* vendors have, as the vending to tourists they practice is not only lucrative but also favors their labor over males due to tourists' perceptions of Maya females as more "authentic" cultural representatives than males. But as Kyomuhendo's (1999) study of working women in poor urban households in Kampala shows, while women's incomes have gone up as a result of informal-sector trading and vending, the proceeds of their labors generally go toward household and education expenses, which replace instead of augment the males' contributions. Males therefore control the extra capital that the females' work provides, and thus, in the case of these female laborers, greater income does not necessarily mean greater power in the household. Wage-earning women's status in the household varies significantly by culture, by class, and by case.

20. While the profit from Roberto's *puesto* is Q3,000, a large figure though not an unprecedented one, it is important to note that this is not his salary. Most of the money went straight to his aunt, as Roberto handed over all income from his kiosk virtually immediately after he took it in.

CHAPTER 5

1. This establishment was not a *comedor*, as *comedores* have tables inside for dining, and this family merely prepared meals and delivered them to vendors, much like a take-out-only restaurant.

2. As I discuss in more detail later, of the forty parents of child street laborers I was able to interview, thirty-one said that it was their child who decided to abandon schooling, and that they did not force their children to do so. While many mentioned many other factors that contributed to the school abandonment, such as the cost of school, the low quality of the education received, problems with migration and school registration, and the moral and educational importance of work, parents were often forced to resolve the contradiction concerning the value they placed on education and the reality that at least one of

their children was denied this valuable experience by explaining that it was the child's decision to do so, often despite their own warnings and protests.

3. It should be noted that Phelan and many other performance theorists draw more heavily from the work of British anthropologist Victor Turner (1967, 1986) than they do from Goffman.

4. Most patrons of street vendors and workers assume that street work is subject to some overhead in the form of rent, either from the municipality in the form of a street vending permit that must be purchased or informally from the formal establishments in front of which they set up. Customers also assume that bribes must be paid to police and ubiquitous private security guards in the area for "protection." Some street vendors working in municipality-sanctioned retail street markets do in fact pay rent to the municipality, but most sidewalk vendors and *ambulantes* in Guatemala City do not pay any formal rent to anyone, as opposed to vendors working in formal markets. Most overhead costs are limited to the price of storing their goods when not selling, as well as small considerations to the police and security guards in the area.

5. Contrary to many of my initial assumptions, virtually no street worker brings his or her own food for meals from home. For many practical reasons, such as the need to stay with their unprotected merchandise and the lack of refrigeration, bringing food from home does not make sense. Many children live with their peers in rented rooms they share with their merchandise, closely packed spaces that have no tools for food preparation. Children also cited the variety of foods available on the street, most as provided by *comedor* delivery girls, as one of the principal benefits of street work.

6. Walter Little (2004) addresses the performance of "Mayanness" in his book on the marketing of Guatemalan crafts to tourists in the markets of Antigua, Guatemala, as does Quetzil Castañeda (1996) in his study of tourism at the Mexican site of Chichén Itzá.

7. Most of my informants had no defined ethnic identity that they would refer to as Maya. Despite some of the claims of a burgeoning pan-Maya movement that seeks to unite all the nation's indigenous inhabitants into a Maya identity group for social and political purposes (see Fischer and McKenna Brown 1996; Warren 1998; and Fischer 2001 for profiles of the pan-Maya movement as it currently exists in Guatemala), very few of my informants would identify specifically as Maya, choosing instead to note the particular village or department they were from or the language they spoke, or to use the designation *de pueblo* or *campesino,* meaning rural small-town farmer. Though most Guatemalans, Maya and Ladino alike, are from rural areas, when my informants identified as either *campesino* or *de pueblo,* it was virtually synonymous with what is considered Maya ethnic identity. Those who did identify as Maya were those who had spent more years in school.

8. Papi-football is soccer played on a hard surface the size of a playground basketball court, usually concrete or Astroturf. The goals are smaller than in stan-

dard soccer, as is the ball itself. The rules are virtually identical to regular soccer, but the skills that are important to success have much more to do with ball
control in tight spaces than the ability to make long speedy runs down the field,
owing to the limited size of the court. There are organized leagues of *papi-fútbol*
throughout Guatemala City, played in the mostly exclusive private soccer clubs.
It is also popular for street games, as it can be played in an alley or a small public
park.

9. "Chino" is perhaps the most common *apodo,* or nickname, for Guatemalan children. It literally means Chinese, and is applied to children whose
eyes and skin color most resemble those of Asians. In popular Guatemalan folk
knowledge, children are thought to grow out of this Asian appearance upon
adolescence and begin to look like true *chapines,* or Guatemalans, though many
retain the yellow tinge to their skin and noticeable epicanthic fold that brought
on their nickname in the first place.

10. As is common throughout the developing world, there is no formal indoor bus station in Guatemala City where passengers purchase seats and wait in
a waiting room for the bus to load. Instead, large intersections and parking lots
are the unofficial headquarters for various regional routes, with some departing
from the large indoor/outdoor market of La Terminal. In both cases, customers board buses directly to get seats, waiting either until the bus is full or until
another identical bus pulls up before departure. Therefore, street vendors do a
good business selling food and newspapers directly to patrons as they sit on the
bus, waiting for departure.

11. While up to seventy individual spot observations of each child were possible, no individual child in my sample was to be found all seventy times, as
they were away from their common job sites for a variety of reasons having to
do with personal as well as work-related matters. As a result, though a total of
4,480 observations were possible (70 days times 64 children), only 3,512 observations were actually recorded, indicating that the children as a group were present for 78 percent of the observations. I did not rely on reports of their whereabouts and activities to fill in these gaps, as this type of reporting would not
have allowed me to gather the kind of spot activity and spot socialization data
that I was looking for.

12. All of these beatings were attributed to students at the Universidad de
San Carlos, who were raising money on the streets for their annual Huelga de
Dolores procession. Students raising funds for the Huelga walk the streets soliciting contributions while wearing hoods *(capuchas)* that both mimic the cowls
worn by religious brotherhoods during the Holy Week processions and offer
them anonymity. Anonymity is considered important because Huelga is a public spectacle whose aim is a critique of the Guatemalan elite, and students have
been attacked and assassinated for their views in the recent past (see Offit 2000
for a complete description of the Huelga). Whether or not it was the actual university students administering the vigilante justice, or others simply adopting

the makeshift hoods of the *huelguistas,* is difficult to determine. Regardless of the identity of the actual perpetrators, many child and adult street vendors were quick to encourage the *encapuchados* (hooded ones) in their beatings.

CHAPTER 6

1. It should be noted that though Salazar does work later than most adult and child street laborers in Zone 1, his *puesto* is five feet from his father's. Their vending location is adjacent to a popular long-distance bus depot, and their good relations with the many nearby food kiosks that cater to the travelers make their work much safer than a typical walking vendor, shoeshiner, or fixed kiosk vendor.

2. While little academic research on the Guatemalan public school system is available, the role of the public educational system in Guatemala, especially as it has impacted rural Maya children and the Mayan language itself, has recently become the focus of much research among linguistic anthropologists and other social scientists concerned with Maya cultural activism or the pan-Maya movement (see especially Cojti Cuxil 1997, Fischer and McKenna Brown 1996, and Warren 1998 for excellent detailed analyses of the pan-Maya movement). Research by linguists on the Maya movement, language, and bilingual education can be found in England 1998, 2003 and Fischer and McKenna Brown 1996. Julia Richards and Michael Richards (1996) provide a fine summary of the history of bilingual education in Guatemala. Also of note is a two-volume study by AVANCSO (1998, 2002) on the Guatemalan educational system and the creation of a Guatemalan national identity.

3. Uniforms for schoolchildren are utilized by virtually all students and required by law, though students who wear either Western street clothing *(vestido)* or indigenous clothing *(traje)* are not refused entry into classes. Students rarely attend school regularly without uniforms, due to the ridicule they face from classmates, teachers, and administrators.

4. The work of Carol Hendrickson (1995, 1996) and Irma Otzoy (1996) sheds a great deal of light on the role of clothing use, especially by women, in the Maya revitalization movement.

5. The PENNAT program has much in common with the informal educational programs for the children of migrant families run by the Mexican government. See Taracena 2003 for a full description of these programs. Informal street education is also tremendously common throughout Latin American cities, and is often a component of programs aimed at helping to "rehabilitate" homeless street children (see, for example, Janowsky 1992 for Guatemala and Honduras and Ortiz de Carrizosa and Poertner 1992). A study of the strengths and weaknesses of all types of informal education programs in Guatemala has been issued by the renowned social science research center AVANCSO (2003).

CHAPTER 7

1. While only 34 of my 108 informants said that they would like to be living in the United States in ten years, many more did desire to spend some time in the States but not be living there in ten years. Thus I know that the majority of my informants do hope to migrate to the United States, even though only one-third want to be living there in ten years.

BIBLIOGRAPHY

Adams, Abigail
1998 Gringas, Ghouls and Guatemala: 1994 Attacks on North American Women Accused of Body Organ Trafficking. *Journal of Latin American Anthropology* 4(1):112–133.

Agar, Michael
1973 *Ripping and Running.* New York: Academic Press.

Altamirano, Teófilo, and Lane Ryo Hirabayashi, eds.
1997 *Migrants, Regional Identities and Latin American Cities.* Washington, D.C.: American Anthropological Association and Society for Latin American Anthropology.

Annis, Sheldon
1987 *God and Production in a Guatemalan Town.* Austin: University of Texas Press.

Anonymous
1999 ¿Ya sabe en qué invertirá su bono 14? *Nuestro Diario* (Guatemala City), June 27, 9.
2000 Un código de la niñez y la juventud que "nació muerta." *Prensa Libre Edición Electrónica* (Guatemala City), February 1.

Aptekar, Lewis
1988 *Street Children of Cali.* Durham: Duke University Press.

Arana Paredes, Edgar Leonel
1998 Gente que vive con menos de Q6.27 al día. *Siglo Veintiuno* (Guatemala City), April 19, 10.

Arellano, Pavel
1998 Comuna reanudará obras en el Parque Concordia. *Prensa Libre* (Guatemala City), March 8, 8.

Arriola V., Luis
1996 *Interacción entre migración internacional e identidad: Aproximación al caso de niños y adolescentes chuj y kanjobales.* Guatemala City: PRONICE.

AVANCSO (Asociación para el Avance de las Ciencias Sociales en Guatemala)

1991   *Vonós a la capital: Estudio sobre la emigración rural reciente en Guatemala.* Guatemala City: AVANCSO.

1996   *Por sí mismos: Un estudio preliminar de las "maras" en la Ciudad de Guatemala.* Guatemala City: AVANCSO.

1998   *Imágenes homogéneas en un país de rostros diversos: El sistema educativo y la confirmación de referentes de identidad nacional entre jóvenes guatemaltecos.* Vol. 1. Guatemala City: AVANCSO.

2002   *Imágenes homogéneas en un país de rostros diversos: El sistema educativo y la confirmación de referentes de identidad nacional entre jóvenes guatemaltecos.* Vol. 2. Guatemala City: AVANCSO.

2003   *Potencialidades y retos de la educacion no formal en Guatemala.* Guatemala City: AVANCSO.

Babb, Florence

1989   *Between Field and Cooking Pot: The Political Economy of Marketwomen in Peru.* Austin: University of Texas Press.

Babenco, Héctor

1981   *Pixote: A Lei Do Mais Franco.* Brazil: Embrafilme. Film.

Bachofen, Johann Jakob

1967   *Myth, Religion and Mother Right: Selected Writings of J. J. Bachofen.* Trans. Ralph Manheim. Princeton: Princeton University Press. (Orig. pub. 1861.)

Bailey, Robert C., and Nadine Peacock

1989   Time Allocation of Efe Pygmy Men and Women of the Ituri Forest, Zaire. In *Cross-Cultural Studies in Time Allocation,* Vol. 4. New Haven: Human Relations Area Files. N.p.

Bales, Kevin

1999   *Disposable People: New Slavery in the Global Economy.* Berkeley: University of California Press.

Barthes, Roland

1981   *Camera Lucida: Reflections on Photography.* New York: Hill and Wang.

Bastos, Santiago, and Manuela Camus

1990   *Indígenas en la Ciudad de Guatemala: Subsistencia y cambio étnico.* Guatemala City: Facultad Latinoamericana de Ciencias Sociales (hereafter FLACSO).

1992   *A la orilla de la ciudad.* Guatemala City: FLACSO.

1995   *Los mayas de la capital.* Guatemala City: FLACSO.

1998   *La exclusión y el desafío: Estudios sobre segregación étnica y empleo en Ciudad de Guatemala.* Guatemala City: FLACSO.

Becker, Gary S.

1976   *The Economic Approach to Human Behavior.* Chicago: University of Chicago Press.

1991   *Treatise on the Family*. Enlarged edition. Cambridge: Harvard University Press.

1999   Bribe Third World Parents to Keep Their Kids in School. *Business Week,* November 22, 15.

Bellingham, Bruce

1983   The Unspeakable Blessing: Street Children, Reform Rhetoric, and Misery in Early Industrial Capitalism. *Politics and Society* 12(1):303–330.

Benedict, Ruth

1934   *Patterns of Culture*. Boston: Houghton Mifflin.

1946   *The Chrysanthemum and the Sword*. Boston: Houghton Mifflin.

Bequele, Assefa

1991   Emerging Perspectives in the Struggle against Child Labor. In *Protecting Working Children,* ed. William E. Myers, 69–86. London: Zed Books Ltd. and United Nations Children's Fund.

Bequele, Assefa, and Jo Boyden, eds.

1988   *Combating Child Labour*. Geneva: International Labour Organization.

Berger, John

1977   *Ways of Seeing*. New York: Penguin Books.

Berkeley Guides

1996   *Central America*. New York: Fodor's.

Bernard, H. Russell

1994   *Research Methods in Anthropology: Qualitative and Quantitative Approaches*. Thousand Oaks: Sage Publishers.

Best, Joel

1990   *Threatened Children: Rhetoric and Concern about Child-Victims*. Chicago: University of Chicago Press.

Black, Maggie

1996   *Children First: The Story of UNICEF, Past and Present*. Oxford: Oxford University Press.

Bock, John

2002   Evolutionary Demography and Intrahousehold Time Allocation: School Attendance and Child Labor among the Okavango Delta Peoples of Botswana. *American Journal of Human Biology* 14(2):206–221.

Bogin, Barry, Maureen Wall, and Robert McVean

1992   Longitudinal Analysis of Adolescent Growth of Ladino and Mayan School Children in Guatemala. *American Journal of Physical Anthropology* 89:447–457.

Borque, Susan C., and Kay B. Warren

1981   *Women of the Andes: Patriarchy and Social Change in Two Peruvian Towns*. Ann Arbor: University of Michigan Press.

Bossen, Laurel

1984   *The Redivision of Labor: Women and Economic Choice in Four Guatemalan Communities*. Albany: State University of New York Press.

1988 Wives and Servants: Women in Middle-Class Households, Guatemala City. In *Urban Life: Readings in Urban Anthropology,* ed. George Gmelch and Walter Zenner, 265–275. Prospect Heights, IL: Waveland Press.

Bourdieu, Pierre

1980 *The Logic of Practice.* Stanford: Stanford University Press.

Bourgois, Philippe

1996 *In Search of Respect: Selling Crack in El Barrio.* Cambridge: Cambridge University Press.

Brett, Rachel, and Irma Specht

2004 *Young Soldiers: Why They Choose to Fight.* Geneva: International Labour Organization; Boulder, CO: Lynne Reinner.

Bromley, Ray

1997 Working in the Streets of Cali: Survival Strategy, Necessity, or Unavoidable Evil? In *Cities in the Developing World: Issues, Theory and Policy,* ed. Josef Gugler, 124–139. New York: Oxford University Press.

Bucholz, Mary

2002 Youth and Cultural Practice. *Annual Review of Anthropology* 31:525–555.

Burns, Allan F.

1993 *Maya in Exile: Guatemalans in Florida.* Philadelphia: Temple University Press.

Butler, Judith

1990 *Gender Trouble.* New York: Routledge.

Caballeros, M. E.

1993 *Niñas y adolescentes prostituidas: Caso Guatemala.* Guatemala City: UNICEF/Childhope/PRONICE.

Cain, Mead

1977 The Economic Activities of Children in a Village in Bangladesh. *Population and Development Review* 3(3):201–227.

CALDH (Centro para la Acción Legal en Derechos Humanos)

1999 ¿Se pueden negar los derechos humanos a los niños? Guatemala City: CALDH/UNICEF.

Camus, Manuela

2002 *Ser indígena en la Ciudad de Guatemala.* Guatemala City: FLACSO.

2005 *La colonia Primero de Julio y la "clase media emergente."* Guatemala City: FLACSO.

Carey, David, Jr.

2001 *Our Elders Teach Us: Maya-Kaqchikel Historical Perspectives.* Tuscaloosa: University of Alabama Press.

Carmack, Robert M., ed.

1988 *Harvest of Violence: The Maya Indians and the Guatemalan Crisis.* Norman: University of Oklahoma Press.

Casa Alianza

2006 Honduras: Análisis mensual sobre problemáticas de la niñez hondureña: Noviembre 2006. Tegucigalpa, Honduras: http://www.casa-alianza.org/docs/2006/2006-12-26-hond-ejec.pdf.

2007 Covenant House Guatemala Fighting Poverty and the Buying and Selling of Children. July 5, 2007. http://www.covenanthouse. org/ab_media_sto7_0705_guat_qna.html.

Castañeda, Quetzil

1996 *In the Museum of Mayan Culture: Touring Chichén Itzá.* Minneapolis: University of Minnesota Press.

1997 On the Correct Training of *Indios* in the Handicraft Market at Chichén Itzá: Tactics and Tactility of Gender, Class, Race and State. *Journal of Latin American Anthropology* 2(2):106–143.

CCCS (Center for Contemporary Cultural Studies) Education Group

1981 *Unpopular Education: Schooling and Social Democracy in England since 1944.* London: Hutchinson.

CEH (Comisión para el Esclarecimiento Histórico)

1999 *Guatemala, memoria del silencio.* Informe presentado por la Comisión para el Esclarecimiento Histórico, Guatemala City.

Chaney, Elizabeth, and M. Castro, eds.

1989 *Muchachas No More: Household Workers in Latin America and the Carribbean.* Philadelphia: Temple University Press.

Chayanov, Alexander V.

1966 *The Theory of Peasant Economy.* Ed. Daniel Thorner, Basile Kerblay, and R. E. F. Smith. Homewood, IL: American Economic Association.

Cheal, David

1989 Strategies of Resource Management in Household Economies: Moral Economy or Political Economy? In *The Household Economy: Reconsidering the Domestic Mode of Production,* ed. Richard Wilk, 11–23. Boulder, CO: Westview Press.

Chibnik, Michael

2003 *Crafting Tradition: The Making and Marketing of Oaxacan Wood Carvings.* Austin: University of Texas Press.

Childhope

1993 *Report to Comisión de las Comunidades Europeas.* Guatemala City: Childhope Oficina Norte de Latinoamérica.

CIA (Central Intelligence Agency of the United States of America)

2002 *The World Factbook: Guatemala.* Electronic resource available at http://www.odci.gov/cia/publications/factbook/print/gt.html.

CITGUA (Ciencia y Tecnología para Guatemala)

1991 *Asentamientos precarios y pobladores en Guatemala.* Guatemala City: Ciencia y Tecnología para Guatemala.

Clark, Graciela, ed.

2003 *Gender at Work in Economic Life*. Walnut Creek, CA: Altamira Press and the Society for Economic Anthropology.

Cogsgrove, John G.

1990 Toward a Working Definition of Street Children. *International Social Work* 33:185–192.

Cohen, Jeffrey

2004 *The Culture of Migration in Southern Mexico*. Austin: University of Texas Press.

Cojti Cuxil, Demetrio

1996 The Politics of Maya Revindication. In *Maya Cultural Activism in Guatemala*, ed. Edward F. Fischer and R. McKenna Brown, 208–221. Austin: University of Texas Press.

1997 *Ri Maya' Moloj pa Iximulew: El Movimiento Maya*. Guatemala City: Editorial Cholsamaj.

Comisión Jurídica

1998 *Código de la niñez y la juventud*. 3 vols. Guatemala City: Coordinadora Institucional de Promoción por los Derechos de la Niñez (CIPRODENI).

Connolly, Mark

1990 Adrift in the City: A Comparative Study of Street Children in Bogotá, Colombia, and Guatemala City. In *Homeless Children: The Watchers and the Waiters*, ed. Nancy Boxhill, 129–139. New York: The Hayworth Press.

Cressey, Paul

1969 *The Taxi Dance Hall: A Sociological Study in Commercialized Recreation and City Life*. Montclair, NJ: Patterson Hall. (Orig. pub. 1932.)

Cross, John

1998 *Informal Politics: Street Vendors and the State in Mexico City*. Stanford, CA. Stanford University Press.

Cumes Salazar, Heliodoro, and Teresa Chocoyo Chile

1997 ...*Nos hacen llorar: Jóvenes trabajadoras en las maquilas coreanas de San Lucas, Sacatepéquez a El Tejar, Chimaltenango*. Guatemala: Programa de Apoyo para la Salud Materno Infantil (PAMI).

Cuzzort, R. P., and Edith W. King

2002 *Social Thought into the Twenty-first Century*. New York: Harcourt.

Delphy, Christine

1984 *Close to Home*. Amherst: University of Massachusetts Press.

de Oliveira, Tania Chalhud

1995 Being with Street Children: Political, Romantic, and Professional Lived Experiences in Youthwork. Ph.D. diss., School of Social Work, University of Minnesota.

de Oliveira, Walter F.

    1995   We Are in the Streets Because They Are in the Streets: The Emergence and Praxis of Street Youth Work in Sao Paulo, Brazil. Ph.D. diss., Department of Education, University of Minnesota.

de Oliveira, Walter F., Michael Baizerman, and Lea Pellet

    1992   Street Children in Brazil and Their Helpers: Comparative Views on Aspirations and the Future. *International Social Work* 35(2):163–176.

Dubois, Cora

    1944   *The People of Alor.* Minneapolis: University of Minnesota Press.

Durkheim, Emile

    1963   *Suicide.* Glencoe: The Free Press.

Ehlers, Tracy Bachrach

    1990   *Silent Looms: Women and Production in a Guatemalan Town.* Boulder, CO: Westview Press.

    1991   Debunking Marianismo: Economic Vulnerability and Survival Strategies among Guatemalan Wives. *Ethnology* 30(1):1–16.

Engels, Friedrich

    1969   *The Origin of the Family, Private Property and the State.* New York: International Publishers. (Orig. pub. 1884.)

England, Nora C.

    1998   Mayan Efforts toward Language Preservation. In *Endangered Languages,* ed. Leonore A. Grenoble and Lindsay Whaley, 99–116. Cambridge: Cambridge University Press.

    2003   Mayan Language Revival and Revitalization Politics: Linguists and Linguistic Ideologies. *American Anthropologist* 105(4):733–743.

Fall, M.

    1986   Street Children. *Populi* 13(4):47–53.

Felsman, J. K.

    1981   Street Urchins in Colombia. *Natural History* 4:41–48.

    1984   Abandoned Children: A Reconsideration. *Children Today* 13:13–18.

Field, Norma

    1995   The Child as Laborer and Consumer: The Disappearance of Childhood in Contemporary Japan. In *Children and the Politics of Culture,* ed. Sharon Stephens, 51–78. Princeton, NJ: Princeton University Press.

Finch, Janet

    1985   Work, Family and the Home. *International Journal of Social Economics* 12:26–35.

Fischer, Edward F.

    2001   *Cultural Logics and Global Economics: Maya Identity in Thought and Practice.* Austin: University of Texas Press.

Fischer, Edward F., and R. McKenna Brown, eds.

    1996   *Maya Cultural Activism in Guatemala.* Austin: University of Texas Press.

Flanz, Gisbert H.

1997 *Constitutions of the Countries of the World.* New York: Oceana Publications.

Fleisher, Mark S.

1995 *Beggars and Thieves: Lives of Urban Street Criminals.* Madison: University of Wisconsin Press.

Fortes, Meyer

1945 *The Dynamics of Clanship among the Tallensi.* London: Oxford University Press.

1949 *The Web of Kinship among the Tallensi.* London: Oxford University Press.

Foster, George

1966 Peasant Society and the Image of Limited Good. *American Anthropologist* 67:293–314.

Frank, Andre-Gunder

1972 Economic Dependence, Class Structure and Underdevelopment. In *Dependence and Underdevelopment: Latin America's Political Economy,* ed. James D. Cockcroft, 19–45. New York: Doubleday.

Franko, Patrice

1999 *The Puzzle of Latin American Economic Development.* Lanham, MD: Rowan and Littlefield.

Freire, Paulo

1970 *Pedagogy of the Oppressed.* New York: Seabury Press.

1983 *Acción cultural para la libertad.* Mexico City: Casa Unidad de Publicaciones.

Freud, Sigmund

1920 *A General Introduction to Psychoanalysis.* Trans. G. Stanley Hall. New York: Boni and Liveright.

Fyfe, Alan

1989 *Child Labor.* Cambridge: Polity Press.

Garrard-Burnett, Virginia

1998 *Protestantism in Guatemala: Living in the New Jerusalem.* Austin: University of Texas Press.

Geertz, Clifford

1973 *The Interpretation of Cultures.* New York: Basic Books.

Gellert, Gisela

1995 *Ciudad de Guatemala: Factores determinantes en su desarrollo urbano.* Guatemala City: FLACSO.

Godoy, Angelina Snodgrass

1999 Our Right Is the Right to Be Killed: Making Rights Real on the Streets of Guatemala City. *Childhood* 6(4):423–442.

Goffman, Erving

1959 *The Presentation of Self in Everyday Life.* Garden City: Doubleday, Anchor Books.

1961   *Asylums: Essays on the Social Situation of Mental Patients and Other Inmates.* Garden City, NJ: Anchor Books.

1967   *Interaction Ritual: Essays on Face-to-Face Behavior.* Garden City: Doubleday, Anchor Books.

1971   *Relations in Public: Microstudies of the Public Order.* New York: Basic Books.

Goldín, Liliana

1985   Organizing the World through the Market: A Symbolic Analysis of Markets and Exchange in the Western Highlands of Guatemala. Ph.D. diss., State University of New York, Albany.

1987   The "Peace of the Market" in the Midst of Violence: A Symbolic Analysis of Markets and Exchange in the Western Highlands of Guatemala. *Ethnos* 53(3–4):368–383.

2001   Maquila Age Maya: Changing Households and Communities of the Central Highlands of Guatemala. *Journal of Latin American Anthropology* 6(1):30–57.

Goldstein, Daniel

2004   *Spectacular City: Violence and Performance in Urban Bolivia.* Durham: Duke University Press.

Góngora, R.

1998   El Concordia revela sus secretos. *Nuestro Diario* (Guatemala City), November 17, 5.

González, Nancie L.

1988   *Sojourners of the Carribbean: Ethnogenesis and Ethnohistory of the Garifuna.* Urbana: University of Illinois Press.

González Díaz, Donald

1998   Cuidarán niños de la calle. *Siglo Veintiuno* (Guatemala City), March 24, 54.

Goode, Judith

1987   *Gaminismo: The Changing Nature of the Street Child Phenomenon.* USFI Field Reports No. 28. N.p. Photocopy.

Gramsci, Antonio

2000   *The Antonio Gramsci Reader.* Ed. David Forgacs. New York: New York University Press.

Grinnell, George

1923   *The Cheyenne Indians.* New Haven: Yale University Press.

Gutmann, Matthew C.

1998   *Mamitas* and the Traumas of Development in a Colonia Popular of Mexico City. In *Small Wars: The Cultural Politics of Childhood,* ed. Nancy Scheper-Hughes and Carolyn Sargent, 130–148. Berkeley: University of California Press.

Hagan, Jacqueline Maria

1994   *Deciding to Be Legal: A Maya Community in Houston.* Philadelphia: Temple University Press.

Hall, Kathleen

1995 "There's a Time to Act English and a Time to Act Indian": The Politics of Identity among British-Sikh Teenagers. In *Children and the Politics of Culture,* ed. Sharon Stephens, 243–264. Princeton, NJ: Princeton University Press.

Hall, Stuart, and Tony Jefferson, eds.

1975 *Resistance through Rituals.* London: Hutchinson.

Hamilton, Nora, and Norma Stoltz Chinchilla

2001 *Seeking Community in a Global City: Guatemalans and Salvadorans in Los Angeles.* Philadelphia: Temple University Press.

Hannerz, Ulf

1980 *Exploring the City: Inquiries toward an Urban Anthropology.* New York: Columbia University Press.

Hardman, Charlotte

1973 Can There Be an Anthropology of Children? *Journal of the Anthropological Society of Oxford* 4(1):85–99.

Hebdige, Dick

1979 *Subculture: The Meaning of Style.* London: Routledge.

Hecht, Tobias

1998 *At Home in the Street: Street Children of Northeast Brazil.* Cambridge: Cambridge University Press.

———, ed.

2002 *Minor Omissions: Children in Latin American History and Society.* Madison: University of Wisconsin Press.

Hendrickson, Carol

1995 *Weaving Identities: Construction of Dress and Self in a Highland Guatemala Town.* Austin, University of Texas Press.

1996 Women, Weaving, and Education in *Maya Revitalization. In Maya Cultural Activism in Guatemala,* ed. Edward F. Fischer and R. McKenna Brown, 208–221. Austin: University of Texas Press.

Hervik, Peter

1998 The Mysterious Maya of *National Geographic. Journal of Latin American Anthropology* 4(1):166–197.

Hill, Robert M.

1989 *The Pirir Papers.* Vanderbilt University Publications in Anthropology No. 37. Nashville, TN: Vanderbilt University Press.

1992 *Colonial Cakchiquels: Highland Maya Adaptations to Spanish Rule 1600–1700.* Fort Worth, TX: Harcourt, Brace, Jovanovich.

Hirabayashi, Lane Ryo

1993 *Cultural Capital: Mountain Zapotec Migrant Associations in Mexico City.* Tucson: University of Arizona Press.

Hull, T.

1975 *Each Child Brings Its Own Fortune: An Enquiry into the Value of Children in a Javanese Village*. Canberra: Australian National University.

Impelizieri, Flavia

1995 *Street Children and NGOs in Rio*. Rio de Janeiro: AMAIS/IUPERJ.

Inter-American Development Bank (cited as IADB)

1990 *Economic and Social Progress in Latin America: 1990 Report*. Baltimore, MD: Johns Hopkins University Press.

International Labour Organization (cited as ILO)

1973 *C 138: Minimum Age Convention, 1973*. Geneva: ILO. http://ilolex.ilo .ch.1567/scripts/convde.pl?C138

1998 *How Globalization Affects Child Labour*. Geneva: ILO International Program on the Elimination of Child Labour. http://www.ilo.org/ public/english/standards/ipec/intinit/how_glob.hmm.

1999a *C 182: Worst Forms of Child Labour Convention, 1999*. Geneva: ILO. http://ilolex.ilo.ch.1567/scripts/convde.pl?C182.

1999b Child Labour: Targeting the Intolerable. International Labour Conference, 86th Session, 1998. Report VI, Part 1. Geneva: ILO.

1999c IPEC Implementation Report 1998–1999. Geneva: ILO International Program on the Elimination of Child Labour. http://www.ilo.org/ public/english/standards/ipec/publ/imprep99/report.htm.

2002 *Children at Work: Health and Safety Risks*. Geneva: ILO.

James, Allison, and Alan Prout, eds.

1990 *Constructing and Reconstructing Childhood*. Basingstoke, UK: Falmer Press.

James, Allison, Chris Jenks, and Alan Prout

1998 *Theorizing Childhood*. New York: Columbia Teacher's College Press.

Janowsky, Erik

1992 Street Children and Street Education in Guatemala City and Tegucigalpa, Honduras. M.A. thesis, School of Public Health and Tropical Medicine, Tulane University.

Jenks, Chris, ed.

1993 *Cultural Reproduction*. London: Routledge.

Jenks, Chris

1996 *Childhood*. London: Routledge.

Jocano, F. Landa.

1969 *Growing Up in a Philippine Barrio*. New York: Holt, Rinehart and Winston.

Johnson, Alan

1975 Time Allocation in a Machigüenga Community. Ethnology 14:310–321.

Johnston, Francis E., and Setha Low

    1995   *Children of the Urban Poor: The Sociocultural Environment of Growth, Development, and Malnutrition in Guatemala City.* Boulder, CO: Westview Press.

Jonas, Susanne

    2000   *Of Centaurs and Doves: Guatemala's Peace Process.* Boulder, CO: Westview Press.

Karabanow, Jeff

    2003   Creating a Culture of Hope: Lessons from Street Children Agencies in Canada and Guatemala. *International Social Work* 46(3):369–386.

Kardiner, Abraham

    1939   *The Individual and His Society.* New York: Columbia University Press.

    1946   *The Psychological Frontiers of Society.* New York: Columbia University Press.

Kearney, Michael

    1986   Integration of the Mixteca and the Western U.S.-Mexico Region via Migratory Wage Labor. In *Regional Impacts of U.S.-Mexico Relations,* ed. Ina Rosenthal Urey, 71–102. San Diego: Center for U.S.-Mexican Studies.

    1996   *Reconceptualizing the Peasantry: Anthropology in Global Perspective.* Boulder, CO: Westview Press.

Kemper, Robert Van

    1977   *Migration and Adaptation: Tzintzuntzan Peasants in Mexico City.* Beverly Hills, CA: Sage Publications.

Kidd, Dudley

    1906   *Savage Childhood: A Study of Kafir Children.* London: Macmillan.

Kiefer, C. W.

    1970   The Psychological Interdependence of Family, School and Bureaucracy in Japan. *American Anthropologist* 72:66–75.

Kirschenblatt-Gimblett, Barbara

    1975   A Parable in Context: A Social Interactional Analysis of Storytelling Performance. In *Folklore,* ed. Dan Ben-Amos and Kenneth S. Goldstein, 105–130. The Hague: Mouton.

    1999   Playing to the Senses: Food as a Performance Medium. *Performance Research* 4(1):1–30.

Kyomuhendo, Grace Bantebya

    1999   Decision-making in Poor Households: The Case of Kampala, Uganda. In *Urban Poverty in Africa: From Understanding to Alleviation,* ed. Sue Jones and Nici Nelson, 113–125. London: Intermediate Technology Publications.

Leacock, Eleanor, ed.

    1971   *The Culture of Poverty: A Critique.* New York: Simon and Schuster.

Lee, Richard B., and Irven DeVore

    1968   *Man the Hunter.* New York: Aldine Publishing.

Lee, Ronald D., and Karen L. Kramer

2002 Children's Economic Roles in the Maya Family Life Cycle: Cain, Caldwell and Chayanov Revisited. *Population and Development Review* 28(3):475–499.

Leis, Philip E.

1972 *Enculturation and Socialization in an Ijaw Village.* New York: Holt, Rinehart and Winston.

Lem, Winnie

2002 Regulating Women and Managing Men: Regimes of Control in Languedoc Family Enterprises. In *Social Dimensions in the Economic Process,* ed. Norbert Dannehauser and Cynthia Werner, 163–186. Oxford: JAI Press.

Lerer, Leonard B.

1998 Who Is the Rogue? Hunger, Death and Circumstance in John Mampe Square. In *Small Wars: The Cultural Politics of Childhood,* ed. Nancy Scheper-Hughes and Carolyn Sargent, 228–249. Berkeley: University of California Press.

Lewis, Oscar

1951 *Life in a Mexican Village.* Urbana: University of Illinois Press.

1959 *Five Families: Mexican Case Studies in the Culture of Poverty.* New York: Basic Books.

1965 *La Vida.* New York: Random House.

1974 *The Culture of Poverty in Contemporary Cultures and Societies of Latin America: A Reader in the Social Anthropology of Middle and South America.* Ed. Dwight B. Heath. New York: Random House.

Little, Walter E.

2004 *Mayas in the Marketplace: Tourism, Globalization, and Cultural Identity.* Austin: University of Texas Press.

Lloyd, Peter

1980 *The Young Towns of Lima: Aspects of Urbanization in Peru.* Cambridge: Cambridge University Press.

Lomnitz, Larissa

1978 The Survival of the Unfittest. In *Urbanization in the Americas from Its Beginnings to the Present,* ed. Richard Schaedel and Jorge Hardoy, 537–568. The Hague: Mouton.

López Ovando, Olga

2000 Trabajos en parque Concordia están paralizados. *Prensa Libre Edición Electrónica.* Guatemala City.

Loucky, James Peter

1988 Children's Work and Family Survival in Highland Guatemala. Ph.D. diss., Department of Anthropology, University of California, Los Angeles.

Loucky, James, and Marilyn M. Moors, eds.

2000   *The Maya Diaspora: Guatemalan Roots, New American Lives.* Philadelphia: Temple University Press.

Low, Setha M.

2000   *On the Plaza.* Austin: University of Texas Press.

Low, Setha M., and Denise Lawrence-Zúñiga, eds.

2003   *The Anthropology of Space and Place: Locating Culture.* Malden, MA: Blackwell Publishing.

Lucchini, Riccardo

1994   *The Street Girl: Prostitution, Family and Drug.* Fribourg, Switzerland: Institute for Economic and Social Sciences.

Lusk, Mark W.

1989   Street Children Programs in Latin America. *Journal of Sociology and Social Welfare* 16(1):55–77.

1992   Street Children of Rio de Janeiro. *International Social Work* 35(3):293–307.

Lutz, Catherine A., and Jane Collins, eds.

1993   *Reading* National Geographic. Chicago: University of Chicago Press.

MacLachlan, Morgan, ed.

1987   *Household Economies and Their Transformations.* Lanham, MD: University Press of America and Society for Economic Anthropology.

Maine, Henry Sumner

1913   *Ancient Law.* London: George Routledge and Sons. (Orig. pub. 1861.)

Malinowski, Bronislaw

1955   *Sex and Repression in Savage Society.* New York: The Noonday Press. (Orig. pub. 1927.)

1961   *Argonauts of the Western Pacific.* New York: Dutton. (Orig. pub. 1922.)

1963   *The Family among the Australian Aborigines: A Sociological Study.* New York: Schocken Books.

Márquez, Patricia C.

1999   *The Street Is My Home: Youth and Violence in Caracas.* Stanford, CA: Stanford University Press.

Marx, Karl

1967   *Capital.* 3 vols. New York: International Publishers.

Mauss, Marcel

1990   *The Gift: The Form and Reason for Exchange in Archaic Societies.* New York: W.W. Norton.

Maxwell, Judith M.

2001   *Textos chujes de San Mateo Ixtatán.* Palos Verdes, CA: Fundación Yax Te. (A collection of folktales and personal narratives in Chuj, with translation into English.)

McBryde, Felix Webster

1933   *Sololá: A Guatemalan Town and Cakchiquel Market Center.* Middle

American Research Series, Publication 5, Pamphlet 3. New Orleans, LA: Middle American Research Institute of Tulane University.

McKenna, James J.

1996   Sudden Infant Death Syndrome in Cross-Cultural Perspective: Is Infant-Parent Cosleeping Protective? *Annual Review of Anthropology* 23:201–227.

McRobbie, Angela, and McCabe Trisha, eds.

1981   *Feminism for Girls: An Adventure Story.* London: Routledge.

Mead, Margaret

1928   *Coming of Age in Samoa.* New York: Morrow.

Mead, Margaret, and Martha Wolfenstein, eds.

1955   *Childhood in Contemporary Cultures.* Chicago: University of Chicago Press.

Menchú, Rigoberta

1987   *I, Rigoberta Menchú: An Indian Woman in Guatemala.* New York: Verso.

Mills, Mary Beth

1999   *Thai Women in the Global Labor Force.* New Brunswick, NJ: Rutgers University Press.

Minge-Kalman, Wanda

1984   Household Economy during the Peasant-to-Worker Transition in the Swiss Alps. In *Work in Non-Market and Traditional Societies,* ed. Herbert Applebaum, 355–362. Albany: State University of New York Press.

Ministerio de Trabajo y Previsión Social

1996   *Código de trabajo de la República de Guatemala.* Guatemala City: Ministerio de Trabajo y Previsión Social.

Moerat, F.

1989   *A Study of Child Labour with Regard to Newspaper Vendors in the Cape Peninsula.* Cape Town, South Africa: University of Cape Town.

Morgan, Lewis Henry

1877   *Ancient Society; or, Researches in the Lines of Human Progress from Savagery through Barbarism to Civilization.* New York: Henry Holt.

1962   *League of the Ho-de-no-sau-neeb, or Iroquois.* New York: Corinth Books. (Orig. pub. 1851.)

Nardinelli, Charles

1990   *Child Labor and the Industrial Revolution.* Bloomington, IN: Indiana University Press.

Nash, June

1970   *In the Eyes of Ancestors: Belief and Behavior in a Maya Community.* New Haven: Yale University Press.

Nash, June, ed.

1993   *Crafts in the World Market.* Albany: State University of New York Press.

Nash, June, and Elizabeth Fernández-Kelly, eds.

1983   *Women, Men and the International Division of Labor.* Albany: State University of New York Press.

Nash, June, and Helen Safa, eds.

1976   *Sex and Class in Latin America.* New York: Praeger.

Nelson, Diane

1999   *Finger in the Wound: Body Politics in Quincentennial Guatemala.* Berkeley: University of California Press.

Netting, Robert M., Richard Wilk, and Eric J. Arnould, eds.

1984   *Households: Comparative and Historical Studies of the Domestic Group.* Berkeley: University of California Press.

Nieuwenhuys, Olga

1994   *Children's Lifeworlds: Gender, Welfare and Labour in the Developing World.* London: Routledge.

1996   The Paradox of Child Labor in Anthropology. *Annual Reviews in Anthropology* 25:237–251.

Offit, Thomas

1993   The Selling of Guatemala at Home and Abroad. *Human Mosaic* 25(1):72–79.

2000   Cien Años de Inquietud: The Huelga de Dolores as a Guatemalan Social Drama. American Anthropological Association Meetings, San Francisco, November.

Oldham, David

1994   Childhood as a Mode of Production. In *Children's Childhoods: Observed and Experienced,* ed. Berry Mayall, 153–167. London: Falmer Press.

Oloko, Beatrice Adenike

1991   Children's Work in Urban Nigeria. In *Protecting Working Children,* ed. W. E. Myers, 11–23. London: Zed Books and United Nations Children's Fund.

Opie, Iona, and Peter Opie

1977   *The Lore and Language of Schoolchildren.* London: Paladin.

1984   *Children's Games in Street and Playground.* Oxford: Oxford University Press.

Ortiz, Sutti, ed.

1983   *Economic Anthropology: Topics and Theories.* New York: Society for Economic Anthropology and University Press of America.

Ortiz de Carrizosa, Susana, and John Poertner

1992   Latin American Street Children: Problem, Programmes and Critique. *International Social Work* 35(4):405–413.

Otterbein, Charlotte S., and Keith Otterbein

1973   Believers and Beaters: A Case Study of Supernatural Beliefs and Child Rearing in the Bahama Islands. *American Anthropologist* 75:1670–1681.

Otzoy, Irma

1996 Maya Clothing and Identity. In *Maya Cultural Activism in Guatemala,* ed. Edward F. Fischer and R. McKenna Brown, 208–221. Austin: University of Texas Press.

Panter-Brick, Catherine

2002 Street Children, Human Rights, and Public Health: A Critique and Future Directions. *Annual Review of Anthropology* 31: 147–166.

Paul, Benjamin

1950 Symbolic Sibling Rivalry in a Guatemalan Indian Village. *American Anthropologist* 52:205–218.

Peterson, Kurt

1996 *The Maquiladora Revolution in Guatemala.* Occasional Paper Series, No. 2. New Haven: Center for International Human Rights at Yale University Law School.

Phelan, Peggy

1997 *Mourning Sex.* New York: Routledge.

Piaget, Jean

1926 *Language and Thought of the Child.* New York: Harcourt, Brace.

Plattner, Stuart, ed.

1985 *Markets and Marketing.* Monographs in Economic Anthropology No. 4. Lanham, MD: University Press of America.

Polanyi, Karl

1944 *The Great Transformation.* New York: Rinehart.

1968 *Primitive, Archaic and Modern Economies: Essays of Karl Polanyi.* Boston: Beacon Press.

1977 *The Livelihood of Man.* New York: Academic Press.

Pollak, Robert A.

2002 Gary Becker's Contributions to Family and Household Economics. Working Paper 9232. Cambridge, MA: National Bureau of Economic Research.

Porio, Emma, Leopold Moselina, and Anthony Swift

1994 Philippines: Urban Communities and Their Fight for Survival. *In Urban Children in Distress,* ed. Cristina Szanton-Blanc, 101–150. Luxembourg: UNICEF/Gordon and Breach.

Porres Castejón, Gustavo

1995 *Déjennos trabajar: Los buhoneros de la zona central.* Guatemala City: FLACSO.

Porter, Karen

1999 An Anthropological Defense of Child Labor. *The Chronicle of Higher Education,* November 19, B11.

Radcliffe-Brown, Alfred Reginald

1964 *The Andaman Islanders.* New York: The Free Press.

1987 *African Systems of Kinship and Marriage.* London: Kegan Paul International.

Redfield, Robert
1941 *The Folk Culture of Yucatan.* Chicago: University of Chicago Press.

REMHI (Project for the Recovery of Historical Memory)
1999 *Guatemala: Never Again.* Maryknoll, NY: Orbis Books.

Reynolds, Pamela
1991 *Dance Civet Cat: Child Labor in the Zambezi Valley.* Athens: Ohio University Press.

Richards, Julia Becker, and Michael Richards
1996 Maya Education: A Historical and Contemporary Analysis of Mayan Language Education Policy. In *Maya Cultural Activism in Guatemala,* ed. Edward F. Fischer and R. McKenna Brown, 208–221. Austin: University of Texas Press.

Richardson, Miles
1982 Being-in-the-Market versus Being-in-the-Plaza: Material Culture and the Construction of Social Reality in Spanish America. *American Ethnologist* 9(2):421–436.

Rizzini, Irene, Irma Rizzini, Monica Munoz-Vargas, and Linda Galeano
1994 Brazil: A New Concept of Childhood. In *Urban Children in Distress,* ed. Cristina Szanton-Blanc, 55–99. Luxembourg: UNICEF/Gordon and Breach.

Roberts, Brian
1973 *Organizing Strangers: Poor Families in Guatemala City.* Austin: University of Texas Press.

Rodríguez, Luisa F.
1999 Educación: Solicitan Q4,500 millones. *Prensa Libre Edición Electrónica* (Guatemala City), November 4.

2000a Educación: Alertan por inscripción. *Prensa Libre Edición Electrónica* (Guatemala City), January 4.

2000b Educación: Maestros no son suficientes. *Prensa Libre Edición Electrónica* (Guatemala City), January 5.

2000c Escuelas del país sin el desayuno escolar. *Prensa Libre Edición Electrónica* (Guatemala City), February 28.

2000d Polémica por dinero asignado a educación. *Prensa Libre Edición Electrónica* (Guatemala City), January 22.

Rothstein, Frances A., and Michael L. Blim
1991 *Anthropology and the Global Factory: Studies of the New Industrialization in the Late Twentieth Century.* New York: Bergin and Garvey.

Rutz, Henry J.
1989 Fijian Household Practices and the Reproduction of Class. In *The Household Economy: Reconsidering the Domestic Mode of Production,* ed. Richard Wilk, 119–148. Boulder, CO: Westview Press.

Safa, Helen I.

    1964   From Shantytown to Public Housing: A Comparison of Family Structure in Two Urban Neighborhoods in Puerto Rico. *Carribean Studies* 4(1).

    1974   *The Urban Poor of Puerto Rico.* New York: Holt, Rinehart and Winston.

Sahlins, Marshall

    1972   *Stone Age Economics.* Chicago: Aldine.

Sassen, Saskia.

    1991   *The Global City: New York, London and Tokyo.* Princeton, NJ: Princeton University Press.

Scaglion, Richard

    1986   The Importance of Nighttime Observations in Time Allocation Studies. *American Ethnologist* 13:537–545.

Scheper-Hughes, Nancy, and Daniel Hoffman

    1997   Brazil: Moving Targets. *Natural History* 106(6):44–54.

    1998   Brazilian Apartheid: Street Kids and the Struggle for Urban Space. In Small Wars: The Cultural Politics of Childhood, ed. Nancy Scheper-Hughes and Carolyn Sargent, 352–388. Berkeley: University of California Press.

Scheper-Hughes, Nancy, and Carolyn Sargent

    1998   Introduction: The Cultural Politics of Childhood. In *Small Wars: The Cultural Politics of Childhood,* ed. Nancy Scheper-Hughes and Carolyn Sargent, 1–34. Berkeley: University of California Press.

Scheper-Hughes, Nancy, and Loic Wacquant, eds.

    2002   *Commodifying Bodies.* London: Sage Publications.

Schmink, Marianne

    1984   Household Economic Strategies: Review and Research Agenda. *Latin American Research Review* 19(3):87–101.

Schwartzman, Helen B.

    1976   The Anthropological Study of Children's Play. *Annual Review of Anthropology* 5:289–328.

    ——, ed.

    2001   *Children and Anthropology: A Century of Studies in Children and Anthropology: Perspectives for the 21st Century.* New York: Bergin and Garvey.

Scott, James C.

    1976   *The Moral Economy of the Peasant: Rebellion and Subsistence in Southeast Asia.* New Haven: Yale University Press.

    1985   *Weapons of the Weak: Everyday Forms of Peasant Resistance.* New Haven: Yale University Press.

    1990   *Domination and the Arts of Resistance.* New Haven: Yale University Press.

Seabrook, Jeremy

    2001   *Children of Other Worlds: Exploitation in the Global Market.* London: Pluto Press.

Selby, Henry A., Arthur D. Murphy, and Stephen A. Lorenzen
  1990   *The Mexican Urban Household: Organizing for Self-Defense.* Austin: University of Texas Press.
Simmel, Georg
  1950   The Metropolis and Mental Life. In *The Sociology of Georg Simmel,* ed. and trans. Kurt Wolff, 409–424. Glencoe, IL: The Free Press.
Small, David B., and Nicola Tannenbaum, eds.
  1999   *At the Interface: The Household and Beyond.* Lanham, MD: University Press of America and Society for Economic Anthropology.
Smith, Carol
  1972   The Domestic Marketing System of Western Guatemala. Ph.D. diss., Anthropology Department, Stanford University.
  1974   Economics of Marketing Systems: Models from Economic Geography. *Annual Review of Anthropology* 3:167–201.
  1976   *Regional Analysis.* Vols. 1 and 2. New York: Academic Press.
  1984   El desarrollo de la primacia urbana en Guatemala. *Mesoamerica* 5(8):195–278.
  1985   Class Relations and Urbanization in Guatemala: Toward an Alternative Theory of Urban Primacy. In *Urbanization in the World Economy,* ed. Michael Timberlake, 121–167. Orlando, FL: Academic Press.
  1988   Destruction of the Material Bases for Indian Culture: Economic Changes in Totonicapán. In *Harvest of Violence: The Maya Indians and the Guatemalan Crisis,* ed. Robert M. Carmack, 206–231. Norman: University of Oklahoma Press.
  1990   Social Relations in Guatemala over Time and Space. In *Guatemalan Indians and the State, 1540–1988,* ed. Carol. A. Smith, 1–30. Austin: University of Texas Press.
Smith, Gavin
  1989   *Livelihood and Resistance: Peasants and the Politics of Land in Peru.* Berkeley: University of California Press.
Snow, David A., and Leon Anderson
  1993   *Down on Their Luck: A Study of Homeless Street People.* Berkeley: University of California Press.
Sontag, Susan
  1977   *On Photography.* New York: Picador Books.
Stephen, Lynn
  2002   *Zapata Lives! Histories and Cultural Politics in Southern Mexico.* Berkeley: University of California Press.
Stephens, Sharon, ed.
  1995   *Children and the Politics of Culture.* Princeton, NJ: Princeton University Press.

Sterk, Claire E.

    2000   *Tricking and Tripping: Prostitution in the Era of AIDS.* Putnam Valley, NY: Social Change Press.

Stoll, David

    1982   *Fishers of Men or Founders of Empire? The Wycliffe Bible Translators in Latin America.* Cambridge, MA: Cultural Survival.

    1990   *Is Latin America Turning Protestant? The Politics of Evangelical Growth.* Berkeley and Los Angeles: University of California Press.

Sutton-Smith, Brian

    1972   *The Folk Games of Children.* Austin: University of Texas Press.

Swetnam, John

    1975   The Open Gateway: Social and Economic Interaction in a Guatemalan Marketplace. Ph.D. diss., Anthropology Department, University of Pennsylvania, Philadelphia.

Szalai, Alexander, ed.

    1972   *The Use of Time: Daily Activities of Urban and Suburban Populations in Twelve Countries.* The Hague: Mouton.

Szanton-Blanc, Cristina, ed.

    1994   *Urban Children in Distress.* Luxembourg: UNICEF/Gordon and Breach.

Tacon, Peter

    1981   My Child Minus One. Teaneck, NY: UNICEF. Unpublished ms.

Tannenbaum, Nicola

    1984   Chayanov and Economic Anthropology In *Chayanov, Peasants and Economic Anthropology,* ed. E. Paul Durrenberger, 27–38. New York: Academic Press.

Taracena, Elvia

    2003   A Schooling Model for Working Children in Mexico. *Childhood* 10(3):301–318.

Tax, Sol

    1953   *Penny Capitalism: A Guatemalan Indian Economy.* Washington, D.C.: United States Government Printing Office.

Thomas, J. J.

    1995   *Surviving in the City: The Urban Informal Sector in Latin America.* London: Pluto Press.

Thompson, Edward P.

    1966   *The Making of the English Working Class.* New York: Vintage Books.

    1971   The Moral Economy of the English Crowd in the Eighteenth Century. *Past and Present* 50:76–136.

    1980   *The Making of the English Working Class.* London: Penguin. (Orig. pub. 1963.)

Thrasher, Frederick

    1963   *The Gang.* Chicago: University of Chicago Press. (Orig. pub. 1927.)

Tierney, Nancy
1997   *Robbed of Humanity: Lives of Guatemalan Street Children.* Saint Paul, MN: Pangaea.
Tumax, L., and V. Morales
1998   Diagnóstico situacional de las niñas y adolescentes de y en la calle de la ciudad de Guatemala. Guatemala City: Childhope.
Turner, Victor
1967   *Forest of Symbols: Aspects of Ndembu Ritual.* Ithaca, NY: Cornell University Press.
1986   *The Anthropology of Performance.* New York: PAJ Publications.
UNICEF (United Nations Children's Fund)
1996   *State of the World's Children.* Oxford: Oxford University Press.
2000   *State of the World's Children.* Oxford: Oxford University Press.
2002   *State of the World's Children.* Oxford: Oxford University Press.
United Nations
2007   Convention on the Rights of the Child. Electronic resource from UNICEF Web site: http://www.ohchr.org/english/law/pdf/crc.pdf.
Urwick, E. J.
1904   *Studies of Boy Life in Our Cities.* London: Georges.
U.S. Department of Labor Bureau of International Labor Affairs (cited as USDLBILA)
1998   By the Sweat and Toil of Children, Vol. 5: Efforts to Eliminate Child Labor. Washington, D.C.: U.S. Department of Labor Bureau of International Labor Affairs.
Valentine, Charles A.
1968   *Culture and Poverty.* Chicago: University of Chicago Press.
Van Esterik, Penny
2002   Contemporary Trends in Infant Feeding Research. Annual *Review of Anthropology* 31:257–279.
Velásquez, Doménica
2000   Educación: Lo que más varió. *Prensa Libre Edición Electrónica* (Guatemala City), January 31.
Vélez-Ibáñez, Carlos
1983   Bonds of Mutual Trust: The Cultural Systems of Rotating Credit Associations among Urban Mexicans and Chicanos. New Brunswick, NJ: Rutgers University Press.
Villarreal, María Eugenia, and Carlos Peralta Chapetón
1997   *Trabajo infantil: Concepción y realidad.* Guatemala City: PAMI.
Vittachi, Anuradha
1990   *Stolen Childhood.* Cambridge, UK: Polity Press.
Wallerstein, Immanuel
1974–1989   The Modern World-System. 3 vols. New York: Academic Press.

Wallerstein, Immanuel, and Joan Smith
2000   Households as an Institution in the World Economy. In *The Essential Wallerstein*, 234–252. New York: The New Press.
Wallman, Sandra
1979   Introduction. In *Social Anthropology of Work*, ed. Sandra Wallman, 1–24. London: Academic Press.
1984   *Eight London Households*. London: Tavistock.
1986   The Boundaries of the Household. In *Symbolising Boundaries*, ed. Anthony Cohn. Manchester, UK: Manchester University Press.
Walvin, James
1982   *A Child's World: A Social History of English Childhood, 1800–1914*. Hammondsworth, UK: Penguin.
Warren, Kay B.
1989   *The Symbolism of Subordination: Indian Identity in a Guatemalan Town*. Rev. Ed. Austin: University of Texas Press.
1998   Indigenous Movements and Their Critics: Pan-Maya Activism in Guatemala. Princeton, NJ: Princeton University Press.
Weber, Max
1958   *The City*. New York: The Free Press.
White, Benjamin
1975   The Economic Importance of Children in a Javanese Village. In *Population and Social Organization*, ed. M. Nag, 127–146. The Hague: Mouton.
1982   Child Labour and Population Growth in Rural Asia. *Development and Change* 13(4):587–610.
Whiting, Beatrice
1963   *Six Cultures: Studies of Child Rearing*. New York: John Wiley and Sons.
Whiting, John, and Irving Child
1953   *Child Training and Personality: A Cross-Cultural Study*. New Haven: Yale University Press.
1969   A Borneo Childhood: Enculturation in Dusun Society. New York: Holt, Rinehart and Winston.
Wilk, Richard R., ed.
1989   *The Household Economy: Reconsidering the Domestic Mode of Production*. Boulder, CO: Westview Press.
Wilk, Richard R.
1996   *Economies and Cultures: Foundations of Economic Anthropology*. Boulder, CO: Westview Press.
1997   *Household Ecology: Economic Change and Domestic Life among the Kekchi Maya in Belize*. DeKalb: Northern Illinois University Press.
Willis, Paul
1977   *Learning to Labor: How Working-Class Kids Get Working-Class Jobs*. New York: Columbia University Press.

Wilson, William Julius
  1997   *When Work Disappears: The World of the New Urban Poor.* New York: Vintage Books.
Winton, Aisla
  2007   Using "Participatory" Methods with Young People in Contexts of Violence: Reflections from Guatemala. *Bulletin of Latin American Research* 26(4):497–515.
Wirth, Louis
  1938   Urbanism as a Way of Life. *American Journal of Sociology* 44:1–24.
Wittig, Martha
  1997   Culture of Poverty or Ghetto Underclass? Women and Children on the Streets of Honduras. Ph.D. diss., Department of Sociology, Tulane University.
Wolf, Diane Lauren
  1994   *Factory Daughters: Gender, Household Dynamics, and Rural Industrialization in Java.* Berkeley: University of California Press.
Wolf, Eric
  1982   *Europe and the People without History.* Berkeley: University of California Press.
Wolf, Margery
  1972   *Women and the Family in Rural Taiwan.* Stanford, CA: Stanford University Press.
World Bank
  1991   *World Development Report.* Baltimore, MD: Johns Hopkins University Press.
  1999   *The World Bank Annual Report 1999.* Electronic Resource available at http://www.worldbank.org/html/extpb/annrep99/.
  2007   *The World Bank Annual Report 2007.* Electronic Resource available at http://www.worldbank.org/html/extpb/annrep07/.
Wright, James D., Donald Kaminsky, and Martha Wittig
  1993a   Health and Social Conditions of Street Children in Honduras. *American Journal of Diseases of Children* 147(March):279–283.
  1993b   Street Children in North and Latin America: Preliminary Data from Proyecto Alternativos in Tegucigalpa and Some Comparisons with the U.S. Case. *Studies in Comparative International Development* 28(2):200–212.
Yanagisako, Sylvia Junco
  1979   Family and Household: The Analysis of Domestic Groups. *Annual Review of Anthropology* 8:161–205.
  2002   *Producing Culture and Capital: Family Firms in Italy.* Princeton, NJ: Princeton University Press.
Zorbaugh, Harvey W.
  1929   *Gold Coast and the Slum.* Chicago: University of Chicago Press.

INDEX

abandoned/abandoning children, 111–113
abduction. *See* child abduction
achimeros, 50, 61–62, 107, 109, 127, 155
Adams, Abigail, 180n8
adult street vendors: child street laborers working for, 1–2, 13, 27–29, 44–45, 80, 93–94, 110–111, 116–117, 121, 135, 162–163; contraband and stolen goods sold by, 51–52, 125; daily routine of, 27–28; and exclusive use of area for sales, 28–29; ideal location for, 29; income of, 14, 66; at intersection of Sexta Avenida and 18 Calle, 35, 37–38; as Maya Indians, 49, 50; municipal licenses and permits for, 28, 41; as parents of child street laborers, 23–24, 65–66, 69, 87, 100, 102–103, 139, 155, 190n1; and personal services, 73–74; relatives of, as unpaid child street workers, 102, 103, 113; statistics on, 48; theft from, by child street laborers, 111; vendors in interior markets compared with, 49; women as, 44–45, 66, 69–70, 93–94, 96, 111, 113, 187n19. *See also individual adult street vendors*
Africa, 55, 56, 57
agricultural work, 56, 102, 103, 104–105, 149, 163, 167, 185n11, 186n16

Américo (child street laborer), 79, 102–103
Annis, Sheldon, 184n8, 186n17
anthropological research: on childhood, child work, and child labor, 54–57; on child street laborers, 57–59; on households, 96–97, 183n2; on markets, 183nn6–7; on street children, 55–56; and time-allocation studies, 140
Antigua Guatemala, 180n6, 180n13
Argentina, 167
Arzú, Álvaro, 39
Asylums (Goffman), 119
Aycimena y Irigoyen, Juan Fermín, 32

Babb, Florence, 183n6
Bachofen, J. J., 96
bares (illicit bars), 52
Barthes, Roland, 180n10
Bartolomé (child street laborer), 152–154
Bastos, Santiago, 181n2
Becker, Gary, 58, 110, 182n6
begging, 72
Berger, John, 180n10
Berger, Óscar, 39
Best, Joel, 182n7
birth order, 99–100, 184n7
birthplace of child street laborers, 103
Bock, John, 140

Bolivia, 180n6
bordellos. *See* prostitution
Bossen, Laurel, 187n17
Bourgois, Philippe, 101
Brazil, 5, 56, 76–77, 187n18
Bromley, Ray, 12, 71–75
bultos (loads of cargo), 51, 67–70
buses: Chino combining entertainment and candy sales on, 139–140; cost of bus ride, 27; customers boarding of buses and waiting for departure, 189n10; at intersection of Calzada Aguilar Batres and Calzada Roosevelt, 47; pedestrians hit by, 150; route of, along 18 Calle, 34, 42–43
Butler, Judith, 122

Caballeros, M. E., 179n5
Camus, Manuela, 181n1
cargadores. See porters (*cargadores*)
car park attendants and car parkers: age as immutable prop of, 130; children and youth as, 61, 62; duties of, 75; income of, 62, 74, 79; initial capital outlay by, 78, 79; in market areas generally, 76; social interactions of, 144, 145; work-related physical activities of, 143, 146–147
car repair service, 51–52
car washing, 61, 62, 75, 79
Casa Alianza (Covenant House), 6
Castañeda, Quetzil, 180n6, 180n10, 188n6
Castro, Don Diego, 102–103
CEDC (children in especially difficult circumstances), 55, 182n3. *See also* street children
Chayanov, Alexander V., 186n16
Cheal, David, 23, 97, 110
Chibnik, Michael, 184n8
Chichén Itzá, 180n6

chicleros (gum and candy merchants), 50
child abduction, 11, 180n8
Childhope, 8
child labor: agricultural work, 56, 102, 103, 104–105, 149, 163, 167, 185n11, 186n16; anthropological research on, 54–57; contextualization of, 53–59; domestic servants, 116, 149, 153; as exploitation, 56, 58–59, 182n7; and gender, 56; Guatemalan laws on, 174–178; International Labour Organization (ILO) conventions on, 120, 171–173, 174, 177; in *maquiladoras*, 149, 166–167; as marginalization, 58, 181–182n6; Marx on, 166; moral condemnation of, 56; national and global factors related to, 165–168; structural causes of, 4–5, 25–26, 120–122, 165–169; United Nations Convention on the Rights of the Child (CRC) on, 173–174, 177; U.S. Department of Labor on, 178. *See also* child street laborers; child street workers
Child Labor (Fyfe), 21
children: anthropological research on, 54–57; CEDC (children in especially difficult circumstances), 55, 182n3; Guatemalan laws on, 174–178; international conventions on, 120, 152, 171–173, 174, 177; nickname for, in Guatemala, 189n9. *See also* education; *and headings beginning with child*
Children and Anthropology (Schwartzman), 55
Children and the Politics of Culture (Stephens), 55
child street laborers: as abandoned/abandoning children, 111–113; abusive behavior toward, 110–113, 116; age as immutable prop of, 12–30;

age of, at beginning of work life, 61, 66; anthropological research on, 57–59; and birth order, 99–100, 184n7; birthplace of, 103; categories of jobs performed by, 12, 70–76; common beliefs and misconceptions about, 2–3, 53, 76–77, 81, 90, 95, 129, 143–144, 161–162; contradictions regarding, 120–122, 125–126; customers of, 121, 125–126, 133, 144; daily routine of, 27–28, 43–45, 63, 68; definition of, 5–7; demographic data on, 23, 103–104; distinguished from child street workers, 6, 15, 57; distinguished from street children, 5–6, 57; employment of, by adult street vendors, 1–2, 13, 27–29, 44–45, 80, 93–94, 110–111, 116–117, 121, 135, 162–163; ethics concerning research on, 16–22; ethnicity of, 50, 103, 108, 132–134, 163, 185n10, 187n18; family assistance for, in gaining entry to street labor, 100–101; family structure and composition of, 97–100; food for, 28, 45, 105, 107, 117, 121, 125, 128, 148–149, 186n14, 188n5; future plans of, 65, 93, 113–114, 153, 162–165; and hierarchy of increasingly lucrative positions, 162–163; and household economic diversification, 101–103, 184–185n8; illness of, 128; immutable props of, 129–134; independent child street laborers, 65–67, 112, 113–114; independent versus dependent workers, 105–107, 109–111; initial capital outlay by, 78, 79; in interior markets, 49; manner, appearance, and scripts of, 134–140; money carried by, 128–129; neighborhoods with, 3, 9, 22, 32–43, 45–53; photographs of, 18–22, 82–89, 180nn10–12; physical activities of, 143, 145–149; physical props of, 126–129; recreation and social life of, 62, 93–96, 127, 136, 143, 146, 147, 148, 188–189n8; religious life of, 92–93; research perspectives and methods on, 7–15, 140–149; residence of, 62–63, 104, 117, 121, 125, 153; resistance strategies of, 111; rural homes of, 90–93, 98–99; safety of, 138, 144–145, 149–151; sex-based divisions among, 21, 74, 75, 78, 79–80, 131, 141; sex of, as immutable prop, 130–132; skills and knowledge of, gained by street education, 4, 25, 65, 117–118, 161–165, 168; social skills of, 24–25, 58, 115–122, 124–151; statistics on, 2, 7, 9; and street setting, 124–126; time-allocation studies of, 14, 140–149, 189n11; and work ethic, 24, 58, 107–108, 155; work schedule of, 1, 10, 24, 81, 153. *See also* car park attendants and car parkers; delivery persons; economic contributions of child street laborers to families; education; families; females; income; part-time child street laborers; porters (*cargadores*); shoeshiners; *and specific children*

child street workers: data gathering among, 15; definition of, 6, 57; as first step to becoming child street laborers, 15, 61, 104; part-time work for, 7; photographs of, 82, 85; of street-vending parents, 102, 103

Chino (child street laborer), 138, 140–141, 189n9

Christianity. *See* evangelical Christianity

cincos (marbles game), 95–96

civil war in Guatemala, 34, 101

clothing: of girl street laborers, 127, 128, 131; of shoeshiners, 137; traditional Mayan clothing, 128, 132, 190nn3–4; uniforms for schoolchildren, 156, 158, 190n3 clothing vendors: adults as, 139; children and youth as, 50, 72, 102–103; customers of, 133; in 18 Calle, 35; females as, 117–118; in El Guarda, 50, 51; income of, 81; physical props of, 127–128

Collins, Jane, 180n10

Colombia, 71, 112

Combating Child Labor (International Labor Organization), 20–21

comedores (food stalls): delivery girls for, 62–65, 75, 127, 132, 144–146; description of, 187n1; in 18 Calle, 43; girls working in, 49; in La Guarda interior market, 49; in Parque Concordia, 39; produce for, 51; women as proprietors of, 62–64, 132

contraband, 51–52, 125

Cortez (child street laborer), 67–70

Costa Rica, 180n6

Crafts in the World Market (Nash), 184–185n8

CRC. *See* United Nations Convention on the Rights of the Child (CRC)

crime, 16, 41, 51–52, 75, 149–151, 182n3. *See also* drug sales; prostitution; theft and robbery; violence

Cross, John, 183n6

culture of poverty, 58, 181–182n6

customers of child street laborers, 121, 125–126, 133, 144

Cutzal, Julio Héctor, 13

delivery persons: clothing of, 127, 131; girls as, 62–65, 75, 79, 84, 127, 131, 132, 144–146; income of, 62, 74, 79, 153–154; initial capital outlay by, 78, 79; photograph of, 84; physical props of, 127; social interactions of, 144–145; work-related physical activities of, 143, 145–146; work schedule of, 153

despotic regime of control, 96–97, 111, 112

DeVore, Irven, 140

domestic service, 116, 149, 153

dramaturgical model of social interaction: definition of front, 124; definition of manner, 134; Goffman's model, 118–119, 122–124, 126; and immutable props, 129–134; and manner, 134–140; and physical props, 126–129; and street setting, 124–126; three aspects of performance, 124

drug sales, 7, 18, 71, 179n5, 180n7, 182n3

earthquake (1976), 33–34, 40, 41, 47, 101

economic contributions of child street laborers to families: amounts of, 45, 62, 92, 106, 107, 153; coercion regarding, 110–111, 116; failure of child street laborers to contribute their income, 111–114; and household economic diversification, 101–103; and household regimes of control, 23, 96–97, 108–111, 112; necessity of, 4–5, 17, 45, 60, 92, 153; role of child street laborers in household economy, 100–101; specific case examples, 45, 60, 62, 92, 102–103, 105, 153; and work ethic of Maya Indians, 24, 58, 107–108, 155. *See also* income

economic diversification in households, 101–103, 184–185n8

Ecuador, 21

education: abandonment of, by child street laborers, 91–92, 120, 154–155, 158–159, 161, 186n15, 187–188n2; bilingual education, 190n2; child street laborers' educational histories, 152–154, 157–160; cost of sending children to school, 25, 156–157; disadvantages of public education for child street laborers, 4, 180n9; ele-

mentary school in Mercado Sur 2, 35; enrollment and attendance statistics on, 155–156; evening classes attended by young adult street laborers, 94, 180n9; of *fresas* (middle- and upper-class children), 7, 179n4; funding for, 155, 167; Guatemalan laws on, 161, 174–175, 177–178; informal education for child street laborers, 4, 94–95, 144, 147, 148, 159–160, 161, 183n1, 190n5; international conventions on, 161, 171–174; parents' and children's belief in value of, 120, 153–154, 187–188n2; for part-time child street workers and laborers, 7; PENNAT educational program, 8–12, 15, 64, 136, 152–155, 159–160, 190n5; percentage of time spent on, by child street laborers, 146; problems with public education system, 15, 25, 154–159, 167; skills and knowledge gained by street education, 4, 25, 65, 117–118, 161–165, 168; and teacher absenteeism, 156; and uniforms for schoolchildren, 156, 158, 190n3
Ehlers, Tracy, 186n17
Eileen, Doña, 117, 121, 135
Emiliana (child street laborer), 111
Engels, Friedrich, 96
England, Nora C., 190n2
entertainers. *See* street entertainers
errand-running duties, 44, 68
ethics, 16–22
ethnicity of child street laborers, 50, 103, 108, 132–134, 185n10, 187n18. *See also* Ladinos; Maya Indians
ethnography, 9, 54, 76, 96, 180nn6–7, 180n10, 182n3
evangelical Christianity, 92–93, 186n17

families: and abandoned children, 111–113; abusive behavior of, toward child laborers, 110–113, 116; anthropological research on households, 96–97, 183n2; birth order in, 99–100, 184n7; children's unpaid work for, 102, 103, 104–105; and deceased parents, 98, 113, 184n6; economic diversification of households, 101–103, 184–185n8; Maya parents, 24; number of children in, 99; parents as adult street vendors, 23–24, 65–66, 69, 87, 100, 102–103, 139, 155, 190n1; parents' belief in value of education, 120, 187–188n2; poverty of, 4–5, 17–18; regimes of control in, 23, 108–111, 112; resource management within households, 97; Rey's family, 90–93; in rural areas, 90–93, 98–99; and safety of child street laborers, 151; structure of, and multilocale households, 90–93, 98–102, 114; vocations for parents in, 100; wage-earning women's status in, 187n19; women's work in, 96; and work ethic, 24, 58, 107–108, 155. *See also* economic contributions of child street laborers to families
family-run businesses, 96–97, 184n5
farming. *See* agricultural work
females: abusive behavior toward girl street laborers, 110–113, 116; as adult street laborers, 44–45, 66, 69–70, 93–94, 96, 111, 113, 187n19; clothing of girl street laborers, 127, 128, 131; as clothing vendors, 117–118; and *comedores* (food stalls), 62–64, 132; as delivery girls, 62–65, 75, 79, 84, 127, 131, 132, 144–145; disadvantages of, due to biological sex, 130–132; as domestic servants, 116, 153; and *fletero* business, 69–70; as food vendors, 37, 49–50, 80, 116, 128, 139; gender stereotypes against, 131–132; income of girl street laborers, 77,

80, 116; lottery ticket sales by, 65–67, 80; manner of girl street laborers, 134–135; photographs of girl street laborers, 82, 84; and sex-based divisions among child street laborers, 21, 74, 75, 78, 79–80, 131, 141; as shoeshiners, 21–22. *See also* prostitution; *and specific street laborers and street vendors*

Fernández-Kelly, Elizabeth, 186–187n17

Fernando, Don, 1–2, 27–29

fertility rate, 99

Fischer, Edward F., 190n2

fixed vendors: definition of, 73; food for, 148–149; income of, 74, 81; physical and work-related activities of, 143, 146, 148–149; sex-based divisions among, 78; social interactions of, 145

fletes, fleteros (trucks, truck owners), 51, 68–70

food for child street laborers, 28, 45, 105, 107, 117, 121, 125, 128, 148–149, 186n14, 188n5

food vendors: beverage sales, 1–2, 28; child street laborers assisting, 68, 80, 116; females as, 37, 49–50, 80, 116, 128, 139; in El Guarda, 50; of Parque Concordia, 39; physical props for, 128; *salchicha* (hot dog) vendors, 34; *taquerías* (taco stands), 41

Fortes, Meyer, 181n5

fresas (middle- and upper-class children), 6–7, 179n4

Freud, Sigmund, 181n5

friendships. *See* recreation; social skills

Fyfe, Alec, 21

gambling, 71–72

gangs, 2, 24, 57, 112, 126, 131, 133, 179n5

garbage dump, 72, 183n5

García Gallont, Fritz, 39, 40

Geertz, Clifford, 150, 151

Gellert, Gisela, 181n3

gender stereotypes and gender socialization, 56, 96, 131–132. *See also* females; sex-based divisions of child labor

girls. *See* females

Gladys, Doña, 48

globalization, 166–168

Goffman, Erving, 24, 118–119, 122–124, 126, 188n3

Goldstein, Daniel, 180n6

El Guarda market, 3, 9, 43–53, 61–65, 67–70, 73, 93–94, 181n4

Guatemala: child labor and education laws in, 161, 174–178; civil war in, 34, 101; earthquake (1976) in, 33–34, 40, 41, 47, 101; economy of, 17–18, 30, 166; illiteracy in, 155; income and income distribution in, 30, 166; and International Monetary Fund (IMF), 167; land distribution in, 166; migration to United States from, 163–165, 167–168, 191n1; population of, 30–31, 132, 166; poverty in, 30, 166; trade between United States and, 167; urbanization in, 31, 33. *See also* Guatemala City, Guatemala; Ladinos; Maya Indians

Guatemala City, Guatemala: earthquake (1976) in, 33–34, 40, 41, 47; economy of, 30; 18 Calle area of downtown (Zone 1), 3, 9, 22, 32–43, 65–68, 73; garbage dump in, 183n5; El Guarda market in, 3, 9, 43–53, 61–65, 67–70, 73, 93–94, 181n4; history of street vending in Zone 1 of, 31–34; intersection of Sexta Avenida and 18 Calle in, 35, 37–38; maps of, 36–37, 46; Maya Indian population in, 30–31; Mercado Central in, 32, 33, 40; Mercado Peatonal (Pedestrian Market) in,

38, 40; Mercado Sur 2 in, 9, 35, 139; migration to, 33–34, 46–47; municipal offices in, 41–42; Municipal Plaza in, 42; Parque Concordia in, 38–40; Plaza Major (Central Plaza) in, 31–32, 41; population of, 30–31, 32, 33, 46–47; La Sexta and La Quinta in, 40–41, 132, 136–138; La Terminal market in, 133, 181n4, 189n10; Trébol area of Zone 11 of, 3, 9, 22, 45–53; El Viejo Guarda in, 45, 48, 49

Guatemalan National Telephone Company (GUATEL), 182n1

Haiti, 155
Hardman, Charlotte, 54
Hecht, Tobias, 16, 55–56, 187n18
hegemonic regime of control, 96–97, 110, 112
Hendrickson, Carol, 190n4
Hernando (child street laborer), 162–164, 168
Hervik, Peter, 180n10
Hoffman, Daniel, 76–77
homeless children. *See* street children
Honduras, 8, 101, 151
hormigas (smugglers), 52
households. *See* families
Huelga de Dolores procession, 189–190n12

illiteracy, 155. *See also* education
ILO. *See* International Labour Organization (ILO)
IMF. *See* International Monetary Fund (IMF)
immutable props, 129–134
income: of adult street vendors, 14, 66; of car park attendants and car parkers, 74, 79; of child street laborers, 1, 3–4, 14, 23, 61, 66–70, 76–81,

105–107, 116, 168; control of income earned by child street laborers, 110; of delivery persons, 62, 74, 79, 153; of domestic servants, 116; of girl street laborers, 80, 116; in Guatemala, 30, 166; minimum wage in Guatemala, 3, 29–30, 45, 181n1, 183n8; of nomadic versus fixed vendors, 74, 81; of porters (*cargadores*), 68–69, 74, 79; of shoeshiners, 74, 78, 79; from street sales, 74, 78, 79–81, 112; variables affecting, 77–81. *See also* economic contributions of child street laborers to families; poverty
independent child street laborers, 65–67, 112, 113–114
International Labour Organization (ILO), 21, 56, 120, 166, 167, 171–173, 174, 177
International Monetary Fund (IMF), 167
Iroquois, 54
Isabela (child street laborer), 115–118, 121, 134–135
Italy, 110, 184n5

James, Allison, 54
Japan, 55
Java, 184n4
Jenks, Chris, 54
Johnson, Alan, 140
Josefina, Doña, 111
Julio, Don, 69, 107–108

Kirschenblatt-Gimblett, Barbara, 122
Kramer, Karen, 185n11, 186n16
Kyomuhendo, Grace B., 187n19

Labor Department, U.S., 178
Ladinos: and car repair service, 51–52;

as child street laborers, 103, 108, 132, 133, 187n18; and *fletero* business, 69–70; population of, 132; and public education system, 158–159; in La Terminal wholesale market, 133; as vendors, 49, 69, 94, 132–133
Lagos, 57
Lawrence-Zúñiga, Denise, 180n6
Lee, José Ángel, 41
Lee, Richard B., 140
Lee, Ronald, 185n11, 186n16
Lem, Winnie, 23, 96–97, 110, 111
Lewis, Oscar, 140, 181n6
literacy. *See* education
Little, Walter, 108, 180n6, 180n13, 182n2, 187n17, 187n19, 188n6
Lone Star, 72
lottery ticket sales, 65–67, 71, 80
Loucky, James Peter, 140, 141, 186nn16–17
Low, Setha, 180n6
Lucchini, Riccardo, 179n5
lucha libre (wrestling), 70
lustradores. See shoeshiners
Lutz, Catherine A., 180n10

Maine, Henry Sumner, 96
malandros (bad street children), 126, 127, 133. *See also* gangs; street children
Malaysia, 111
Malinowski, Bronislaw, 181n5
manner, 134–140
maquiladoras, 149, 166–167
Maradona (child street laborer), 128–129
marginalization, 58, 181–182n6
María, Doña, 62–64
markets. *See* adult street vendors; child street laborers; El Guarda market; Mercado Central; Mercado Peatonal (Pedestrian Market); Mercado Sur 2
Márquez, Patricia, 56

Marx, Karl, 166
Matador (child street laborer), 109–110
Maxwell, Judith, 180n11
Maya Indians: advantages of Maya ethnicity for child street laborers, 131–134; as child street laborers, 103, 108, 132–133, 163, 185n10, 187n18, 188n7; and ethnic identity as immutable prop, 132–134; kin-based pooling of economic resources for, 101; languages of, 2, 132, 190n2; migration of, to United States, 163–165; and pan-Maya movement, 188n7, 190n2; population of, 30–31, 132; poverty of, 30; prejudices against, 133; and public education system, 158, 190n2; as street vendors, 49, 50, 180n13; and tourism industry, 188n6; traditional clothing of, 128, 132, 190nn3–4; and work ethic, 24, 58, 107–108, 155
Mayas in the Marketplace (Little), 182n2
McKenna Brown, R., 190n2
Mercado Central, 32, 33, 40
Mercado Peatonal (Pedestrian Market), 38, 40
Mercado Sur 2, 9, 35, 139
Mexico, 55, 165, 167, 183n6, 190n5
migration: rural-to-urban migration, 33–34, 46–47, 98–99; to United States, 163–165, 167–168, 191n1
Mills, Mary Beth, 110, 184n4
Minge-Kalman, Wanda, 186n16
minimum wage. *See* income
Minor Omissions (Hecht), 55
Mónica, Doña, 69, 70
moral economy model of households, 23, 97, 110
Morales, V., 179n5
Morgan, Lewis Henry, 54, 96
multilocale households, 90–93, 98–102, 114. *See also* families
municipal offices, 41–42
Municipal Plaza, 42

Nash, June, 186–187n17
Nelson, Diane, 180n8
newspaper vendors, 1–2, 22, 27–28, 37,
    39, 66, 80
New York University, 122
Nieuwenhuys, Olga, 56, 59
Nigeria, 7
night watchmen, 75
nomadic vendors: bus accidents injur-
    ing, 150; definition of, 73; income of,
    74, 81; photograph of, 86; physical
    and work-related activities of, 143,
    146; sex-based divisions among, 78;
    social interactions of, 144, 145
Northwestern University, 122

Oaxaca, 184n8
Oldham, David, 184n4
Oloko, Beatrice, 7, 11–12
organ thievery, 180n8
Otzoy, Irma, 190n4
overhead costs, 125, 188n4

pan-Maya movement, 188n7, 190n2
papi-fútbol, 136, 147, 188–189n8
parents. See families
Parque Concordia, 38–40
part-time child street laborers: data
    gathering among, 15; distinguished
    from full-time child street labor-
    ers, 11–12; education of, 7; Oloko on,
    11–12
patriarchy, 96, 184n4
PENNAT (Educational Program for
    the Child and Adolescent Laborer),
    8–12, 15, 64, 136, 152–155, 159–160,
    190n5
Penny Capitalism (Tax), 101
performance. See dramaturgical model
    of social interaction
performance studies, 122

Perla (child street laborer), 65–67, 110,
    112, 113
personal services. See service trades
Peru, 183n6
Phelan, Peggy, 122, 188n3
phone cards, 66, 182n1
photographs of child street laborers,
    18–22, 82–89, 180nn10–12
physical props, 126–129
Piaget, Jean, 181n5
"pirated" goods, 51–52
Pixote: Law of the Weakest, 182n7
Pizarro (child street laborer), 60–64
Plattner, Stuart, 183n6
Plaza Major (Central Plaza), 31–32, 41
police, 144, 151
political economy model of households,
    97, 110
Ponce (child street worker), 102, 103,
    104
Porres Castejón, Gustavo, 132, 181n3
porters (cargadores): age as immutable
    prop of, 130; duties of, 51; income of,
    68–69, 74, 79; initial capital outlay
    for, 78, 79; males as, 67–70, 75, 78;
    photograph of, 85; physical props of,
    127; social interactions of, 144, 145;
    work-related physical activities of,
    143, 146, 147
poverty: culture of, 58, 181–182n6; of
    families of child street laborers, 4–5,
    17–18; in Guatemala, 30, 166; of Maya
    Indians, 30; vocational patterns of
    working poor, 101
The Presentation of Self in Everyday Life
    (Goffman), 118
Programa Educativo del Niño, Niña y
    Adolescente Trabajador (PENNAT).
    See PENNAT (Educational Pro-
    gram for the Child and Adolescent
    Laborer)
prostitution, 7, 18, 46, 52–53, 57, 71, 131,
    179n5, 180n7, 182n3

Protestantism. *See* evangelical
Christianity
Prout, Alan, 54
Proyecto Alternativos (Alternatives
Project), 8
public education. *See* education
public transportation. *See* buses
punchboards, 71, 183n4

Quinta Avenida, 40–41

Radcliffe-Brown, A. R., 181n5
rape, 113, 131
recreation, 62, 95–96, 127, 136, 143,
146–148, 188–189n8
recuperation activities, 72, 183n5
recycling, 72, 183n5
regimes of control, 23, 96–97, 108–111, 112
Reina (child street laborer), 62–65, 79,
105, 110
religion, 92–93, 186n17
relojeros (watchmakers), 73–74
research methods: categories of jobs
performed by child street laborers,
12, 70–76; data gathering among
child street laborers, 12–15; data
gathering among other groups,
15; description of, 7–15; and ethics, 16–22; interviews, 13, 14–15, 123;
participant observation, 12–15, 123;
random-interval instantaneous sampling (spot observation), 140–141,
189n11; selection of informants,
11–12; time-allocation studies, 14,
140–149, 189n11
residence of child street laborers, 62–63,
104, 117, 121, 125, 153
resistance strategies, 111
retail sales. *See* street sales
Rey (child street laborer), 1–3, 27–30,
90–93

Reynolds, Pamela, 56, 186n16
Richards, Julia, 190n2
Richards, Michael, 190n2
Richardson, Miles, 180n6
Rizzini, Irene, 55–56
robbery. *See* theft and robbery
Roberta (child street laborer), 112–113
Roberto (child street laborer), 112–113,
187n20
Ronaldo (child street laborer), 135–138
Roxana, 2, 28
rural-to-urban migration, 33–34, 46–47,
98–99

Safa, Helen, 186–187n17
safety issues, 128–129, 138, 144–145,
149–151
Sahlins, Marshall, 140
Salazar (child street laborer), 154–155,
190n1
sales. *See* street sales
Sami, Doña, 117
Sapo (child street laborer), 138–139
Sargent, Carolyn, 54, 55
Sayles, John, 72
Scaglion, Richard, 140
scavenging, 72, 183n5
Scheper-Hughes, Nancy, 54, 55, 76–77,
180n8
schools. *See* education
Schwartzman, Helen, 55
Scott, James, 110, 111
Sebastián (child street laborer), 113–114
security services, 74, 75
self-presentation. *See* dramaturgical
model of social interaction
service trades, 73–74, 79, 80. *See also*
delivery persons; shoeshiners
sex-based divisions of child labor, 21, 74,
75, 78, 79–80, 131, 141. *See also* gender
stereotypes and gender socialization
Sexta Avenida, 41, 132, 136–138

shoe repair, 1, 29, 73
shoeshiners: age as immutable prop
of, 130; children and youth as, 28,
29, 33–34, 39, 51, 73, 76, 113, 138–139,
163; clothing and appearance of, 137;
common beliefs and misconceptions
about, 129; girls as, 20–22; income of,
74, 78, 79; initial capital outlay by, 78,
79; manner and scripts of, 135–139;
photographs of, 20–22, 89; physical
props of, 126–127; social interactions
of, 144, 145; work-related physical
activities of, 143, 146, 147–148
small-scale transportation, 73, 74–75.
See also delivery persons; porters
(*cargadores*)
Small Wars (Scheper-Hughes and
Sargent), 55
Smith, Carol, 31, 186n17
soccer, 95, 127, 136, 147, 188–189n8
socialization process, 58, 142–145, 181n5
social marginalization, 58, 181–182n6
social skills: of child street laborers,
24–25, 115–122, 124–151; dramaturgical model of social interaction,
118–119, 122–124; and immutable
props, 129–134; and manner, 134–140;
and physical activities of child street
laborers, 143, 145–149; and physical
props, 126–129; and safety issues,
144–145, 149–151; and social interaction categories, 142–145; social life of
child street laborers, 62, 93, 94–96;
and street setting, 124–126; and
time-allocation studies, 140–149
soda sales. *See* food vendors
Sontag, Susan, 180n10
South Africa, 55, 57
Stephens, Sharon, 55
street children: abandoned children
as, 112; anthropological studies of,
55–56; CEDC (children in especially
difficult circumstances), 55, 182n3;

data gathering among, 15; definition
of, 5–6, 57; difficulties of, 18, 150;
ethnographic studies on, 180n7; and
gangs, 112; informal education for,
190n5; and mother love and child
obedience, 187n18; and Parque Concordia, 39, 40; physical props of, 126;
police brutality against, 151; popular
conception of, 2; Ronaldo as, before
becoming street laborer, 137–138;
statistics on, 5–6, 56
street education. *See* education
street entertainers, 8, 39, 75–76
street sales: by *achimeros*, 50, 61–62,
107, 109, 127, 155; of clothing, 35, 50,
51, 72, 81, 102–103, 117–118, 127–128,
133, 148; of consumer products,
50, 60–62, 76, 127, 148; entertainment combined with, 139–140; food
vendors, 34, 37, 39, 41, 49–50, 68, 80,
116, 128, 137; girls in, 65–67, 80, 131;
and haggling, 64–65, 80; hierarchy
of increasingly lucrative positions
in, 162–163; income from, 74, 78,
79–81, 112, 187n20; of lottery tickets,
65–67, 71, 80; newspaper vendors,
1–2, 22, 27–28, 37, 39, 66, 80; nomadic
versus fixed vendors, 73, 74, 78, 81,
86, 143, 144, 145, 148–149; physical
props of street vendors, 127–128; of
"pirated" and stolen goods, 51–52,
125; statistics on, 72, 73; transition
from service trades to, 79, 80. *See
also* adult street vendors; child street
laborers
street setting, 124–126
Susana, Doña, 66, 113

Taiwan, 184n4
Tax, Sol, 101
taxis and taxi drivers, 43, 74, 131
Tejada, Marie Román de, 13

Index   227

telephone service, 66, 182n1
La Terminal market, 133, 181n4, 189n10
Thailand, 110, 184n4
theft and robbery, 7, 52, 57, 71, 111, 126, 149–151, 182n3, 189–190n12
Thompson, E. P., 110
time-allocation studies, 14, 140–149, 189n11
Tonga, 56
transportation. *See* buses; *fletes, fleteros* (trucks, truck owners); small-scale transportation
trash-collecting duties, 44–45, 105
trucks. *See fletes, fleteros* (trucks, truck owners)
Tumax, L., 179n5
Turner, Victor, 188n3
typists, 73

Ubico, Jorge, 33
UNESCO, 155
UNICEF, 180n12
United Nations, 55, 94
United Nations Convention on the Rights of the Child (CRC), 173–174, 177
United Nations Year of the Child (1979), 182n7
United States: migration to, 163–165, 167–168, 191n1; trade between Guatemala and, 167
U.S. Department of Labor, 178

Velásquez (child street laborer), 43–45, 93–96, 105, 110, 183n1
vendors. *See* adult street vendors; child street laborers; street sales
Venezuela, 56
vice. *See* contraband; prostitution
El Viejo Guarda, 45, 48, 49
violence, 16, 113, 131, 150–151, 189–190n12. *See also* crime

Wacquant, Loic, 180n8
Wallman, Sandra, 97
watchmakers (*relojeros*), 73–74
Wilson, William, 101
Wittig, Martha, 101
Wolf, Diane, 184n4
Wolf, Margery, 184n4
women. *See* females
work ethic, 24, 58, 107–108, 155
working poor. *See* child street laborers

Ximena, Doña, 69–70

Yanagisako, Sylvia, 184n5
Yoli, Doña, 44–45, 93–94, 96
Yucatan, 185n11, 186n16

Zimbabwe, 56